Developing a Pedagogy of Teacher Education

Developing a Pedagogy of Teacher Education demonstrates how teacher educators genuinely need to understand that a pedagogy of teacher education must go way beyond the transmission of information about teaching. The book purposefully portrays and explores the complex nature of teaching and learning about teaching and illustrates how important teacher educators' professional knowledge is and how that knowledge must impact teacher education practices.

The book comprises two main parts. Part I is concerned with the notion of teaching about teaching and highlights important aspects of the knowledge and skills about practice that require teacher educators to be more than just good teachers. Loughran shows that the distinction between teaching student-teachers and teaching them *about* teaching is crucial. Teacher educators, he says, must unpack for student-teachers the pedagogical expertise that allows practice to push beyond the technical-rational, or tips-and-tricks approach, to teaching about teaching in a way that displays the appropriate attitudes, knowledge and skills of teaching itself.

Part II focuses on learning about teaching drawing attention to how student-teachers must recognize and respond to two competing agendas as they learn about teaching. Student-teachers need to not only concentrate on learning what is being taught but also the way in which that teaching is conducted. These two competing agendas demand that teacher educators respond appropriately in the way they teach about teaching so that both agendas are simultaneously addressed.

This is a challenging but exciting book that overtly values teaching about teaching and pushes the knowledge of practice in teacher education in such a way as to enhance the va. iing of teacher educators' knowledge, skills and ability in shaping the learning about teaching that they attempt to create for their student-teachers.

John Loughran is a senior member of the Faculty of Education at Monash University as the Foundation Chair in Curriculum and Professional Practice. He has written and edited several books for Routledge, Teachers' College Press and Kluwer.

Developing a Pedagogy of Teacher Education

Understanding teaching and learning about teaching

John Loughran

Routledge
Taylor & Francis Group

LONDON AND NEW YORK

First published 2006
by Routledge
2 Park Square, Milton Park, Abingdon, Oxon OX14 4RN

Simultaneously published in the USA and Canada
by Routledge
270 Madison Ave, New York, NY 10016

Routledge is an imprint of the Taylor & Francis Group

© 2006 John Loughran

Typeset in Sabon by
Integra Software Services Pvt. Ltd, Pondicherry, India
Printed and bound in Great Britain by
The Cromwell Press, Trowbridge, Wiltshire

British Library Cataloguing in Publication Data
A catalogue record for this book is available from the British Library

Library of Congress Cataloging in Publication Data
Loughran, J. John.
  Developing a pedagogy of teacher education : understanding
  teaching and learning about teaching / John Loughran.
    p.   cm.
  Includes bibliographical references.
  ISBN 0–415–36730–1 (hardback)—ISBN 0–415–36727–1 (pbk.)
  1. Teachers—Training of.   2. Teacher educators.
  3. Education—study and teaching (Higher)   4. Teaching.
  I. Title.
  LB1707.L68 2006
  370′.71′1—dc22   2005014702

ISBN 10: 0–415–36730–1 (hbk)
ISBN 10: 0–415–36727–1 (pbk)

ISBN 13: 978–0–415–36730–1 (hbk)
ISBN 13: 978–0–415–36727–1 (pbk)

To Jeff Northfield (14 August 1938–23 May 2004), a much missed mentor and colleague who developed and shared his wisdom of teaching and teacher education in ways that encouraged others to better value and respect the expertise and skills of practice.

Contents

Acknowledgements

To Airlie, Holly, Allister and Sophie for their ongoing support and patience which are never taken for granted but always enormously appreciated.

To Vanessa Davidson and the many other students of teaching who so graciously allowed me to use their anecdotes, assignments and papers to highlight their perspectives on teaching and learning about teaching. Theirs is a voice that continually needs to be sought in *developing a pedagogy of teacher education*.

To PEEL for allowing Donna Fox's case to be summarized and used in this book.

1 Introduction: Developing a pedagogy of teacher education – What does that really mean?

> [B]eing a teacher educator is often difficult ... in most places, there is no culture in which it is common for teacher education staff to collaboratively work on the question of how to improve the pedagogy of teacher education.
> – Korthagen (2001a, p. 8)

Developing a pedagogy of teacher education – What does that really mean? An answer may be found in the importance of the three parts that comprise the whole: developing, pedagogy and teacher education. First, it is important to understand the nature of the term *pedagogy*. As has been demonstrated in the literature many times, sometimes seemingly familiar terms develop a life of their own as a diversity of definitions, understandings and interpretations emerge over time. Such terms, like that of, for example, reflection, tend to "ring true" with people in ways that carry meaning through the tacit understandings inherent in them. Such tacit understandings can be so strong that they lead to the term being adapted and adjusted to suit a range of contexts and situations. In such situations, ironically, the meaning may then become less definitive, less purposeful and more easily misunderstood so that what may once have seemed obvious can no longer be assumed or taken for granted. As a result of the growing range of interpretations, it may become necessary to (re)define the term so that that which is intended, and that which is not, can be made more explicit. In so doing, acceptance (or rejection) of the arguments, ideas and practices associated with the use of the term may more easily be made.

The term *reflection* has spawned a number of related terms such as reflective teaching, reflective learning and reflective practice. It has also led to the creation of terms that are sometimes confused with one another because of the similarity in meaning, for example reflexion and reflectivity. Thus the descriptor reflection has led to the underlying concept being adjusted, adapted and changed as individuals have sought to use it to signify issues and practices important to them and so that they might be grasped more easily by others through the link with the original term. Pedagogy, it could well be argued, has suffered in ways similar to that of reflection.

Pedagogy, as described in some of the educational literature (e.g. in the US, Australia, the UK, Canada and New Zealand), is sometimes used as a synonym for teaching. In this sense, pedagogy is seen as a catch-all term for such things as teaching procedures, teaching practice, instruction and so on. Van Manen (1999) explained this trend in some detail when he revisited Simon's (1981) lament: "Why no pedagogy in England?" (p. 14). However, as he goes on to explain, if one draws more on the roots of European traditions (e.g. The Netherlands, Belgium, Germany and Scandinavia), pedagogy can be seen to encompass much more than simply teaching (van Manen, 1999). Pedagogy is the art and science of educating children and as van Manen makes clear, focusing on the relationship between learning and teaching such that one does not exist as separate and distinct from the other is crucial to such education.

Importantly, drawing on this European tradition, teaching and learning are seen as being linked in powerful and important ways such that the intention implicit in the use of the term is that teaching purposefully influences learning and vice versa. Therefore, pedagogy is not merely the action of teaching (which itself can easily be misinterpreted as the transmission of information), more so, it is about the relationship between teaching and learning and how together they lead to growth in knowledge and understanding through meaningful practice.

Korthagen (2001b), in building further on the place of relationship in conceptualizing an understanding of pedagogy, goes beyond issues associated with teaching and learning *per se* and focuses on the importance of self-understanding and connectedness. In so doing, he places emphasis on the development of self-identity and the manner in which that impacts pedagogy. For example, he suggests that he "follow[s] Kohnstamm (1929), who stated that many durable learning experiences are rooted in the I–you relationship between teacher and student, in genuine personal encounters in which both are, within the here-and-now, in contact with their inner selves" (p. 264). Thus, in educational encounters, a teacher's norms and values, and the extent to which they are enacted in practice, influence the manner which students might develop their own. Thus personal relationship between teachers and students is crucial as identity formation and personal growth combine to shape the nature of pedagogy itself.

Next, consider the term *teacher education*. In most contexts, the use of the term teacher education is synonymous with pre-service teacher preparation. In pre-service teacher preparation programs, students of teaching (Bullough and Gitlin, 1995, 2001) seek to develop knowledge and skills of teaching and to learn how to competently apply these in practice. So in teacher education, students of teaching enter their programs with a natural concern to learn about teaching while their teacher educators (those associated with teaching in the program) clearly have a major responsibility for, and hopefully, an interest in their teaching about teaching. Hence, teacher education itself has two important foci: learning about teaching and, teaching about teaching, each of which involves complex skills, knowledge, abilities and competences (Koster *et al.*, 2005).

These foci are further complicated by the competing cognitive and affective tensions that influence learning and growth through experiences in the practice setting. In fact, it could well be argued that in much of what we do in teacher education, attention to the cognitive domain too often dominates. Such domination can be to the detriment of the importance of recognizing and responding to one's emotions, feelings and reactions, all of which are so enmeshed in the experiences of learning and teaching about teaching.

Finally, *developing*. This is an interesting term as it suggests neither a point of beginning nor an end. *Developing* implies a sense of "coming to be" or pushing ahead toward a more "advanced state." If one is developing, then one is growing in understanding, moving forward, purposefully building on that which is already present. Developing then hints at the value in extending that which one already knows (and is able to do) such that questioning and challenging that which might normally be overlooked, or taken for granted, will be reconsidered in such a way as to offer new insights to an open-minded inquirer. Being open-minded is important because "It includes an active desire to listen to more sides than one; to give heed to facts from whatever source they come; to give full attention to alternative possibilities; to recognize the possibility of error even in the beliefs that are dearest to us" (Dewey, 1933, p. 30).

Taken together, the intention is that *developing a pedagogy of teacher education* signifies that the relationship between teaching and learning in the programs and practices of learning *and* teaching about teaching might be purposefully examined, described, articulated and portrayed in ways that enhance our understanding of this complex interplay. In so doing, our knowledge of, and practice with, students and teachers of teaching might then be nurtured in ways that can positively influence the manner in which such work is conducted, understood and valued. From this perspective, two crucial aspects of a pedagogy of teacher education need to be fully grasped: teaching about teaching and learning about teaching.

Content and pedagogy in teacher education

In a teaching and learning situation there is an obvious focus on both the content to be taught and the learning to be experienced. In teaching and learning about teaching, the content, or subject matter, comprises at least the "theoretical" aspects of the "knowledge" of teaching (some might describe it as the *discipline of teaching*). Typically, much of this subject matter is distilled and offered through some form of curriculum (e.g. the knowledge of classroom management, wait time, higher order questioning, learning theories, gender issues, constructivism, co-operative learning, etc.) and is what Russell (1997) has described as the *content turn* in teacher education. However, an issue that is often easily overlooked in teaching and learning about teaching is the concurrent need to also pay careful attention to the practices employed in presenting the subject matter – the *pedagogical turn* (Russell, 1997). Hence, for both the teacher and the student of teaching, ongoing and conflicting roles continually complicate the competing agendas of *teaching and learning* about teaching. Not only must both teachers and students of teaching pay careful attention to the subject matter being taught, they must also simultaneously pay attention to the manner in which that knowledge is being taught; and both must overtly be embraced in a *pedagogy of teacher education.*

Learning about teaching

> Preservice teachers also should be encouraged to be metacognitive and become more aware of how they learn in teacher education courses with the intention of informing their decision-making as they construct their personal pedagogies. (Hoban, 1997, p. 135)

At first Hoban's suggestion sounds quite straightforward; perhaps more a subtle point rather than an outstanding revelation and so it is not difficult to see why it might initially be viewed as self-evident. However, on closer examination, the requirements for, and expectations about, appropriate actions and responses are far from simple. What Hoban's suggestion really means for the student of teaching is that at any given time in the teaching and learning environment there is a need to be learning that which is being taught while at the same time questioning, examining and learning about the way in which it is actually being taught: asking questions about the nature of the teaching; the influence of the practice on the subsequent learning (or lack thereof); the manner in which the teaching has been constructed and is being portrayed; how the teaching-learning environment has been created and so on.

For a student of teaching, to consistently pay attention to these competing agenda (learning about the particular content that is being taught and learning about teaching) is difficult; to respond to both is demanding. It is clearly much easier for a learner to pay attention (or not) only to the content that is being taught. For most students of teaching, that is what 13 years of formal schooling has encouraged. More so, for the large majority of students of teaching, that is also what traditional university teaching has more than likely further reinforced. Therefore, for students of teaching to shake themselves out of their well-established comfort zone of (perhaps passive) learning and to begin to question the taken for granted in their learning about teaching at both levels requires energy. It also requires an expectation, or belief, that there is real value and purpose for so doing. This is then where metacognition begins to play an important role.

In learning about teaching, students of teaching need to be conscious of their own learning so that they overtly develop their understanding of the teaching practices they experience in order to purposefully link the manner in which they learn in a given situation with the nature of the teaching itself.

Therefore, for students of teaching, their learning agenda includes learning about the specific content being taught, learning about learning and learning about teaching. All of these inevitably shape their developing understanding of the complexity of teaching and learning but may not be fully apprehended if not explicitly linked to their learning agenda. I would argue that there is little doubt that creating such an agenda is important because:

> Student teachers' expectations of their preservice programs are strongly influenced by their prior experiences as learners, together with popular stereotypes about teachers' work. Student teachers commonly enter their teacher education with a view of teaching as simple and transmissive. They believe that teaching involved the uncomplicated act of telling students what to learn. (Berry, 2004a, pp. 1301–1302)

At the same time the teacher of teaching also has a competing agenda to manage.

Teaching about teaching

> becoming a teacher educator (or teacher of teachers) has the potential (not always realized) to generate a second level of thought about teaching, one that focuses not on content but on *how* we teach...This new perspective constitutes making the '*pedagogical turn*', thinking long and hard about how we teach and the messages conveyed by how we teach...I have come to believe that learning to teach is far more complex than we have ever acknowledged... (Russell, 1997, p. 44)

Just as the student of teaching is confronted by the need to pay attention to both the content and the manner of teaching, so too the teacher of teaching is confronted by a similar situation. The need to teach the given content is obvious but, sadly, it is all too often the only focus of attention. However, if students of teaching are to genuinely "see into teaching," then they require access to the thoughts and actions that shape such practice; they need to be able to see and hear the pedagogical reasoning that underpins the teaching that they are experiencing (Loughran, 1996). For the teacher of teaching this raises similar competing agenda as that which students of teaching experience as there is the need to simultaneously pay attention to two different things.

It has been well illustrated in the literature how difficult this can be to do (Berry, 2001; Hutchinson, 1998; Nicol, 1997) because the manner in which a teacher educator might come to know that which is worth investigating in teaching about teaching, and for whom it is helpful (the teacher educator and/or the student-teacher), is exceptionally challenging.

Learning how to teach about teaching can be confusing as the purpose and value of "unpacking" the teaching is buffeted by recognizing and responding to the needs of the learner as well as the learning needs of the teacher educator. Thus making "the right decisions" about that which might be seen as a teachable moment can be exceedingly difficult for the teacher of teaching, especially when complicated by needing to know when and how to respond in the crucible of practice.

> I have therefore sought to develop a pedagogy of teacher education that seriously attempts to address the prior beliefs that prospective teachers bring with them to the course by expanding teachers' visions of what is desirable and what might be possible in teaching...The pedagogical challenge for me then has been to develop instructional moves, activities, tasks, and problems which will encourage and open prospective teachers to asking questions, analysing, taking new perspectives, and considering alternatives as well as developing defensible arguments for teaching practices that move beyond their personal experiences of studenting...But the challenge is also for me to do this in a way which authentically represents the nature of teaching, its inherent uncertainty and complexity....I want my prospective teachers to be investigating genuine pedagogical problems through which they might develop reasoned arguments about the problems and dilemmas of practice. However, this is no simple task. (Nicol, 1997, pp. 97–98)

Teaching about teaching should not be confused with modeling teaching practice. Teaching about teaching goes beyond the traditional notion of modeling, for it involves not just teaching in ways congruent with the expectations one has of the manner in which pre-service teachers might teach, it involves unpacking teaching in ways that gives students access to the pedagogical reasoning, uncertainties and dilemmas of practice that are inherent in understanding teaching as being problematic. It involves helping to make clear how the teaching approach purposely encourages learning and how learning influences teaching in action such that the responsive interplay might be explicit and able to be critiqued in an honest and meaningful manner; it is thoughtfully knowing how and when to make the:

> experimenting and the inevitable "mistakes" and confusions that follow [be] encouraged, discussed, and viewed as departure points for growth... [so that] a climate of trust, as well as the disposition to take learning seriously...begin[s] with the [teacher educator's] own capacity for reflection on teaching, together with his or her ability to make this evident to the student teacher. (MacKinnon, 1989, p. 23)

Teaching and learning about teaching

Together then, both the students of teaching and the teachers of teaching need to consciously be operating on two levels: the first is on the nature of the "content" being examined in the teaching and learning environment; the second is on the nature of the teaching that is being employed. It is for this reason that teaching and learning about teaching requires such careful attention for, "...the teacher education profession is unique, differing from, say, doctors who teach medicine. During their teaching, doctors do not serve as role models for the actual practice of the profession i.e., they do not treat their students. Teacher educators, conversely, whether intentionally or not, teach their students as well as teach about teaching" (Korthagen, Loughran and Lunenberg, 2005, p. 111). It is this dual role that so complicates teaching and learning about teaching. And, keeping these roles to the fore requires vigilance that is perhaps not so easily apprehended in the normal day-to-day expectations and experiences of teacher education programs.

Unlocking the knowledge of practice that illustrates the importance and complexity of these dual roles for both teachers and students of teaching is difficult, and the existing teacher education literature is far from replete with examples. However, some strong cases have begun to emerge through the research efforts of many of those involved in self-study of teaching and teacher education practices (see Hamilton *et al.* (1998); Loughran *et al.* (2004) for a detailed explanation of self-study). For example, Tidwell (2002) noted how in her teaching about literacy education a focus on individual differences needed to be integral to her own practice in teaching about that content, that is she needed not only to teach the content, but to teach in ways commensurate with the "messages and practices" that was the content.

Tidwell described in detail how she came to see the importance of her teaching about teaching at two levels and how she responded to her desire to develop her practice by embarking on a rich self-study in order to learn more about her teaching and her students' learning. In so doing, she began to better see not only the content to be taught, but the manner in which it needed to be taught and made that more explicit to her students. She there-fore began to better conceptualize her teaching about teaching whilst also seeing how her enhanced views of practice impacted in new and different ways on her students' learning about teaching: "What I find most fulfilling, intriguing, and difficult about this type of self-study is that it requires me to get very close to my own teaching and to my own thinking. It forces me to ask questions that are not always easy to answer, and this can be a painful process" (Tidwell, 2002, p. 41).

The complexity of learning about teaching for students of teaching (from their perspective) has not traditionally been extensively reported in the literature although in recent times, some have begun to explore this important facet of teacher education. For example, a student-teacher and teacher educator working together (Russell and Bullock, 1999) have illustrated well how carefully observing, questioning and unpacking a teacher educator's practice can be a powerful way of learning about one's own teaching. And, it does so by creating the impetus for pursuing the necessary risk-taking that is so important in shaping learning:

Tom [teacher educator] was adept at not giving the 'right answer'...
instead he would ask more questions...I now realize that he was
avoiding the pitfalls associated with...'Answerland'...he could have just
as easily said 'I disagree because'...but instead he asked me questions
that required me to look at deeper issues. I have since explored the
notion of interpreting experiences in different ways...[I now see that]
'How we teach is the message.' It is a concept I have taken very much
to heart. If I want students to construct an understanding of the world
around them, I must create an environment rich in experience. (Russell
and Bullock, 1999, pp. 138–140)

Further to this, it is difficult to find studies that examine in detail both
teaching *and* learning about teaching yet it is the focus on each of these
aspects of practice from a teacher educator's and student-teacher's perspective
that is crucial to generating, articulating and portraying a pedagogy of teacher
education. One useful framework for considering the nature of teaching
and learning about teaching then as an entrée to better articulating and
portraying a pedagogy of teacher education is through the concepts of
episteme and phronesis (Korthagen *et al.*, 2001).

Developing knowledge: Episteme and phronesis

Most teacher educators will recognize the example: A student teacher
formulates a problem from practical experiences, which leads the other
students or the teacher educator to come up with possible solutions...
Sometimes such a sharing of thoughts seems to help...But sometimes –
more often than we wish – it does not seem to help. What seems
obvious to the teacher educator is not so to the student teacher. What
to us seems directly applicable in practice appears to be too abstract,
too theoretical, and too far off to someone else. What to us seems
evident and easy to understand does not get through to the student. No
matter how carefully we consider the problem, we do not find a way
into it...there is an unbridgeable gap between our words and the
student's experiences. (Kessels and Korthagen, 2001, pp. 21–22)

This unbridgeable gap is an excellent way of conceptualizing the impact of
the difference between episteme and phronesis in teacher education.
Episteme, as described by Korthagen *et al.* (2001), is propositional knowledge,
consisting of assertions of a general nature that apply to many different
situations and problems. Episteme then is traditional, scientifically derived
knowledge that is often described in abstract terms and considered to be
objective and timeless. On the other hand, phronesis is a form of practical
wisdom that is derived through understanding specific situations and cases
(Korthagen *et al.*, 2001). Phronesis is often understood as being developed
through experience whereby the knowledge gained may not be immediately

generalizable, but it is certainly appropriate to the given situation. In teacher education, this distinction can be an important way of better understanding how knowledge of practice might then be developed and shared by both teacher educators and students of teaching.

Korthagen (2001a) describes teacher education as a "problematic enterprise," and it is in coming to view both teaching and teaching about teaching as problematic that is crucial to grasping the full extent of the value of the frames of episteme and phronesis. For students of teaching, epistemic knowledge is not immediately helpful in addressing their problems of practice. This is not to demean such knowledge, rather to recognize that in the absence of teaching experience, generalizable knowledge about practice (no matter how "right" it might be) does not necessarily help neophytes see into their actions and teaching behaviors in ways that lead to constructive (at that given time) solutions. So, although a teacher educator may be able to recognize the problems with which their students are confronted and offer solutions, as such solutions are not drawn from the students' own experiences, they struggle to align the problem with the stated solution. This may well be because students do not always see the problem in the same way as the teacher educator, or more so, that they do not see the problem as being a problem. Thus being told about a solution is akin to absorbing propositional knowledge but not knowing how or why to apply it, because the problem and solution are not purposefully linked (yet) in the students' mind (or able to be played out in their actions).

In a similar vein, the teacher educator is also confronted by the distinction between episteme and phronesis. The knowledge of teaching that the teacher educator has developed over time, and that may well be framed in the form of episteme, is not necessarily immediately helpful to their emerging problems of teaching about teaching. In many ways, just as the student of teaching needs to experience the tensions, dilemmas and problems of practice in order to learn through the accumulation of knowledge of practice, so too the teacher educator is confronted by a similar situation in learning through the accumulation of knowledge of teaching about teaching. The often tacit knowledge of teaching needs to be made explicit in order to enhance teaching about teaching. A teacher educator needs to be challenged about the "why" of practice not just the "how" of practice in order to be able to articulate their own understandings for it is through this articulation that problem and solution may become much clearer as noted so long ago by Dewey (1933), "If we knew just what the difficulty was and where it lay, the job of reflection would be much easier than it is...we know what the problem *exactly* is simultaneously with finding a way out and getting it resolved. Problem and solution stand out *completely* at the same time. Up to that point, our grasp of the problem has been more or less vague and tentative" (p. 108, emphasis in original).

Hence, phronesis can be a conduit to episteme for as the knowledge of practice develops through phronesis, it is almost inevitable that similarities and differences between situations will encourage thoughts about tentative generalizations and abstractions of practice such that "big ideas" of teaching and teaching about teaching begin to emerge in ways that are able to be tested, refined and verified. Thus rather than the difference between theory and practice appearing as a chasm, approaching the development of knowledge as learning through experience can bridge the two in a meaningful way.

Clearly then, this is the task confronted by those teacher educators concerned to describe, articulate and share in meaningful ways their knowledge of teaching and learning about teaching. It is also what could be described as developing a pedagogy of teacher education and is something that has been lacking for far too long. If teacher education is to positively influence the way in which beginning teachers view the profession, if teacher education is to appropriately support a growing knowledge of teaching and learning and if teacher education itself is to be more highly valued, then articulating a pedagogy of teacher education is crucial for it is at the heart of challenging teaching as telling and fundamental to enhancing teaching for understanding. If teaching for understanding is not central to teacher education, then how can such practice truly be expected in schools?

> A coherent pedagogy of teacher education...requires considering how teachers learn about teaching and what it means to know and understand teaching and learning [about teaching]. (Northfield and Gunstone, 1997, p. 55)

Overview

This book works from the basis of the argument established in this chapter to outline in detail some of the elements that might comprise a pedagogy of teacher education.

At the "big picture" level, the distinction between teacher educators' teaching about teaching and student-teachers' learning about teaching is important for drawing attention to these two different but complimentary aspects of teacher education, thus the division of the book into these two sections. Within these sections, the underlying frames of episteme and phronesis are important in shaping understandings about not only the nature of knowledge that influences teaching and learning, but also the way in which that knowledge might be identified, portrayed, applied and shared in developing a pedagogy of teacher education.

I trust the following chapters help you to consider carefully your own approach to teaching about teaching and encourage you to research, document and share your learning with others so that a pedagogy of teacher education might become an articulable and defining aspect of the knowledge, skills and practices of teacher educators.

Part I

Teaching about teaching

> For a variety of reasons, not least among them the training orientation of
> teacher education, teacher educators frequently ignore what they tacitly
> understand: As with other teachers, what they teach will be filtered through
> and made more or less meaningful based on a set of biographically embedded
> assumptions, beliefs, or preunderstandings held by their students ... Some
> of what is taught will be ignored and discarded as meaningless because it does
> not fit current understanding, and recognized as self-confirming, other
> content, perhaps even less significant content, will be embraced eagerly.
> Ignoring the past does not make it go away. It lingers, ever present and quietly
> insistent.
>
> (Bullough and Gitlin, 2001, p. 223)

Teaching about teaching demands a great deal from teacher educators.
There is a continual need for teacher educators to be conscious of not
only what they are teaching, but also the manner in which that teaching is
conducted. It is imperative that in their own teaching, teacher educators
continually invite students of teaching to see into the teaching being experienced so that a serious examination of teaching is always a central
element of practice. Therefore, the complexity of teacher educators' work
hinges around recognizing, responding and managing the dual roles of
teaching *and* teaching about teaching concurrently. Approaching teacher
education in this manner can indeed be challenging and confronting, but
if teacher education programs are to do more than simply convey tips and
tricks about practice, then thoughtful and sustained examination of
teaching must begin and be encouraged to grow in teacher preparation
programs.

This first part of *Developing a Pedagogy of Teacher Education* is organized
in such a way as to focus on the nature of the work of the teacher educator
and is designed to illustrate how challenging and complex such work is
when viewed as comprising these two purposes (teaching *and* teaching
about teaching). By concentrating on ways of conceptualizing the demands
and expectations of teacher educators' work, it is anticipated that a deeper

understanding of approaches to teaching and researching teaching about teaching might be realized so that they are viewed as part of a holistic understanding of scholarship in teacher education practices rather than as separate, distinct and independent tasks.

2 Being a teacher educator: A focus on pedagogy

When we began as assistant professors, we already had extensive experience as teachers, both in public schools and at university level. From the beginning, we knew how to construct curriculum, carry out evaluation, use a variety of teaching strategies, and counsel students. Unfortunately, having and using this knowledge did not give us the edge we hoped it would. Because we teach teachers, concerns with and about teaching could not be easily or systematically resolved . . . In our case, our teaching and the teaching of our students was and is representative of all aspects of our responsibilities as university professors – research, teaching, and service.

(Guilfoyle *et al.*, 1995, p. 36)

It has been well documented that, in the transition from school teacher to teacher educator, many have struggled (Ducharme, 1993). One aspect of this struggle is associated with the change in demands and expectations in teaching about teaching as opposed to teaching *per se* (Smith, 2003). Whilst a school teacher's main role is often viewed as "just teaching," a teacher educator's role encompasses other expectations beyond "doing teaching." These additional expectations can be perceived as threatening to the ongoing links to the school sector as well as carrying the tag of "ex-schoolteacher" which can frame one's professional identity (Lanier and Little, 1986). One difficulty associated with framing professional identity through the lens of "ex-schoolteacher" is that the teacher educator may be viewed as simply being a teacher teaching in teacher preparation rather than as a teacher educator with an expertise in teaching and learning *about* teaching. The distinction being that knowledge, skill and ability in teaching needs to be able to be taught not just demonstrated.

The transition from teacher to teacher educator is under-represented in the research literature but the issues are well foregrounded by Dinkleman *et al.* (2001) in their extensive study:

Becoming a teacher educator involves more than a job title. One becomes a teacher educator as soon as one does teacher education, but one's professional identity as a teacher educator is constructed over time. Developing an identity and practices in teacher education is best understood as a process of becoming. Though the work of teaching shares much in common with the work of teacher education, the two positions are significantly divergent in important ways. (p. 1)

Being a teacher educator requires an understanding of teaching that goes beyond being a good teacher. There is a need to be able to theorize practice in such a way as to know and be able to articulate the what, how and why of teaching and to do so through the very experiences of teaching *and* learning about teaching. This matters because students of teaching need to be able to see into practice in ways that go beyond their initial expectations of learning the script, or developing a recipe, for how to teach. It also matters in terms of the expectations of the work of academia (creating, researching, disseminating and using new knowledge).

Beyond these points, there is also the need for teacher educators to be capable of challenging simplistic views of, and approaches to, teaching as telling or the transmission of information (i.e. rejecting what Freire (1972) described as the "banking" approach to education whereby students are filled with "deposits" of learning; some time later maybe even using them). Teacher Education should be a place where challenging simplistic notions and practices should be normal for it is where the seeds of change for the profession surely reside.

Teacher Education should be a place where the breakthroughs and insights of knowledge and practice in teaching and learning are immediately applicable and constantly questioned and tested. Clearly then, teacher educators carry a heavy responsibility in what they do, how they do it and the manner in which they come to know and develop their own professional knowledge and practice. As Dinkleman *et al.* (2001) suggest, "it is reasonable to believe that the initial experience of doing teacher education is a powerful force in shaping the professional practice of teacher educators over their careers" (p. 49), so making clear the differences between school teaching and teaching about teaching is crucial for creating an environment, expectations and practices that will foster the development of a pedagogy of teacher education.

Teaching: A discipline in its own right?

In the dailiness of school teaching (Loughran and Northfield, 1996), there is little time for teachers to reflect on their practice. There is always another class waiting to be taught and a pile of student work to assess. There is urgency in teaching as lessons are relatively short and classroom management concerns constantly arise requiring careful (and skillful) attention – even though it may not be obvious to the casual observer.

School teachers constantly juggle the needs and concerns of a diverse range of individuals (students, colleagues and administration). There is little downtime in which to withdraw from the hectic pace of schooling as the need to be responsive to the range of demands creates an expectation of immediate action. It can feel as though everything needs to be done "now" as the consequences for being less than well-prepared loom large and are personal. If a lesson is not thought through, if papers have not been corrected, if background research on a topic is not done, then the consequences are experienced immediately and directly by the teacher. Like a spotlight, the harsh glare of the classroom can quickly focus on argument, cross-examination, critique and judgment and create a real sense of stress and tension. Not surprisingly then, the nature of teachers' thinking (Clark and Peterson, 1986) and the myriad of decisions needing to be made keep teachers busy "doing teaching" in order to maintain their students' interest in learning.

It is little wonder then that teachers' professional knowledge is largely tacit such that their skills and knowledge appear to be the result of the accumulation of experience, as routines and procedures are developed and refined over time. However, as has been demonstrated by many researchers (Clandinin and Connelly, 2000, 1995; Cochran-Smith and Lytle, 2004; Hamilton, 2004; Lytle and Cochran-Smith, 1991), such a view ignores (even if inadvertently) the reality of teachers' knowledge as "a fluid, social construction that is more extensive than can be articulated...[it] is elusive because teachers may not have the language to articulate it...[and] Duckworth (1991) points out that teachers seem to lack a seriousness about their knowledge and often do not critically examine it" (Hamilton, 2004, pp. 388–389). Hence, it may well be that arguments surrounding the nature of teachers' professional knowledge are more a reflection of the difficulties associated with uncovering and articulating it in such a way as to fully appreciate that which it genuinely comprises.

Despite the fact that the research literature is replete with a diversity of competing descriptions of teachers' knowledge, little of that research information is of immediate value or use to teachers in the rush and bustle of the dailiness of teaching. Teaching comprises a vast array of skills and knowledge which teachers display but may not so readily recognize in practice. Sadly, this lack of recognition can reinforce the notion of a theory–practice gap and detract from other conceptualizations of teaching implicit in the real working knowledge and skill of the expert pedagogue. Combined with transmissive views of teaching and learning, it is not difficult to see how some may equate teaching with simply doing rather than seeing teaching as being carefully structured, thoughtfully created and deliberately informed in order to engage students in learning for understanding; as opposed to learning by rote.

Perhaps a contributing factor supporting these dichotomous views is caught up in a teacher's need for activities that work. Activities that work may easily be misinterpreted or misrepresented in arguments about the nature of teachers' professional knowledge. Too great a focus on activities can be to the detriment of the pedagogical reasoning that underpins the activities. Yet, students' meaningful learning may well be as a result of the pedagogical reasoning underpinning successful activities while the lack of a shared language of practice may limit broader understanding.

Clearly, teaching, like any other subject or content area, can be delivered as a series of rules, facts and strategies, to be learnt, applied and technically mastered. But, such an approach is to the detriment of teaching itself. However, if teaching is more than simply doing, then teaching about teaching requires an understanding of the complex nature of teaching and learning, unpacking the relationship between each with due reference to theory and practice in ways that does not detract from the impact and value of each on the creation of a wisdom of informed practice. And, it is through the changed conditions and expectations of teaching in a university setting (as opposed to a school) that the possibilities for making such a view more real and alive should emerge – a view whereby theory and practice are partners in knowledge creation, not combatants defending unquestioned or taken-for-granted assumptions and positions.

One way of demonstrating how to unpack the complexity of teaching is through the work of Jeff Northfield (Loughran and Northfield, 1996), an experienced teacher educator who returned to school teaching. Jeff's understanding of the nature of teachers' professional knowledge was from the perspective of both an educational researcher and a high school teacher. Jeff was well aware of the difference between teachers' views of their knowledge (individual, idiosyncratic, context dependent *Personal* knowledge – often seen as low status) and that of educational researchers (abstract, generalizable, verifiable and reliable *Public* knowledge). Through his return to school teaching, he was not only aware of these differences, he also felt them as he experienced the tensions created by each in his own practice:

> While teachers may acknowledge external knowledge as having higher status than their own knowledge, they are quick to point out that educational theories and ideas are often irrelevant in assisting them to address day-to-day concerns. After returning to school teaching I can identify closely with the teacher feelings about the educational knowledge that matters. From the perspective of an educational researcher I had to come to terms with the teacher knowledge I was gaining. It was extremely powerful but closely linked to a particular class of students in particular contexts. It was difficult to analyse and communicate to others. My day-to-day concerns did not seem to fit with the diverse range of ideas and theories I had in my background. . . . the return to teaching was often a confusing and unsettling experience. . . . The dailiness of teaching and its unpredictability appeared to dominate my reflections. . . . I was experiencing the earlier observations made about teachers and their knowledge, yet feeling that I should have been able to better understand and use my experience. I would [now] argue that teacher knowledge has different characteristics in the way it is developed and

used.... [in addition to this it is also important to realize that] students see their schooling experience in different ways to the intended purposes for our [teachers'] classroom activities. (Loughran and Northfield, 1996, pp. 135–136)

What Jeff came to articulate was an understanding of classroom teaching whereby alternative perspectives (particularly students' and teachers') must be apprehended and respected if the dilemmas, issues and concerns of teaching and learning are to be better managed – and managed they must be for, by definition, dilemmas are not resolved. Jeff described this through two alternative views of teaching and learning (Tables 2.1 and 2.2).

The importance of understanding these alternative perspectives is demonstrated through both an ability of the teacher to respond appropriately to students' expectations and responses to pedagogic episodes whilst still helping them to make progress in their learning; despite them often holding contrary views about the very intent of the activities in the first place. To manage the inherent uncertainty of practice created by managing these

Table 2.1 A personal view of teaching and learning

- Where possible, students should have opportunities to be active and think about their learning experiences.
- Students should experience success in learning and gain the confidence and skills to become better learners.
- Linking experiences from both within and outside school greatly assists learning.
- Effort and involvement are important outcomes of school activities and students need to gain credit and encouragement for their efforts.
- Enjoyment and satisfaction with learning are important outcomes.
- Learning involving the above features requires learner consent.

Source: Loughran and Northfield (1996, p. 137).

Table 2.2 Some student views of teaching and learning

- Learning is associated with gaining right answers and thinking and personal understanding are just different and often frustrating ways of achieving the required outcomes.
- The learning process and thinking is difficult to associate with school work, and texts and notes are important indicators that school learning is occurring.
- Linking experiences is very demanding and unreasonable when added to the classroom demands for students.
- The final grade is the critical outcome and the basis by which progress is judged.
- Enjoyment is not always associated with school learning – real learning is hard and not usually enjoyed.
- Learning is done to students and teachers have major responsibility for achieving learning.

Source: Loughran and Northfield (1996, p. 137).

alternative perspectives simultaneously requires a knowledge, understanding and sensitivity to (at least) the environment, the subject matter and the students in such a way as to demonstrate that teaching comprises much more than simply delivering information. Hence, the expert pedagogue must surely display a familiarity with the ability to massage the relationship between teaching and learning in ways that dismiss teaching as telling as a model for practice. Therefore, expert teachers' knowledge of pedagogic cause and effect, the ability to be responsive in the moment to changes in the environment, the amalgamation of content, teaching and learning into a coherent whole, all combined with dealing with a class of individual learners equates with a knowledge of teaching that is real in practice, evolutionary in development and productive in terms of students' learning outcomes. To *teach* about teaching that is conceptualized in this way requires an acute understanding of practice that goes way beyond a store of tips and tricks or the simple delivery of information about teaching.

The research literature demonstrates an enormous array of skills, knowledge, competencies, conceptualizations and practices that have been uncovered as comprising teaching. Beyond these being viewed as checklists for determining technical proficiency, they demonstrate that teaching is complex and messy and that it can be approached, interpreted and practiced in a diversity of ways, any of which when used by a skilled teacher may lead to successful learning outcomes for students. It is not difficult to see that teaching can be viewed as comprising a knowledge of theory in and through practice and that each gently moulds the other in the creation of purposeful pedagogical experiences. The ability to make all of this clear and helpful to students of teaching through the experiences of teaching and learning in teacher education requires a genuine scholarship of teacher education and demands much more than simply "demonstrating good teaching."

In teaching about teaching, the fundamental specialization that must consistently be displayed, practiced and developed is the teacher educator's advanced knowledge of the field of teaching: "the content of teacher education is teaching – a subject matter area with very different characteristics than content such as mathematics" (Richardson, 1997, p. 11). If advanced knowledge of the field of teaching is to be recognized, encouraged and developed, then practices of teacher preparation cannot be conceptualized in terms of teacher training, they must be based on notions of teacher education.

Knowing yourself: Questioning assumptions

Many teacher preparation programs begin with activities designed to help students of teaching begin to reflect on the manner in which they personally respond to ideas, issues and events. In essence, there is a purposeful focus on encouraging novices to begin to "better know themselves." One reason for drawing attention to "knowing oneself" is linked to the maxim: "by better knowing yourself you are more likely to know how to help others" and, in teaching, there is little doubt that helping others is fundamental to enhancing students' learning.

Brookfield (1995) outlined in detail not only the value of "learning to know ourselves" but also the ways in which such learning might be encouraged. Like Cole and Knowles (1998a), he made a strong case for learning to trust in personal experience as a way of developing insights into knowledge, or, as Beck *et al.* (2004) suggested: "Coming to understand one's own life history is essential in grasping what one believes and why in making appropriate modifications to one's beliefs and practices" (p. 1261). In teacher education, such views are consistently put forward as being important in shaping the learning about teaching of our students of teaching. It stands to reason then that they must also be important in shaping teacher educators' learning of teaching about teaching.

Knowing ourselves means searching for, revealing and, "owning" up to the assumptions and taken-for-granted aspects of practice that quietly lurk in the depths of our subconscious; but quickly surface through the ways in which we teach. Such assumptions are not always so readily apparent to us because they are often implicit rather than intentional in our actions; observers see them in our actions more easily than we see them in ourselves. Therefore, there is a need to learn to be conscious of our assumptions and to confront them in real ways.

Trumbull (2004) captures the essence of the difficulties created by our often hidden assumptions in teacher education practices and the manner in which they imply particular views about knowledge, learning and schooling. Through the use of five adages she offered a framework for identifying and spelling out ways of thinking about teacher education:

- Good teachers are born not made.
- Experience is the best teacher.
- Good teachers have been trained to master the proper techniques.
- Good teachers are those who best facilitate learning.
- Carefully structured and analyzed experiences produce the best teachers.

Trumbull describes the first two adages as conservative for they limit what teacher educators need to do (can do?) by imposing a predisposition to teaching and minimizing the value, or impact, of any theoretical framework on teaching. Therefore, these first two adages carry the assumption that all that teacher educators need to do is to "spot talent" and "place it in the right environment" so that that talent can grow to meet its preordained potential. Obviously then, such an assumption also suggests that there is little need to concentrate any attention on teaching about teaching for it would have little impact on development, as development itself presupposes a linear path which the capable can follow – with minimal need for assistance.

The adage "Good teachers have been trained to master the proper techniques" carries an assumption that technical training in the use of particular skills and procedures guarantees successful student learning outcomes. Clearly, implicit in this adage is the assumption that teacher educators are expert trainers and that their role is to appropriately prepare beginning teachers with the most up-to-date teaching procedures and correct "tips and tricks." Accompanying this is the weight of expectations on students of teaching and teacher educators alike that at the completion of teacher preparation, beginning teachers will be fully prepared for all the challenges that teaching will offer up. A difficulty with this is related to Freire's (1972) critique of the "banking" model of teaching – an assumption being that the "deposits" of learning might one day be drawn upon and used (with interest!). Thus, this adage also offers a view of teaching and teacher education that is quite limited, reliant on teaching as a *solely* systematic process (although it does at least suggest that there is something teacher educators can do to assist in the developmental process).

Trumbull describes her final two adages ("good teachers are facilitators of student learning;" "carefully structured and analyzed experiences produce the best teachers") as reforming views although she highlights concerns related to the likely proliferation of the theory–practice gap through the assumptions underpinning each. For example, with regard to teachers as facilitators she notes: "it is not clear how teacher educators can help their students learn to implement these reforms...there is some tendency to focus on helping students understand pupil learning in all its complexity, which entails a thorough grasp of content areas and learning theory and research... [but] imagines teacher education as a highly intellectual enterprise in which experts well grounded in current theories...help learners to understand the theories. The assumption is that students will then use these theories to guide their actions....Indeed, the theory–practice distinction has not worked in teacher education" (pp. 1214–1215).

She also draws attention to the manner in which theory and practice might be conceptualized through the final adage whereby Korthagen *et al.*'s (2001) explication of episteme and phronesis is seen as helpful in understanding learning through experience. However, she makes it clear that one is not necessarily more important than the other and that it is essential to recognize that: "[This adage] emphasizes experience, but emphasizes equally systematic thinking about experience. The addition of an emphasis on phronesis helps us to think about the design of teacher education programs and about how teacher educators can structure the reflection central to this view. This adage also suggests the complexity of scholarship in teacher education" (pp. 1215–1216).

The importance of thinking about the interconnectedness of assumptions, beliefs and practices through adages is not an attempt to assign blame to particular positions, or to suggest that "choosing correctly" from the possibilities will resolve the tensions and dilemmas of teaching about teaching. Rather, it is to draw attention to the fact that many views of teaching and teacher education are underpinned by assumptions that can surface in practice in ways that may inadvertently limit our intentions for, and responses to, students' learning. Further to this, it is not as if our assumptions themselves comprise a simple choice between competing alternatives (an either/or position). Rather, it is that the extremes are easier to recognize and characterize yet such a simple differentiation (either/or) may be to the detriment of the possibilities along the continuum between. The reality is that depending on the context, we may move between the extremes along the continuum. Therefore, knowing "where we are" at a given time in a given context – while experiencing given pressures, tensions or dilemmas – is important in shaping how we might respond to (and in) situations so that our assumptions do not blindly lead our practice.

It is not difficult to envisage instances in which each of Trumbull's adages quickly spring to life in response to various situations. For example, in teaching about teaching, teacher educators are consistently confronted by those students of teaching who are already well aware of their strengths as presenters and who are more than capable of capturing their students' attention. At such times, it is easy to inadvertently fall back on the "born teacher" adage and be influenced by the hidden assumptions that implicitly accompany that position. Therefore, considering the implicit assumptions which underpin these adages, and others, is important in really "knowing oneself" for they become starkly apparent when teaching about teaching. Clearly, the link between assumptions and practice is significant and requires careful attention in teacher education practices.

Using the lens of critical reflection, Brookfield (1995) offered interesting insights into the influence of assumptions on practice:

> One of the hardest things teachers have to learn is that the sincerity of their intentions does not guarantee the purity of their practice … and the way power complicates all human relationships (including those between students and teachers) mean that teaching can never be innocent. Teaching innocently means thinking that we're always understanding exactly what it is that we're doing and what effect we're having. Teaching innocently means assuming that the meanings and significance we place on our actions are the ones that students take from them. … In many ways we *are* our assumptions [emphasis in original]. Assumptions give meaning and purpose to who we are and what we do. Becoming aware of the implicit assumptions that frame how we think and act is one of the most challenging intellectual puzzles we face in our lives. It is also something we instinctively resist, for fear of what we might discover. Who wants to clarify and question assumptions she or he has lived by for a substantial period of time, only to find that they don't make sense? What makes the process of assumption hunting particularly complicated is that assumptions are not all of the same character. (pp. 1–2)

As Brookfield makes clear, unquestioned taken-for-granted aspects of our practice can convey messages that are not intended. For example, behind the practice of running an interpretive discussion may be the teaching view that students need to hear their own and others' ideas out loud in order to reconsider and construct their own position; or that putting up and defending arguments between peers minimizes the power relationship between the teacher and the students; or, withholding the teacher's opinion discourages passive compliance – the game of "guess what's in the teacher's head." However, from a student's perspective, it is not difficult to see how interpretive discussions could be viewed as unstructured tasks designed to consume time in order to cover the teacher's lack of knowledge or uncertainty about "what to do and where to go" in a pedagogic situation. The assumptions underpin each perspective matter not in terms of which is right or wrong, they matter in terms of recognition of the possibility that each (and indeed others) exist. Again, in teaching about teaching, being able to bring assumptions to the surface and to confront them in meaningful ways is one way of jointly exploring the complexity of teaching while simultaneously inviting a questioning of the likely misunderstandings associated with "allocating" intentions to actions. In developing a pedagogy of teacher education, it is essential that such practice be continually pursued.

Experience precedes understanding

It is a curious thing in teacher education that although the place of experience is seen as central *to* learning it can equally be argued that experience is also easily mistaken *as* learning. Perhaps the assumption that learning occurs in experience sometimes masks the reality so that there is an expectation that a *good* experience is a *learning* experience and, that by setting up appropriate experiences, the learning will take care of itself.

Long ago Dewey (1938) drew attention to the need for experience to be seen as a shaping force in the development of thoughtful and alert students of education as opposed to an entrée to a rudimentary proficiency in teaching. He also highlighted the danger of confusing experience with education when he noted that: "the belief that all genuine education comes about through experience does not mean that all experiences are genuinely or equally educative. Experience and education cannot be directly equated to each other" (p. 25). Therefore, just as it is important to pay attention to the relationship between experience and learning with regard to the programmatic features of teacher education (something which is considered in more detail in Part II of this book), it is equally important to make similar links in the teaching in teacher education.

Clarke and Erickson (2004), in reconsidering Schwab's contribution to curriculum and pedagogical practices (see for example Schwab (1978) in Westbury and Wilkof's (1987) *Joseph J Schwab: Science, curriculum, and liberal education – selected essays*), intimate the centrality of the nature of learning *through* experience when they state:

> Schwab's enduring focus on the importance of dialogue and deliberation stems from his strong commitment to action accompanied by reflection on those actions...[and] although he claimed that the reflective process could be accomplished at the individual level, he argued that the deliberation within a 'learning community' was a more powerful means for generating the necessary insights to deal with many educational problems....He wrote about the 'situated nature of curriculum knowledge' and the crucial role of teacher as an active creator of knowledge... [whereby] the complexity of translating curricular intents into classroom actions and practices led him to propose the four 'commonplaces' of pedagogical practice – the learner, the teacher, the educational milieu, and the subject matter. (pp. 204–205)

Teacher educators' knowledge of, and familiarity with, the four commonplaces of pedagogical practice are important in shaping learning through experience not only for students of teaching but also for teacher educators. In so doing, it is not *just* the experience that matters, it is the learning through experience that needs to be reflected upon and shared, as the nature of the deliberations within the teacher education learning community is critical to the development of a pedagogy of teacher education.

Clarke and Erickson (2004) take this point further by suggesting that self-study of teacher education practices should be viewed as the fifth commonplace. In so doing, they draw attention not only to the place of experience in teaching about teaching, but also to the importance of sustained inquiry into practice, which begs the question: "What is in the nature of experience that might warrant such careful attention and what outcomes might be insightful for teaching about teaching?" One possible response is explored through the following vignette.

Learning to make the abstract concrete

As a science teacher educator I was concerned to teach my student teachers in ways that did not reinforce the traditional "science is all about facts and figures" approach that they had all no doubt experienced – and probably successfully mastered, through their own schooling. I had lots of interesting teaching procedures that, when used with appropriate science content, could engage them in learning and for the most part, they (and I), found these activities to be quite entertaining and seemingly useful in their learning to teach science.

Even though I thought I taught these procedures quite well, I was not consciously aware of the fact that I was not really a part of the learning when using these procedures. I was very familiar (and comfortable) with what was happening during these teaching episodes and so was not really personally confronted by either the intellectual or pedagogical challenges inherent in the use of the procedures – I did the teaching, my students did the learning.

One of these activities was the use of role-plays. I had set up situations for my student teachers to act out role-plays a number of times – although I was not all that keen on them myself – because I thought it was important for them to experience this teaching procedure. Maybe somewhere in the back of mind I thought I was dutifully completing that part of the teacher education curriculum described as "introducing student teachers to a range of innovative teaching approaches." Anyway, whatever the reason (intended or not), I directed the role-play episode and observed my student teachers "doing the learning."

One session that is vividly etched in my mind was the time I decided to use a role-play that I hadn't used before. I had noticed that, in the past, most of the role-plays only involved a small number of students and so I was conscious of the need to have more participants involved in doing things – to have less observing with no specified task to complete.

At the time, I was involved in a project that was documenting exemplary science teaching and so decided to use a role-play from that project that I knew would involve the whole class. On paper it was a good role-play. It ensured that all students did something and in our research group we had had some interesting discussions about the activity. Therefore, I felt relatively confident that I could successfully teach this particular role-play to my class.

The role-play was designed to explore the way the Moon revolves around the Earth. I remembered that one of my colleagues had made a big point of the difference between the Moon *revolving* around the Earth as opposed to it *rotating* on its axis. It seemed a big point at the time, one of those "scientific language" issues, so I was sensitized to something that was apparently an important learning point for my class.

I started off in the normal way by getting students' prior views, listing them on the board, pushing and probing their ideas and generally trying to create a sense of interest in the topic. That went well, as expected – after all it was the very approach to introducing a new topic that I had always modelled and encouraged my student teachers to use.

The next phase was to set up the problem. This was not difficult either, it was something like: "The Moon rotates on its axis once during its revolution of the Earth, so how is that we only ever see the same face?" I'm not sure that before encountering this role-play I was ever aware of this myself (at least not beyond some esoteric link to my childhood and Pink Floyd's Dark Side of the Moon), so at first I think it probably made me stop and think, but not for too long as the problem was directed at the class (not me as the teacher). Besides, I was already fully occupied in teaching as I expertly stumbled through a teaching procedure (that I usually did not like) in a content area (with which I was unfamiliar).

Acknowledging to myself that the increasing pressure I was under in the class was due to the barrage of students' questions about procedures (that were all new to me), actions and reactions to what was happening, it finally dawned on me that we had to go outside if we were to have enough space to do the role-play; we would never manage the role-play in the confines of the classroom.

"Phew, some breathing space at last." I thought as we meandered down the corridor on our way outside.

When we spread out under the Oak trees next to the Faculty I quickly organized everybody into their positions. I knew it couldn't be too hard. All I needed was a small group (4–5 students) to make a circle by linking their arms while standing back to back – so that they would all be looking outwards – that group would be the Moon. Then the same formation was needed for the remainder of the students and they would be the Earth. So far, so good.

"O.K. Earth, start revolving (or should that be rotating? A little quiver in my voice." I wondered if anyone noticed!). "Let's see how that goes." I said. The role-play had begun.

It was a bit messy so I told the Earth to rotate a little more slowly. This was met by complaints about the pace of rotations necessary for them to manage a month in the time that the Moon would take to get back to its starting point – 28 rotations.

"Hmm! I hadn't thought about that. Did it really matter?" I wondered to myself. "You'll work something out." I blithely responded.

"Now Moon, start a revolution around the Earth, but while you do it, you have to organise yourselves to do only one rotation on your own axis. So Janet, from where you are now, you need to be facing the Earth again when you get back to that spot. Put a mark on the ground so you know where that will be. O.K., off you go." I said with great confidence.

I stood back and watched the role-play unfold. As the Moon slowly rotated in its revolution of the Earth I tried to visualize how it could be that if it rotated only once on its axis that only one side of the Moon would be seen from the Earth. I couldn't do it though. I just could not manipulate that in my mind to understand how it could be possible. But as I stood there watching it, I could see it happening before me. The abstract became very concrete.

When the Moon arrived back at its starting point I asked how the role-play had worked – I was now moving away from the prescribed script; my curiosity piqued. Liz (a part of the Earth) and Athena (a part of the Moon) said they didn't get it. Having just watched it unfold before me, I decided that they would "get it" if they could see it happening so

I got them to stand out and watch while we repeated the role-play and I took Athena's place in the Moon.

As the role-play unfolded again, I actually felt what it was like to be the "dark side" of the Moon and although in my mind I still couldn't really visualize what was happening, being a part of the action made it very real for me. Suddenly I got what it meant to be involved in a role-play. Suddenly I saw a number of important pedagogical insights. Suddenly content matter started to take new shape as a developing understanding slowly emerged. Suddenly, our class became alive with learning; and I was part of it.

Together we pushed around ideas about teaching and learning as new and interesting insights into the nature of role-play became clear to all of us. Questions, issues and ideas about astronomy were also initiated and different role-plays were envisaged as the students discussed the fundamentals of this approach in relation to other topics (summer and winter; day and night, etc.).

After the class I mused over the episode again. I reflected on the previous weeks and how in the research group we had discussed this role-play when considering it for inclusion in the "exemplary practice folder." At the time, I was satisfied with my grasp of the ideas – I was certainly able to suggest advice for other teachers about how they could use the role-play and the value it offered as a teaching and learning tool. However, what I knew – or thought I knew – before the experience was dramatically different to what I knew after the experience. Being involved in the experience was different to directing it for others. Abstracting the learning from this experience to other situations was intellectually challenging and engaging. What I saw in my students' approach to learning about teaching was new and different. What I began to see in teaching about teaching was a revelation. What I previously knew, I now understood.

Although it appears obvious that understanding is enhanced through experience, it is curious how often in teaching information is substituted for experience. More so, although the value of experience is commonly acknowledged, there seems to be an implicit view that such experience is for the students, not for the teacher. The vignette (above) illustrates how important experience was for the teacher educator and how understanding emerged as a result of the experience. Knowing about role-play was not sufficient to teach about role-play. Experiencing teaching using role-play and being a learner in a role-play created a situation in which new understandings of teaching about teaching were catalyzed.

Recognition of the place of experience in *learning* about teaching about teaching which, as Clarke and Erickson (2004) suggest is enhanced through the fifth commonplace (self-study), carries with it an invitation to teacher educators to purposefully study *their* teaching and learning about teaching.

However, perhaps an invitation might be accepted only if, through experiences such as those portrayed in the vignette, they are valued for the possibilities they create for reframing teaching about teaching for the problem needs to be apprehended if the situation is to be an impetus for inquiry.

It seems reasonable to suggest that inquiry into one's own teaching about teaching shapes one's understanding of the nature of a pedagogy of teacher education. Examples of such inquiry are demonstrated through the work of many involved in self-study (Fitzgerald *et al.*, 2002; Pereira, 2000; Schuck and Segal, 2002) whereby their own inquiries into their own classrooms have led to new understandings of their own practice.

Clift (2004) describes self-study research as:

> important to teacher educators seeking to improve their practice and to understand their students' learning. In some instances, it is also an important contribution to understanding overall program impact and how the program and its intentions have evolved over the years. And, to the degree that the similar studies might be aggregated over time, we may be able to derive a common understanding about the nature and influence of selected pedagogies, curricula, and philosophies within similar courses. (p. 1362)

With these purposes and benefits in mind, the following brief glimpse of one self-study is offered to help demonstrate how learning *about* teaching about teaching might be enhanced; especially when embedded in personal experience. In the following self-study, experience well and truly preceded understanding and, the teacher educator accepted the challenges created as a result of allowing an experience to direct his inquiry.

Dinkleman (1999) was teaching a social studies course when he was confronted by the following:

> as the class moved away from a discussion of the appointed topic, multicultural education, and toward a forum for airing grievances with the course, one class member began her contribution by saying, "I don't feel safe in this classroom...." and burst into tears. I was taken aback... That our classroom had become a less than welcoming environment for some was an unsettling sentiment I had detected in the prior weeks, but try as I might to figure out what was so threatening about our class, I had few answers. (p. 1)

There may be many ways one might react to a situation such as the one which confronted Dinkleman; no doubt responses surge forth quickly in the reader. Not surprisingly, the experience was somewhat troubling and lingering in his mind. Then, two months later, during a research interview with a student, he inquired as to why some students did not feel safe to speak their mind in his class. To his absolute surprise, he was informed about the manner in which some students interpreted his "look." They saw it as judgmental and therefore found it very difficult to honestly offer their point of view during class discussion. "I was stunned. This response was truly a revelation to me. Promotion of open discourse was, and is, one of the most valued objectives of my teaching, one that I was unknowingly squelching" (p. 2). He pushed a little further, checking with others and found that the problem truly was linked to students' interpretation of one element of his "style" as a teacher. However, he could not leave it at that because he was shocked into action.

Dinkleman's beliefs and his practice were in conflict; what he intended and what was happening were two different things. As a result of the subsequent self-study he came to see, and respond, to issues and concerns that he previously could not see from his very personal teacher perspective. Had he not had the experience of the student speaking up in class the way she did, he may not have been so receptive to the possibility of there being any incongruity between his practice and his beliefs. If he had not taken the experience and pursued a purposeful inquiry into his teaching he would not have come to understand the nature of interactions within his classes, nor would he have so readily come to learn about the influence of his teacher behaviors on his students' learning.

What he knew about teacher–student interactions before this episode was dramatically different from what he understood afterwards. His experience preceded his understanding. But, it was only because he was receptive to the experience, it was only because he accepted the learning challenge created that his learning about teaching was enhanced. No doubt, Dinkleman came to see his pedagogy of teacher education very differently through his personal and confronting experience. How many such possibilities might we not grasp because in our own teaching about teaching we are not sufficiently sensitive to, or prepared to pursue, inquiries into our own practice?

Dinkleman's learning episode is a reminder to all involved in teaching about teaching just how important it is to question the taken for granted; to be conscious of one's own teaching behaviors; to be a part of the teaching and learning situations with students of teaching; and, to constantly be reminded that the teacher is also a learner. It is through experiences within our own classes that we might begin to value our own developing professional knowledge of teaching about teaching so that we might begin to recognize the importance and value of a pedagogy of teacher education; initially for ourselves, but ultimately for the profession.

Overview

Teaching in any field (e.g. science, history, law, language) should encourage students to dissect and analyze the assumptions, practices and structures that together form the basis of that discipline's approach to the construction and use of knowledge. More than any other field though, the teaching of teaching must not only encourage such an approach, it should overtly display it in practice. There should be an expectation that students of teaching will critically examine their teacher educators' practice and that they will see that their teacher educators similarly examine their own practice.

In developing a pedagogy of teacher education, there is a crucial need to look beyond the ability to perform particular skills and procedures and to aim to critique and analyze the nature of practice in both teachers and students of teaching. Such a stance though requires a need to accept that it carries inherent vulnerability because learning through such means is a risky business. However, if teacher educators do not see teaching as comprising specialized skills, knowledge and practice; if there is not a serious commitment to confront one's own assumptions in order to better align actions and beliefs; and, if the possibilities for understanding derived from experience are not purposefully sought and grasped, then there is little likelihood that teacher education will be more than the transmission of information about practice and the pursuit of technical competency.

Teacher education should be a crucible in which the very practice of teaching *and* learning about teaching is the source of sustained inquiry and development. Exposing one's vulnerability in learning is central to developing practice. It is essential for students of teaching in learning about teaching and is crucial for teacher educators in learning about teaching about teaching. As a consequence, the recognition of, and responses to, the problematic nature of teaching will nurture the growth of a pedagogy of teacher education.

3 Teaching: A problematic enterprise

I can see important changes that have occurred in my practice as a result of confronting the gaps between my rhetoric and the reality of my teaching.... The process of coming to terms with teaching dilemmas is, of course, never-ending. I believe it is important for those of us who say we want to prepare teachers who are reflective practitioners to make more visible to our students our deliberations about our own work. They can then see 'up front' how a teacher experiences the inevitable contradictions and tensions of the work and goes about trying to learn from his or her teaching experience ... We all know that both teaching and teacher education are much more complex than they are often made out to be. We ought to let our stories about our work as teacher educators appear to others to be as complex as they really are.

(Zeichner, 1995, pp. 20–21)

Teaching is problematic. On the surface, teaching can appear to be a well ordered, technically proficient and purposefully directed routine, but, as so much of the growing teacher research literature demonstrates, when teaching is unpacked by teachers, when *their* voice prevails, then the constant undercurrent of choices, decisions, competing concerns, dilemmas and tensions are made clear for all to see. Despite the thoughtful planning that goes into teaching, the very act of teaching churns up the waters of learning and creates situations that, although perhaps able to be anticipated, are not able to be fully addressed until they arise in practice. The image of an "indeterminate swampy zone" (Schön, 1983) conjures up a strong picture of the world of practice. "It is a complex and messy terrain, often difficult to [map and] describe" (Berry, 2004a, p. 1312).

Myers and Simpson (1998) consider that much of what teachers learn about teaching is "by teaching and from teaching," because the range of experiences that comprise teaching are "logged intellectually into a teacher's conceptual framework and built into his or her personalized professional set of knowledge, skills and values" (p. 58). Thus the very nature of teaching and learning to teach is dominated by the journey along an individual path whereby development and growth is dependent on what that person sees and understands as important to his or her practice at that time. Therefore, the time, effort and energy that an individual devotes to inquiry into practice; to discovering new ways of seeing situations; to testing out alternative approaches; and, to understanding teaching and learning from both a teacher's and a learner's perspective, is a matter of choice.

The choice as to how much and/or what to focus on, though, will be dependent on many things, but one thing most central to the array of possibilities is that which the teacher sees as being problematic – for there is clearly little likelihood of paying attention to that which does not appear to need attention. This means then that "teacher learning and professional practice fit better the idea of teaching as a never-ending process of investigating and experimenting, reflecting and analysing what one does in the classroom and school, formulating one's own personal professional theories and using these theories to guide future practice, and deciding what and how to teach based on one's best personal professional judgment" (Myers and Simpson, 1998, p. 58). If such a view of teaching prevails, then a number of important aspects of practice require careful attention in order that some way into and out of the swampy lowland might be possible. And, so that the journey itself might be purposeful, professionally satisfying and educative.

Being sensitive to the problematic

One difficulty with conceptualizing teaching as being problematic is that, for novices, the messiness, the apparent lack of a clear path, and the reliance on individuals to accept responsibility for directing their own learning about teaching can be an impediment. This impediment may create a yearning for a much simpler solution in order to fashion a sense of control over the impending uncertainty of teaching. Avoiding the urge to seek a simple solution to a complex problem is difficult but is crucial in working with teaching as being problematic. Seeing teaching as problematic means that the swamp becomes intellectually challenging and practically engaging so that mapping its terrain becomes professionally rewarding. It is a process through which teachers learn to adapt, adjust and construct approaches to teaching and learning in the ongoing quest to be better informed about practice. It is a quest which ebbs and flows, is sometimes demanding, may sometimes appear simple and routine, but is always present because almost regardless of the outcome of a teaching experience, teaching itself is never completely successful. Again, for the novice, such a view of practice may be far from comforting, but when realized and accepted, opens up a new vista that can be encouraging, inviting and professionally affirming. For the individual, taking the risk to seek to explore answers to the questions yet to be asked can be quite intimidating, yet enlivening and rewarding; especially when considered in retrospect. For example, consider the following *case* (an abbreviated form of the original) of a student of teaching embarking on an approach to teaching that challenged her more traditional view of "teacher as expert telling while students listen."

What do I do with all these questions?

I am sitting in a Year 11 Chemistry class at the beginning of my third and final teaching round. My supervising teacher is tying up a few loose ends and I am due to "go on" in a few minutes....I am using all the techniques I have at my disposal to overcome my nervousness. "Just take it a step at a time, get through the beginning, stand up, introduce yourself, hand out the notes, pray for a miracle."...It's none of the usual things that make the palms of a student teacher sweaty, it's as simple as these notes in front of me....These notes are class handouts... interspersed with "thinking tasks" designed to encourage student processing, further questions and comments, and connections to other content....The difficulty is that I don't know what to do next. The students have all the information they need in front of them and there doesn't seem to be much left for me to do. I feel obsolete, unnecessary, superfluous....To make things worse, I've seen these guys in action. They take nothing for granted. I feel that if I make a suspicious sounding statement, they'll question it, or if I make a reasonable sounding statement, they question that too...my subconscious view of the role of teacher is still purely to stand up and impart irrefutable truths. [However], when the students have all the content on paper [as they have now], the role seems challenged and diminished.

Luckily these students...define my role for me, by generating discussions, questioning content and making associations with theory and their own experiences. Their behaviour allows me to fit into the classroom. The very things I had feared make this class work. I become a mediator, a clarifier and a learner....Many times the direction of a discussion is dictated by the type of questions that are asked and answered by the students. My presence is often only necessary to keep the lesson channelled in the right direction....This is not to say this style of teaching is easy. It is a difficult and demanding format in which to teach, but it is also very satisfying....They move very quickly from one idea to the next, often far more quickly than is comfortable for me....I learn to rely on an often under-used classroom asset, the students.

Obaidullah is a fabulous student to have in this type of classroom situation....We are discussing the "Greenhouse Effect", a topic that at first seems quite straightforward. Laurie is asking about radiation heating the atmosphere. Whatever my answer to his question is, it is not satisfactory, and he keeps asking. I keep re-phrasing my answer, but I'm obviously missing the point. Finally Obaidullah answers in a far more satisfactory manner. In hindsight, I realise that I was not actually listening to what Laurie was saying. This meant that I was answering without understanding or addressing the reasoning that had led to the question....The discussion continues with the types of comments and questions that give an indication of how the students are progressing and what misconceptions they have.

Incidents of this sort could be seen as undermining my control or authority, or as a threat to my role as a "teacher." ...but I must admit I did not perceive them as such. The class format is one that is challenging and demanding, but also one I find desirable. [In my pre-service teacher preparation program] we had spoken many times about approaches like this, but they often seemed abstract, or suited only to experienced teachers. It was a welcome feeling to realise that these things are quite attainable and workable. (Fox, 1997, pp. 45–47)

Cases (Shulman, 1992) are structured around the tensions and dilemmas that teachers experience in their own teaching. In so doing, they invite inquiry into the diversity of possibilities and responses inherent in the problematic situations that arise in teaching and learning. Alternative interpretations to (and within) a case are important in affirming the personal autonomy crucial to understanding teaching as professional practice. By creating opportunities for questioning the taken for granted, cases acknowledge the complexities intrinsic to teaching. As windows into reality, cases help to frame the problematic as liberating; the possibility for learning more about teaching emerges through the diversity of others' experiences. Cases therefore offer ways of articulating the problematic and highlight the importance of seeing into teaching and learning situations in a variety of ways.

Recognizing and building on that which is problematic in practice can be enhanced through what Mason (2002) describes as noticing. An important aspect of noticing is the realization that a situation may not *really* be seen until it is seen differently and so noticing is important in helping to see into practice in such a way. Further to this, for the observant teacher, the ongoing interaction of the myriad aspects of practice (for example, the influence of Schwab's (1978) "commonplaces") suggests that despite superficial commonalities, teaching is rarely the same thing; thus further highlighting the importance of recognizing that teaching is being problematic.

At the heart of all practice lies noticing: noticing an opportunity to act appropriately. To notice an opportunity to act requires three things: being present and sensitive to the moment, having reason to act, and having a different act come to mind. Consequently, one important aspect of being professional is noticing possible acts to try out in the future... A second important aspect is working on becoming more articulate and more precise about reasons for acting. The mark of an expert is that they are sensitised to notice things which novices overlook. They have finer discernment. They make things look easy, because they have a refined sensitivity to professional situations and a rich collection of responses on which to draw. Among other things, experts are aware of their actions... (Mason, 2002, p. 1)

Mason draws attention to the importance of learning from (and through) experience and in so doing illustrates one outcome of such learning – that the "expert makes things look easy." Because some aspects of teaching may look easy, the novice may be lulled into a false sense of security whereby the simple response of developing routines and patterns that mimic the expert's practice may be misconstrued as offering certainity about that which is inherently uncertain; it just does not look that way at the time.

In Fox's case (above), the approach she implemented in her teaching was not necessarily her choice; at least, not her first choice. She had been asked to teach the way she did, to prepare students' work with thinking tasks and to accept the uncertainty of the role that she was about to embark upon. Perhaps, had she written another case about observing a more experienced teacher teaching in a similar manner, it would have been very different, for, as an observer, the teaching may have appeared quite simple to her, that is the teacher prepares the work, allows the students to engage in the task and answers questions. However, through her case, we are given access to her thoughts and feelings as she moves through a seemingly simple process; a process that is far less simple when doing it than it might appear when only observing it. Therefore, Fox's case illustrates well that that which might appear simple can be quite complex, and in teaching, there is little doubt that looking beneath the surface quickly illustrates the real complexity of professional practice.

A focus on complexity: From teaching to teacher education

With so many different things able to be "noticed" in teaching, it can be very difficult to narrow one's focus to just one or two things that might be more easily seen and appreciated (or one or two things that particularly capture one's attention). However, by narrowing the focus on what to notice, some of the complexity of teaching might be peeled back so that one or two isolated aspects of practice might be better analyzed and acted upon thus helping one accept (rather than overlook) the complexity of the big picture whilst maintaining a view of teaching as holistic practice.

One way of conceptualizing complexity in teaching is through a consideration of a systems approach whereby:

> The behaviour of a system is not due to linear cause and effect relationships between independent elements, instead, the behaviour of a system is caused by *non-linear* interactions because of the interrelationships that exist among a combination of elements and groups of elements. Because of this dynamism, the behaviour of a system is difficult and sometimes impossible to predict. . . . Change in a complex system results in dynamic interactions because of a special balance point between chaos and order that has been called the *edge of chaos*, . . . [which] is

when creativity occurs as people experiment with ideas and attempt to change the balance of a complex system. In sum, both chaotic and complex systems display non-linear interactions due to their interrelationships, but a complex system is more likely to develop a sense of order because it carries information within it, although this is not always the case. This does not mean, however, that complex systems can be controlled, rather, they are more inclined to be influenced and managed than chaotic systems. (Hoban, 2002, pp. 23–24, emphasis in original)

Hoban applied a systems approach to teacher learning and demonstrated well how teaching can, or perhaps should, be viewed as a complex system. In many ways, his point about differentiating between control and management is important in thinking about coming to understand the complexity of teaching for it is in managing the many inter-relationships in a pedagogic situation that the skill, knowledge, ability and professional autonomy of teachers comes to the fore. And, it is this management that elicits possibilities for understanding teaching as being problematic and stands in stark contrast to the transmissive approach which is so dependent upon control.

Fox's case illustrates this point well. It demonstrates her thoughts, feelings and actions and how she came to learn about managing the problematic nature of the teaching approach in which she was engaged. She was not able to control it, but she was able to manage it and, in managing rather than controlling, her appreciation of the learning outcomes for both her teaching and her students' learning was considerably enhanced.

Just as understanding teaching is linked to a recognition of the problematic, so too teaching about teaching is equally demanding. For the novice teacher there is a need to see into practice with new eyes, to be open to the possibilities that can emerge when inter-related aspects of practice collide, interact and are brought into sharp focus. In the same way as the novice teacher needs to be sensitive to releasing control in order to manage the complexity of teaching, so too teacher educators need to depart from their well-marked path and approach the *edge of chaos* in order to re-embrace the creativity, experimentation and risk-taking that so shapes a developing understanding of pedagogy.

Teaching about teaching therefore hinges on: supporting students of teaching as they learn to be comfortable about progressively relinquishing control in order to learn to better manage the many competing aspects of teaching through engaging with the problematic; while at the same time, responding similarly to the very same situation in one's own practice. In many ways, seeing anew what one already sees is one way of managing the complexity of teaching about teaching as it requires a familiarity with practice in concert with maintaining a distance from practice in order to see what is happening while it is happening.

Questioning the taken for granted: Learning more about pedagogy

As noted earlier, the teacher research literature is replete with examples of how teachers inquire into, and therefore learn more about, their own teaching. In many ways, it is because teacher researchers see practice as problematic that their inquiries are initiated. They do not usually seek to know "what works best" (and by extension can therefore be generalized and applied henceforth), rather they anticipate increasing their wealth of knowledge about a situation and therefore aim to become better informed about possibilities and ways of acting and responding pedagogically. For example, consider the learning about teaching of many of the PAVOT (Perspective and Voice of the Teacher, see Loughran *et al.*, 2002) teachers. As a result of looking into their classrooms in different ways and seeking data that might shed new light on their teaching, three types of outcomes were apparent across all of their research projects. They were that they:

- challenged their common practice and developed new conceptions of what was possible;
- developed greater understandings of student learning and of student change; and,
- developed new teaching practices.

Challenging existing practice

In challenging their existing practice, the teacher researchers in PAVOT were drawn to puzzling or curious aspects of *their* teaching and *their* responses involved considerable risks; however, there were risks that they considered well worth taking. In examining their existing practice they were able to stand aside from their normal teaching routine and critique their pedagogy. Based on what they considered to be credible and convincing data, new insights were developed. Consequently, meaningful change to practice was initiated as teaching intentions and outcomes were better aligned and the value of pedagogical reasoning and understanding emerged in new and helpful ways. Hence, their professional knowledge became more explicit and the problematic became more obvious, intellectually engaging and manageable.

Student learning and change

In developing greater understandings of student learning and student change, the teacher researchers in PAVOT chose to know what was, and was not, happening in their classes from a student's perspective. They came to see some of the barriers to learning that students face and in so doing, developed a more sophisticated understanding of what might constitute reasonable expectations about student change and the rate of change. Interestingly, they also became much more aware of the lack of learning that occurred in what, hitherto, they had regarded as good teaching and learning episodes. In addition, this focus on learning also enhanced the confidence and support necessary for the increased risk-taking and perseverance necessary to pursue the changes in conditions crucial to enhanced learning outcomes.

Developing new practices

The development of new practices is an outcome of the desire to improve. However, it is not simply improvement for improvement's sake. Rather it is improvement as a result of adapting, adjusting and developing practice in ways that are responsive to a (new) sense of dissatisfaction with existing procedures and routines; new understandings of learning and change therefore impact understandings of what to do and how to do it in both new and familiar circumstances. The articulation of new practices comprises that which might be described as practically sophisticated knowledge and can act as a compass to offer direction (but not prescribe the route) in traversing the swamp and, eventually, enhance possibilities for individual mapping.

Dinkleman *et al.* (2001) offer insights into linking this type of development of knowledge of teaching (i.e. the PAVOT learnings) with being a teacher of teaching. Through the transition from teacher to teacher educator, Dinkleman's colleagues (Jason and Karl) touched on the way in which their vista of the knowledge of the teaching landscape became clearer to them and how their approach to teaching about teaching was being constructed differently to their existing school teaching practice.

> [Through] the practice concerns experienced by Jason and Karl in their transition from teacher to teacher educator.... each expressed a deep interest in making sure their pedagogy as teacher educators matched the ideas of best practice they hoped to develop in their student teachers. Like Loughran (1996), they became keenly aware of the educative power they had via their actions as teacher educators. Such a concern was a departure from their days as classroom teachers in that, at the university, what they were teaching was no longer just social studies or English. *Instead what they were teaching was, essentially, teaching itself.* As a result, each asked himself repeatedly whether he had the professional respect of the student teachers in his charge.... Jason saw the necessity of bringing his knowledge to the table, not merely allowing student teachers to construct it all themselves: "I don't know how to help them become really good in the classroom without modeling for them in seminars and sharing with them ideas from my folders" (interview, 4/3/00).

Karl...opined early on that "it drives me crazy when people employ poor educational practices to try to communicate what good educational practices are" (interview, 9/9/99)....this would become a powerful and durable priority: to practice with his student teachers what he preached to his student teachers. He pointed out that he was "very conscious of trying to be consistent with the principle that I'm teaching" (interview, 5/25/00). In one early assignment, he asked his students to assess one of two seminar sessions in terms of their evolving definitions of good teaching....Karl's sense of mission, and agenda for the class, became sharper as he worked to reach the resistant members of his seminar... "You finally start to get good teaching," Jason observed, "and you want your students to do the same thing" (interview, 1/10/00)....Jason had learned something about good teaching that he wanted his students to understand. Though Jason expressed views of teacher education as providing a "space to facilitate" their own development at their own pace, he also came to see a directive aspect to his efforts to teach through modeling.

...Making the transition from teacher to teacher educator also required Jason and Karl to substantiate their competence as teacher educators.... modeling became a prominent feature of the ways Jason and Karl thought about their emerging identities as teacher educators. (emphasis added, Dinkelman *et al.*, 2001, pp. 38–39)

Dinkleman and his colleagues raise a number of interesting issues that help to highlight the additional layer of complexity in teaching about teaching that is unavoidable when teaching is viewed as being problematic. The issues, dilemmas, concerns and puzzles that are central to practice are also fundamental to teaching about practice and, students of teaching must see and feel these in their learning about teaching. But, so must their teacher educators. Therefore, teacher educators need to: "get beyond the question of whether theories, ideas, and research taught in teacher education programs are evident in the practice of teachers, to focus instead on *how such learning is evident*. [Because] some of the problems of practice might be more clearly explained by examining how theories emerge rather than discussing whether or not they do or do not" (emphasis in original, Pinnegar, 1995, p. 67). More than this though, the problems of practice must emerge and be explained within the experiences of practice so that both students and teachers of teaching together can examine the tacit (Polanyi, 1962, 1966) aspects of teaching.

Elbaz (1991), like many others, describes teachers' knowledge as being holistic, largely tacit in nature, nonlinear, and imbued with personal meaning. Therefore, if teachers' knowledge is to be unpacked, examined, analyzed and understood through teaching about teaching in a way that will carry personal meaning, it must be that in the immediate experiences of teaching *in* teacher education, that episodes from the past be called up, compared and contrasted with possibilities for the future. In this way the dynamic nature of practice is more likely to be viewed as stimulating learning about pedagogy rather than as a threat to one's personal competency. It will also most certainly illuminate the nature of teachers' professional knowledge and how it applies in practice.

Dinkleman and his colleagues (above) offer a glimpse of these possibilities in teaching *and* teaching about teaching. Jason and Karl recognize teaching as the important specialism of which they have advanced knowledge, thus they have a field to teach about ("what they were teaching was, essentially, teaching itself...Jason saw the necessity of bringing his knowledge to the table"). However, they have not yet developed a language to discuss the field ("You finally start to get good teaching," Jason observed, "and you want your students to do the same thing") even though they see their teaching differently as a result of being teachers of teaching. Modeling is the catch-all phrase that they use to hint at understanding their practice differently when they are not just doing teaching, but are teaching about teaching. It could well be that they are approaching the *edge of chaos* as they begin to question the taken for granted in their existing practice; they are appreciating the complexity of teaching as they learn more about their practice and how to teach that to their students of teaching.

Modeling: Looking into practice

The notion of modeling carries the connotation that it is a "demonstration of exemplary practice" and, although that may well be the case, it is also important to recognize that in all that occurs in teaching about teaching "something" is always being modeled; be it good or not so good, intentional or unintentional practice. One way of viewing modeling in teacher education is as an entrée to the ideas and underpinnings of practice so that that which is sought from the analysis of the breaking down then building up again of teaching, might be more purposefully critiqued and discussed.

Just as Jason (above) started to see new things in his teaching and wanted to find ways of bringing those insights to the attention of his students, so too there is a need to develop ways of sharing one's knowledge of practice so that it might be accessible to students of teaching beyond the actions alone. Hence, although modeling is a means for demonstrating practice, modeling alone is not sufficient for learning about practice.

Modeling should be conceptualized as embracing the possibilities for critique and interrogation in learning about teaching experiences, no matter how they arise; be they planned or unplanned. Modeling of this form means that teaching itself is continually being questioned so that both the subtleties and complexities of practice might be viewed and reviewed in order to shed light on pedagogical reasoning, thoughts and actions. This view of modeling carries with it the hope that as students of teaching see their teacher educators teach in this way that they will be encouraged to risk doing the same. As a consequence, there is a greater likelihood that the holistic, nonlinear and personal nature of teaching might be better illuminated while at the same time the notion that knowledge of practice must inevitably be tacit may be challenged. As, for example, the following vignette attempts to demonstrate through the process of one teacher educator teaching a class followed by a colleague de-briefing that teaching episode. In so doing, the unseen aspects of practice are brought to the surface for examination, and teaching itself is the focus of interrogation, not the teacher *per se*; a central issue to the public examination of practice.

Making the problematic explicit

We were doing the initial 'modeling' of teaching with the class and my role was to do the de-brief in such a way as to bring out as much as possible about the teaching, learning and pedagogical reasoning. I wasn't too concerned as we'd decided to use the same teaching approach as last year – John would do a POE and that usually engaged the students quite well.

As the session progressed, things seemed fine, then for some reason which was not clear to me, a student question led John into some ideas on static electricity.

This certainly didn't happen last year and although it was interesting, I couldn't quite see how it was linked to the air pressure topic he was doing, nor why he was spending so much time on it.

As the session came to an end, I moved into the de-briefing mode. After asking John about his purpose in the session and the manner in which he had conducted it, I asked if there was anything in the session that surprised him. He spoke about the level of student engagement and how the POE seemed to work well but he didn't mention the static electricity bit that had caught my attention.

I thought it was worth the risk so said, "Well, what happened with that static electricity bit? You spent ages playing with the balloon trying to get it to 'stick' to the wall and I wasn't sure why you got so caught up with that. What was happening there?"

John then explained how at first, he was simply responding to a student's suggestion about static electricity. He said he did not want to be seen to be discounting a "wrong response" and so took the suggestion seriously and pushed it further. However, at every step of that, he told us that he felt himself getting further and further away from the "real" topic and that he couldn't find a way out of his dilemma and back to the task. He said he felt like he just didn't know how to resolve the situation without making the student's idea seem (now) more unrelated, or how to 'force' a way of making a link back to the topic. Eventually he said he just made a joke of his inability to create static electricity and abruptly went back to the air pressure topic. However, in so doing, he felt as though he'd lost the impetus of the session and from then on things were less than satisfactory – from his perspective.

The students all had a lot to say at this point.

Many were surprised that John thought he had made the situation worse than it was. Others didn't think the static electricity was a side-track at all and that things were going 'as intended'. The student who put the static electricity idea forward said she was pleased that her idea had so much impact on the teacher.

As the de-brief came to a close, I drew the class' attention back to the static electricity one more time. I asked what they made of the examination of the episode and how it might influence their own teaching.

Jacinta said, "Well what you think you are doing as the teacher is not always what the class think you're doing, and it's good to see that happening with our lecturers because it sure as heck happens to us. I think it's good that we see you struggle in ways just like us. But maybe your experience covers it up so that we just don't see the reality often enough. I liked having a chance to talk about it. It's good to see the thinking behind the teaching that we experience." (Berry and Loughran, 2004, pp. 17–18)

As Jacinta (in the vignette above) suggests, students of teaching find great comfort in knowing that their teacher educators experience the same struggles in teaching that they face. Unfortunately though, in far too many instances, what for a teacher educator may well be a difficult or perplexing pedagogical situation is made to look simple to the students of teaching. From a student's perspective, that which is perceived to be modeled is not so much about managing the situation but about knowing how to act to fully resolve it. Understandably, for students of teaching, they tend to see into the situation from their perspective as a learner. They therefore bring to bear their past experiences of teaching and combine them with their experiences of the present in order to anticipate how they might act in the future. However, more often than not, their decisions about how to act in the future are about how to do it "correctly" as they seek a path through which to link their experiences to construct *the* way of acting. Thus, that which is problematic is not always viewed that way, therefore it needs to be modeled.

Opening up teaching in the manner displayed through the vignette demonstrates how the teacher educator did not have a "correct" way of resolving the situation, rather he worked to manage it. And, one interesting aspect of being problematic is that even though the students generally appeared satisfied with their involvement as learners, the teacher educator was not so satisfied with the outcome from his teaching perspective. The vignette highlights the value of teaching about teaching being embedded in the unfolding practices of teaching and learning within the relative safety of teacher education settings. In so doing, students of teaching begin to appreciate the varying perspectives crucial to shaping understandings of that which may be interpreted as problematic in practice.

For the problematic to be seen as problematic, teacher educators must accept the responsibility of teaching in ways that continually focus attention on not only what is being taught, but also on the complexity of how and why it is taught; regardless of the perceived success or otherwise of the practice at that time. In that way, the problematic nature of teaching is more likely to be made more "tangible, real and normal" for students of teaching.

Overview

In fully accepting the challenges associated with teaching about teaching, teacher educators need confidence in their practice in order to display the vulnerability necessary to publicly unpack teaching without carrying the baggage associated with "good" and "bad" teaching. Teaching about teaching needs to focus attention on the dilemmas, puzzles, issues and concerns that comprise the problematic nature of teaching so that that which is so often hidden and therefore implicit in practice is better able to be seen.

Modeling in teacher education means teaching about two things simultaneously; the content under consideration and the teaching employed to convey that content. Modeling is risky business because such things as assumptions, teaching behaviors and perceptions of learning are open to scrutiny. Confidence for all participants (teachers and students of teaching) is dependent on laying out practice for critique and being involved in the learning whilst maintaining the integrity of the individual. Building confidence through the risks associated with learning whilst respecting the learner as an individual is fundamental to any meaningful teaching and learning; all the more so in teaching about teaching and learning. Modeling then requires teachers of teaching to actively make the tacit explicit.

Teacher education is where all students of teaching should learn to challenge their deeply held views of teaching and learning; so often implicit in practice but so rarely articulated, confronted and examined. Teacher education is where teachers of teaching should model such processes, and all that entails, for it is central to an understanding of professional practice, and it is fundamental to developing a pedagogy of teacher education.

4 Making the tacit explicit

The process of teaching and learning itself – that which remains hidden in those "other" courses – must not only come to light but become the substance of the educative endeavour. That is, teaching in teacher education should include more than teaching *about* teaching as content, as an abstract entity, separate and separated from prospective teachers' *own* learning experiences as students preparing to teach. It is the focus on that "hidden" aspect that invites a conversation . . . [through which we might] encourage students to identify and discuss the messages embedded in the explicit, implicit, and null curricula both in and of learning to teach. . . . [However], it is not likely to be comfortable . . . instructors will be asked to subject their practice to critical examination. Students will be placed in the position of publicly questioning the practices of instructors . . . Indeed, asking a teacher education program to promote critical and public reflection on its own practices necessitates a level of educational courage not often evident in current conceptualizations of the teaching/learning environment . . . [but] it is precisely that kind of courage that would result in student teachers becoming students not only of education but of their *own* education.

(emphasis in original, Segall, 2002, pp. 159–160)

What teachers know, need to know and are able to do have been the focus of considerable debate. Although the language associated with describing much of the argument around this debate may have changed over time, in essence the issue itself has remained the same. At the heart of the debate are questions of knowledge, and the nature of knowledge in relation to its influence on teaching.

Munby *et al.* (2001) in their review of *Teachers' knowledge and how it develops* suggest that the literature on teachers' knowledge is: "characterized by a root tension: Different views have developed about what counts as professional knowledge and even how to conceptualize knowledge" (p. 878). Fenstermacher (1994), for example, differentiated between the formal knowledge of teaching (the knowledge created by educational researchers) and the practical knowledge of teaching (the knowledge created by teachers through their experiences of classroom teaching) but, unfortunately, this differentiation has often been interpreted as suggesting a concurrent judgment about the perceived value and importance of each, that is that formal knowledge is high status while practical knowledge is low status.

Sadly, this differentiation (and the baggage it carries) also influences views about the nature of teaching about teaching where, most typically, formal knowledge is thought to be the domain of the universities (world of theory) and practical knowledge is considered to be the domain of schools and teachers (world of practice). Thus, the stereotypical "traditional teacher education program" appears to be constructed on this differentiation through structures that suggest that theory is taught at university so that the knowledge might then be practiced in schools by student-teachers whose job is to "provide the individual effort to apply such knowledge" (Wideen *et al.*, 1998, p. 167).

Despite the arguments and baggage that surround the nature of teachers' professional knowledge, there is much that can be helpful in understanding approaches to constructing teaching about teaching and that can assist in shaping alternative conceptualizations to the theory–practice gap. Shulman's (1987) views of teacher knowledge, of which pedagogical content knowledge was a defining element, helped to concentrate attention on understanding not only what knowledge might be, but also how it might be developed (Shulman, 1986); thus begging exploration of how it might be used in practice.

Grimmett and MacKinnon (1992) proposed the construct of craft knowledge as another way of considering teachers' professional knowledge and suggested that both researchers and teacher educators could learn much through this conceptualization as it: "can act as a sensitizing framework to teachers…[and] such a framework would constitute a broadly conceived set of principles…[which] would provoke discussion and intellectual ferment; they would stimulate teachers to reflect on why they enact certain classroom practices and resist others.…[craft knowledge] has a powerful contribution to make to teacher education programs…" (p. 438).

Cochran-Smith and Lytle (1999) offered another perspective through their explication of knowledge *for* practice, knowledge *in* practice and knowledge *of* practice which led them to suggest the construct of *inquiry as stance* which was "intended to offer a closer understanding of the knowledge generated in inquiry communities, how inquiry relates to practice and what teachers learn from inquiry.…the term *inquiry as stance* describe[s] the positions teachers…take toward knowledge and its relationships to practice.…it involves making problematic the current arrangements of schooling; the ways knowledge is constructed, evaluated and used; and teachers' individual and collective roles in bringing about change" (pp. 288–289). (Inquiry as stance has much in common with the intentions of self-study, hence the idea that the construction and use of knowledge for, in and of practice have much in common with the endeavours of teacher educators and the articulation of professional knowledge of teaching about teaching.)

Central to much of these discussions about knowledge is the relationship between professional knowledge and professional practice for it is through this relationship that access to learning to teach is facilitated. Clearly, teaching about teaching should create real opportunities for this relationship to be laid bare for serious examination so that students of teaching might better appreciate not only what teachers know, need to know and are able to do, but to also be able to actively develop, assess, adjust and articulate such knowledge in relation to their own teaching. Thus making this knowledge explicit is crucial. Therefore, how teacher educators might do this is vital to the development and articulation of their professional knowledge of teaching about teaching.

Looking into teaching

Much of the learning to teach literature demonstrates that students of teaching feel a need to accumulate examples of how to teach in order to develop a "bag of teaching tricks" so that they might feel adequately prepared to embark on their teaching careers. Further to this, there is little to suggest that students of teaching are encouraged to unpack the professional knowledge or beliefs of their teaching mentors (whether they be in school or university) or that their teacher mentors themselves see that unpacking their professional knowledge and beliefs comprises part of their role in teaching about teaching. It is not difficult to see then that the "hunter-gatherer" approach to accumulating teaching procedures may well prevail as a major purpose of, and discernible outcome from, learning to teach.

Zanting *et al.* (2003) set out to challenge this lack of explication of teachers' professional knowledge for students of teaching by creating an expectation that such unpacking is indeed part of the process of learning to teach. They initiated a research program in which students of teaching used a range of methodologies to "access their mentor teachers' [school supervising teachers'] professional knowledge and beliefs." Not surprisingly, like many before (see for example, Carter, 1990) they found that there was great difficulty in eliciting the substance of teachers' professional knowledge, for like the knowledge itself, the elicitation was also problematic. However, despite these difficulties, some of their findings offer important advice for the education of teachers. For example, just as studies in science education have demonstrated that students tend to observe what they "expect to see," so too in learning to teach, students of teaching interpret classroom events in light of their own experiences as learners and so "student-teachers who have experienced group work as rather chaotic during their own school time as a pupil may be inclined to interpret pupils working together as being turbulent and not concentrating on their task while, in fact, the pupils can be discussing their task constructively" (p. 207). Further, to this, some student-teachers "just observed some teaching actions that 'work[ed]' and they could possibly use for their own lessons, and were not interested in the cognitions underlying teaching" (p. 207).

In both of these findings the lack of a serious consideration of teachers' professional knowledge suggests that learning to teach can easily become too personal and not sufficiently balanced by understandings derived from an articulation of practice, underlying beliefs and cognition and, conceptualizations of the development of knowledge in, and/or for, action. Without serious attention to teachers' professional knowledge, despite the best intentions and efforts of all involved, learning to teach may then still be misinterpreted, or unwittingly perceived, as largely comprising technical competency and the accumulation of teaching procedures. Therefore, if such interpretations are to be challenged, teacher educators need to push the boundaries of their own practice in making their professional knowledge clear and explicit for their students of teaching. Making professional knowledge clear and accessible is vital for students of teaching and is a key component of the work of teacher education.

Examples of how teachers' professional knowledge might be made explicit for students of teaching are important, but fundamental to such explication is a recognition of the need for it to be central to teaching and learning about teaching. Zanting *et al.* (2003) offer a number of possibilities that include such things as more focused classroom observation with greater attention to the why of practice, stimulated recall, concept maps, interviews, repertory grids and narratives which Sim (2004) also draws attention to through the notion of *the personal as pedagogic practice*. However, although Zanting *et al.* (2003) and Sim (2004) concentrate on school teachers in their studies, it is equally important to consider the same intentions for teacher educators. So the question arises: "How can the unpacking of the professional knowledge of teaching become an integral aspect of teaching about teaching?" Perhaps a preface to this question should be the challenge for teacher educators to carefully consider the nature of their own knowledge of teaching and to begin to clarify the role that it does, and should, play in their own conceptualization and practice in teaching about teaching.

In the self-study literature, there are interesting approaches to the ways in which teacher educators have attempted to better understand their own professional knowledge and, it is through these explorations that developments in their knowledge of teaching about teaching have been enhanced. In a detailed review of this work (see Loughran, 2004a), a number of approaches have been noted and categorized. These include:

- learning about self (see for example, Bass, 2002; Chin, 1997; Elijah, 1998; Freidus, 2002; Kuzmic, 2002; Wilkes, 1996);
- learning with and through critical friends (see for example, Cole and Knowles, 1995, 1996, 1998a, 1998b; Mitchell and Weber, 1998, 1999, 2000);
- learning by seeing practice from the students' perspective (see for example, Hoban, 1997; Nicol, 1997; Russell and Bullock, 1999; Schuck and Segal, 2002; Senese, 2002);

- teacher educator as student-teacher (Pinnegar, 1995);
- teacher educator on school attachment (He *et al.*, 2000); and,
- teacher educator as school teacher (see, for example, Berry and Milroy, 2002; Heaton and Lampert, 1993; Loughran and Northfield, 1996; Russell, 1995).

In the day-to-day work of teaching about teaching, the following approaches offer possibilities for incorporation into teacher educators' "normal practice".

Thinking aloud

Thinking aloud in teaching about teaching is a valuable way of helping students of teaching to see into their teacher educator's practice. But, as has been well demonstrated by others (e.g. Berry, 2001; Nicol, 1997; White, 2002), it is not necessarily an easy thing to do, for there are many competing and conflicting concerns associated with the practice: "Choosing an appropriate time to explain that I would be 'thinking out loud' and my purpose for doing so was important. I had to have a sense of trust in the class and they with me otherwise my behaviour could appear to be peculiar rather than purposeful. There was a danger that talking aloud about what I was or was not doing, and why, could be interpreted as lacking appropriate direction" (Loughran, 1995, p. 434). Thus, making the purpose for thinking aloud clear is a most important aspect of helping that practice to be understood as a teaching about teaching procedure designed to highlight the professional knowledge of practice *in* practice for students of teaching.

So what does thinking aloud look like? The following excerpt hopefully offers a way of understanding it in practice. However, how it appears on paper is not the same as what it is really like to do, for, as Berry (2004a) illustrates, developing expertise in the use of thinking aloud is a challenging aspect of learning to teach about teaching, but an important way of making professional knowledge of practice accessible to students of teaching.

> An important aspect of my teaching is to encourage student involvement especially through discussion. On occasions, the topic under consideration might provoke group responses whereby everyone has something to say, but, as in any large group situation, everyone can not speak at once. I remember a session where we were discussing different views of student ability and some of the reasons that accompanied those views. As the discussion developed, I could see that more and more members of the class were frustrated at not being able to respond to others' statements, and that some members of the class had considerably more 'air time' than others. As I began to respond to this situation, I interrupted the discussion by saying that I was dissatisfied with the way the session was evolving, not because of the nature of the discussion but because of the structural or procedural constraints; I was pleased with

the content of the debate, but I was not convinced that the format was conducive to good learning. Even though I was not sure what I would do about it, I was verbalizing the feelings that were influencing my thinking. I was able to describe the problem, reason through why it was a problem for me, and hypothesize about the likely outcomes if the discussion continued in the same way. Then, as I verbally sorted through some of the suggestions flashing through my mind which might address the situation, I introduced a different pedagogical approach which I explained as I introduced it and outlined why I was changing the teaching and what I hoped it would achieve.... The introduction of this 'silent discussion'... was a spontaneous shift in pedagogy in response to a problem situation. By talking aloud about the changes in my pedagogy and the influences on these as they were occurring, my students could see beyond the teaching itself to my reflection on practice which guided and directed the learning in which we were so intensely involved. (Loughran, 1996, pp. 33–34)

By talking aloud about teaching in action, a teacher educator develops new ways of articulating their practice and therefore can not only come to making that practice accessible to students of teaching but also begin to develop a shared language for discussing professional knowledge. Importantly, in doing so within pedagogical experiences, the beliefs, knowledge and practices of teaching that influence actions are able to be examined so that the tensions, issues and dilemmas that arise might be better understood within that particular experience.

In the approach to "discussion" in the situation above, the teacher educator was concerned about the way the discussion was evolving. There was a concern that the purpose of discussion was being undermined by the way discussion as a teaching procedure was being conducted. The response to this situation was to change the way the discussion was structured, not to dispense with discussion itself.

The nature of the professional knowledge in this case could be described as, in the first instance, knowing how to recognize and name the tension. In so doing, attention is focused on the problematic whereby the very act of encouraging ideas and issues to be raised can simultaneously silence participants and limit the impact of the intended learning outcomes. The professional knowledge also involves moderating the tension in practice, not simply responding to the simple either/or exclusionary options. The knowledge in practice response (silent discussion) that emerged demonstrated a shift to a teaching procedure that helped to address the tension. However, and more important to teaching about teaching, the concurrent conversation about why the silent discussion was introduced, how it might work and whether or not it was actually needed created opportunities to unpack the tension in a tangible manner so that the professional knowledge underpinning the practice could be understood in ways beyond that of simple propositional knowledge. Therefore, although the professional knowledge examined could well form the basis of further explorations into knowledge *for* practice, the particular aspects of knowing *in* and *of* practice were being developed, unpacked and applied in that particular teaching about teaching situation.

Through the thinking aloud of the teacher educator, an invitation was issued to his students through which they were encouraged to question the what, why and how of teaching. Because their learning about that particular aspect of professional knowledge was a part of their experience of learning about teaching at that time, they were also well aware of other possible responses and how informed decision making is vital to professional knowledge and crucial to teaching as an educative experience. More than this alone, the explication of the questions, issues and concerns associated with the changes to the pedagogic episode also helped to highlight the difference between experience and expertise.

Experience may suggest that in a similar situation the silent discussion teaching procedure might change the dynamics of the discussion and create equal "air time" for all participants. But expertise is embedded in choosing teaching procedures that are appropriate to the intended learning outcomes and knowing not only how to use them, but why, under what changed circumstances and, being able to adjust and adapt them to meet the contextual needs of the time. Thus, in using a talking aloud approach to making the tacit aspects of practice explicit, it is important that teacher educators and students of teaching remember that although experience of a situation may be informing, learning from and through that experience is crucial to developing expertise.

Further to this, an easily overlooked aspect of the development of expertise in teaching is that generalizing and abstracting from one experience to another situation requires the individual to actively process and synthesize the learning so that the knowledge and experience combine to better inform one's future practice. Teacher educators cannot do that for their students of teaching, but they can create the experiences that may be central to facilitating and enhancing such possibilities. Simply being told what to do or seeing what others do is not sufficient in teaching about teaching. Explication is crucial to being better informed about practice and in highlighting the importance of professional knowledge in shaping quality in pedagogy. In teaching about teaching, making the tacit explicit matters.

Journal writing

Professional knowledge of teaching about teaching is inevitably influenced by teacher education program structure, that is context influences the nature of learning. In the one year end on postgraduate diploma in education, I was an advocate for the use of journal writing. Through using a journal myself in the ways that I anticipated my students of teaching might approach their own journal writing, I was able to offer them access to my professional knowledge of teaching (for full description see Loughran, 1996, pp. 29–32). In so doing, the documented accounts of my anticipatory, contemporaneous and retrospective reflections on our teaching and learning offered entry points for the thinking that underpinned my practice so that it could be questioned, examined and critiqued so that that which was being modeled was more than "just the teaching." However, in undergraduate Double Degree programs I have been confronted by the fact that most students quickly become "journaled out" as it can be a somewhat ubiquitous expectation across subjects. Hence, despite what I consider to be a valuable approach to unpacking knowledge of practice, the procedure can also negate the intended learning outcomes. It is therefore not hard to see how teacher education program intentions and actions can be perceived as incongruous by students of teaching.

Berry (2004c), who teaches Biology Method in a postgraduate diploma in education program (as well as teaching in an undergraduate Double Degree program) found her ongoing use of journal writing to be most helpful for her Biology students despite not pursuing the same with her undergraduate students. In her work in the postgraduate diploma in education, Berry found her use of journal writing to be an important tool for helping her students of teaching to better understand her pedagogical reasoning in relation to the teaching and learning experiences they share in their pre-service biology teacher education classes: "Usually there is a multitude of thoughts running through my head as I teach.... Making a choice about what to make explicit ... in my journal entries was a constant dilemma for me. I had to choose carefully what I held up for public examination... [but] I wanted to convince them it is o.k. to be unsure in your own practice, that teaching is problematic" (Berry, 2001, p. 3).

In an attempt to better understand her students' perceptions of her use of journaling, mid-way through the one-year program, she asked them to complete a questionnaire (Berry, 2004b). In an analysis of the open-ended question "What is the purpose or value of the journal to you?" responses were categorized as:

- providing insights into the purposes for the method class;
- highlighting issues that may not have been considered by the learners at the time of the class;
- a model for students' own thinking about teaching;
- an opportunity to continue thinking about biology teaching, that would otherwise be unlikely to occur;
- an empathy connection; and,
- no real value.

The data accompanying these categories suggests that Berry's students were keen to know what she thought she was doing as a teacher and why, and that they found it interesting to see what she found difficult or what played out differently in class compared to what she had anticipated would be the case. Overall, the data suggested that these students valued seeing "common teacher problems and concerns" and that just as they faced such concerns in their own teaching, so too did their teacher educator. Overall, the use of journaling to make the tacit explicit appeared to Berry to serve the purpose well; both for her as a learner of teaching *about* teaching and her students as learners *of* teaching:

> Making a choice about what to make explicit...in my journal entries was a constant dilemma for me. I had to choose carefully what I held up for public examination that would be useful for them...I wanted to show them that uncertainty in teaching practice is usual, that teaching is problematic....Keeping a journal has served as a useful record of my experiences, from which I have begun to explicitly state aspects of practice such as: (i) My intentions for students' learning and my actions to facilitate this learning are not always aligned, and not always obvious to me, (ii) There are 'different worlds' (Perry, 1988) that exist within the same classroom so what individual learners perceive is going on may be quite different to what I (or others) perceive, (iii) There are many thoughts that inform a teaching decision and it can be hard to choose which decision for which moment....My decision to write a public journal was in response to a problem that I experienced and has been a catalyst for self-study. I found it difficult to articulate my pedagogical reasoning during classes, but I needed a quiet space to sort through my experiences, somewhere that was removed from the 'noise' of competing concerns that interfered with my thinking. The Journal was not intended as a substitute for talking about experience in the practice context, but something to use in concert. As I learnt, my students also struggled with the task of hearing messages beyond what immediately concerned them. The Journal offered some of them a quiet place to reconsider their experience, too. As one student put it, *"[the journal] makes me...more aware of what I am doing and why. I have to think about the why when I often don't." (anonymous survey response)...* Helping preservice teachers begin to recognise a problematic and uncertain 'script' is a difficult and demanding task both for the teacher educator (how to do this?) and for the student teacher (why do this?). Perhaps this means that more of those involved in teacher education, including supervising teachers, need to consider making explicit the dilemmas of practice that they face so that student teachers come to challenge their apprenticeship of observation. (emphasis in original, Berry, 2004b, pp. 22–24)

Berry's realizations about the nature of learning to teach illustrate the importance of linking teacher education practices in both universities and schools and how explicating the nature of professional knowledge matters for teacher education regardless of setting. It also illustrates the importance of pursuing a research agenda along the lines that Zanting *et al.* (2003) suggested so that the "educational value of this exploration for student-teachers" (p. 210) might be better understood.

Disturbing practice

What triggers a new phase of personal development? Most frequently there is some form of disturbance which starts things off.... Whatever it is, something startles me out of my current habits. Disturbance can have positive and negative aspects: a small disturbance can usually be encompassed, while a large disturbance may be disruptive. An idea for doing things differently can be seen as an opportunity, or as a pressure. If the disturbance is experienced as negative... [one may deal with it] in characteristic ways such as blaming others or myself, or justifying my actions by showing how I could not actually have done otherwise.... [but] if the disturbance remains, if something positive attracts my attention, something different to try which I hope or believe will make a difference may come to mind. (Mason, 2002, p. 10)

In the Double Degree program at Monash University, the subject *Curriculum and Pedagogy* has been designed to help students of teaching see into practice (their own and that of their teacher educators). The subject has been developed, refined and researched (Berry and Loughran, 2002, 2005; Loughran *et al.*, 2005a, b) and one outcome of this work has been a better understanding of ways in which *disturbing practice* can lead to positive learning outcomes. In Curriculum and Pedagogy, a consistent focus on the practice of both the teacher educators and their students of teaching has been maintained in an overt attempt to make the professional knowledge of teaching, and of teaching about teaching, explicit, articulable and applicable.

Curriculum and Pedagogy models particular aspects of teaching so that they might then be unpacked through honest and professional critique. In this subject, the teacher educators model this process by teaching and having their practice critiqued in advance of developing an ongoing program in which a similar process is initiated for their students of teaching (see the vignette *Making the problematic explicit* in Chapter 3 as an example of this process). All participants are therefore involved in teaching their peers, then having that teaching professionally critiqued[1] before a de-briefing of these shared experiences. Thus, students of teaching develop insights into practice

---

1 Professional critique is an important issue for it is the teaching that must be critiqued not the individual: separating the teacher from the teaching is a learning issue in its own right that the teacher educators pay careful attention to and help to shape views of critique so that there are positive learning about teaching opportunities.

through the range of roles they experience (i.e. teacher, critiquer and de-briefer) and by reviewing the videotape of the session.

The introduction of this subject into the Double Degree program was in response to the need for students of teaching to have a "safe place" to experiment with teaching and to develop understandings of *their* practice in a context that did not carry expectations of "teach like me" (so common in many teacher education courses but perhaps even more so during school practicum).

In this subject the teacher educators purposefully confront pedagogical issues, raise teaching dilemmas and disrupt practice – when it seems appropriate and helpful to the learning about teaching of participants. Disturbing practice is a difficult teaching about teaching approach which requires considerable professional judgment and, as the research reports from the program illustrate, is something that has become increasingly refined and sophisticated over time. The reason for disturbing practice in this way is in accord with Mason's view (above) whereby a positive disturbance can be a catalyst for growth and enhancing understanding of teaching and learning. It also offers a powerful way of teaching about teaching that dramatically contrasts with teaching as telling and all that that suggests about learning. The following vignette offers an illustration of disturbing practice.

Vignette: Disturbing practice

Having done some teaching with the class, de-briefing it and trying to model the importance of having teaching critiqued in order to see not 'just the teaching' but also the pedagogical reasoning, concerns, issues and dilemmas underpinning the teaching, brought us to a point of expectation that our students would be ready to embrace the same in their peer teaching experiences. However, our experience from previous years also reminded us of the difficulty in the first few peer teaching sessions of getting honest feedback on what was really happening from both a teacher's and a student's perspective. This meant that beyond helping to highlight particular situations in the de-briefing sessions that might shed light on different aspects of teaching and learning, that we also had to choose wisely when we disturbed the flow in teaching experiences and to be conscious of why we would be doing it so that the disturbance served a worthwhile purpose. Thus, our teaching about teaching is brought into sharp focus by our need to think, reason and respond as either a teacher or a learner when a teachable moment is apparent; and in some circumstances, to create such moments.

The idea of responding to a teachable moment means that it is not possible to have all things prepared and planned in advance; the ability to be flexible, to respond to the moment, is something we try to encourage in peer teaching sessions and is one way of encouraging experimenting with practice in a "safe environment."

Julie and Scott were up for their peer teaching and the introduction was quite long and convoluted. Scott was clearly nervous and was saying much more than he probably intended as he introduced the topic.

As Scott's monologue relentlessly continued I decided to interrupt just as he was placing yet another transparency on the overhead projector.

"Scott, I can't read that from here, the writing is too small." I blurted from the back of the class.

"That's o.k. you don't have to read it, I'm telling it to you anyway." he quickly responded.

He moved on relatively unperturbed but the look on some of the students' faces suggested they had a problem with what was happening. I sat quietly, watching and listening but feeling more anxious; Scott appeared unaware of the restlessness of the class. His single focus on his notes seemed to be consuming all of his attention. After another few minutes, which seemed like an eternity, I interrupted again.

"Are we supposed to be copying down your notes?" I asked somewhat forcefully hoping that he might draw breath, think about what was happening and maybe wrap it up and pass over to Julie to get on with the task.

"No. It's fine. Just be quiet and listen." was his quick reply.

He started to speak a little faster, then, surprisingly, the volley of overheads stopped and he seemed to be 'ad libbing'.

He asked a few questions but didn't wait for any replies and appeared to be confusing not only us but also himself.

In what was now an almost 20 minute introduction, we had been bombarded with all of the information about the topic, what we would be doing and what we would learn. Julie was looking uncomfortable as she flicked through her papers watching while Scott continued to push on.

After all of the talk and information we were supposed to absorb, it looked as though we were about to embark on a task that now seemed rather pointless: "Why would we want to do this if we have already been told everything about it?" I asked myself and, by the look on the faces of many of the members of the class, they seemed to be questioning it too.

I decided to interrupt again and asked Scott when we would be doing something ourselves rather than just listen to him. I'm not sure how I worded it though as I think by that stage I was as anxious as him.

I had by now persistently interrupted his teaching and, although everyone else seemed to see what was happening and were quietly in agreement with my inquiries, Scott was oblivious to it. I was becoming concerned that my interruptions had served no purpose and so I was already thinking hard about what might happen in the de-brief – if we ever got to it!

Finally, Julie stepped in front of Scott and took over. He seemed somehow relieved as he slowly moved to one side.

Julie told the class that they would be doing an activity and she handed out the sheets that explained the task.

She told us to form small groups and to get started.

After all of the teacher talk from Scott, this was a complete about face. I wondered if she was responding to the situation or whether this was part of her plan.

As I joined in with a group there was much discussion about what had been happening and nothing about the task we were supposed to be doing. I tried to get my group to get started with the task but they were not all that interested.

After a minute or so I put up my hand and although Scott looked right at me, he didn't respond at all. He looked at me but looked past me. After a while I just called out saying we didn't know what to do and could someone tell us. Julie's response was one I really enjoyed.

"John, you have all of the information in front of you. You have had plenty of time to get organised so I suggest you and your group work it out for yourselves and hurry up. You are already falling behind the other groups and we need your results to complete the task as a class. So, do you think you can all get on with it now please?" she said with a strong sense of expectation of compliance in her voice.

As I turned back to my group, they all looked at me.

"So come on, what's the problem, let's get moving." Mischa said.

I couldn't believe it. A minute ago they didn't want to do anything, now I was the culprit.

Julie's confident response had quickly dealt with a number of issues and turned the group around. I felt pleased with her response but wondered if others had noticed what had really happened in that short tête-à-tête. So I risked one last intervention.

"Julie, we're still not sure what to do. Can you come and sort it out for us please?" I called out in a somewhat demanding tone.

Scott was looking a little harassed and started to respond to me in a not so pleasant manner: something along the lines of working more, talking less and minimizing the disruption to those who were trying to do the "right thing". He looked far from pleased as his words surged forth while striding toward my group. But, before he reached our table, Julie gently intervened and directed him to another group that had been patiently waiting for assistance.

As she knelt down next to our table she turned to me and quietly said, "It's o.k., I know what you're trying to do, get on with the task now and we can talk about all of this in the de-brief."

I think I was more relieved than anything else; I was certainly impressed with Julie's manner. Mischa gave me that look of quiet satisfaction, or maybe it was an "I told you so look", and we all got on with the task.

As the de-brief commenced David asked Scott how he felt about what had happened in the session. He initially started off justifying his need to give us all of the information but after a few questions from other members of the class he "fessed up" that he just didn't seem to know what to do at the time, so he just kept on going.

"I think I knew what was happening, like I could see myself doing all this talking and saying to myself slow down, you don't need to keep going, but although I knew what I was doing, I just kept going. Why is that?" he asked rhetorically.

Much discussion followed and many other members of the class talked about things they did when they were nervous or uncertain and how important it was to know how to do something about it. Scott seemed quite pleased that his actions had triggered such an interesting discussion then he turned to Julie and said, "It was lucky you butted in when you did. What if you had done even more talking re-explaining everything they had to do? Good move just giving them the sheets and telling them to work it out for themselves."

Julie smiled knowingly and a most interesting de-brief about teacher directed and student initiated learning ensued all based around what they had all just experienced together.

Mischa had a few interesting points about how our group worked (or didn't) and wondered how she might have dealt with, "a student like John!"

As the class finished I handed the video tape of the session to Scott.

"Thanks for that." he said. "I didn't feel all that good at the time, but now I think it's not so bad. I'm glad we don't get graded on this stuff, but if we did, I can tell you I learnt more doing it wrong than I would've if I'd have got it right!"

I looked across to catch Julie's eye but she was on her way out.

"Don't forget to catch up with Scott to watch the video and do your paper while all of this is fresh in your mind." I called out as she disappeared out the door.

As I packed up the camera and gathered my papers Belinda and Michael approached me.

"That was great. Please don't hold back on me next week. I want you to be like that with me. O.K." said Belinda.

"Yeah, me too." added Michael. "I want you to spot things like that while I'm teaching next week. I'll be ready for you."

As I wondered what Scott and Julie's papers from today's session might be like I also had a niggling doubt about what Belinda and Michael had taken from all of this. "I hope they don't think it's a game." I said to myself as I started to think about how I might respond to their peer teaching if that was the case.

"Disturbing practice disturbs all of us." I muttered to myself.

Disturbing practice is one way of helping to make the tacit explicit. It brings to the surface the reasons (or lack thereof) for acting in a particular way at a particular time and it does so in a way that does not divorce feelings from the actions associated with the confrontation or challenge; it creates powerful learning episodes.

Teaching about teaching issues abound through disturbing practice. So much so that any decision about whether, or how, to intervene in the peer teaching immediately challenges one's own knowledge of practice and focuses attention on one's purposes, intentions and behaviors as a teacher of teaching. Disturbing practice is not intervention for intervention's sake; it is not a game. Disturbing practice is a way of creating real responses to real situations so that learning about teaching will be personal and meaningful, but above all, positive. It is important that the knowledge of teaching embedded in, and uncovered through, disturbing practice is opened up for all participants to see; and, it is understood more fully when the experiences of such knowledge in action are personally felt.

If disturbing practice was to create an environment in which blaming, justifying inappropriate practices and behaviors, or artificially separating teaching from learning was to be the outcome, then it would not be helpful to teaching or learning about teaching. Working with colleagues is one way of being sensitive to approaches to disturbing practice and of gaining advice and feedback on such episodes and of continuing to push to make the tacit explicit.

Collaboration: Teaching together

In his work on change, Fullan (1993) draws attention to "change agentry" which he describes as "being self-conscious about the nature of change and the change process" (p. 12). He depicts change agentry as comprising four capacities: personal vision-building, inquiry, mastery and collaboration. In the preceding chapters, the first three of Fullan's capacities have been touched upon in a variety of ways; learning about the teaching of teaching clearly involves change agentry. However, collaboration is an aspect of teacher education that requires particular attention as it encourages making the tacit explicit and is vital for the development of knowledge, skills and expertise in practice. There is power in collaboration as it is essential for personal learning (Fullan and Hargreaves, 1991) yet in traditional teaching practices, collaboration rarely extends into classroom practice. The isolation of teaching and teacher education tends to reinforce notions of practice as a covert activity (Ginsburg and Clift, 1990).

Teachers working together, collaborating and teaming in ways that provide professional support for one another leads to improvements in practice as the sharing with, and learning from, one another offers meaningful ways of framing and reframing existing practice. Minnett (2003) found that effective collaboration was evident when: "an individual partner is neither the leader nor the follower, but an equal and full participant who will adopt either role as the need arises" (p. 280). Minnett's observation rings true for me in terms of thinking about the foundations for successful collaboration. I have been fortunate to collaborate with a much valued and trusted colleague for a considerable period of time as we have taught together in Curriculum and Pedagogy, and through the process, have learnt many things about the nature of teaching and learning about teaching.

As a result of free and honest discussions of practice, through having an extra set of eyes in the classroom able to offer alternative interpretations of shared experiences, and by teaching and learning together, our tacit knowledge of practice has become increasingly explicit. As a consequence, the possibilities for development, critique, experimentation, articulation and consolidation of our knowledge of practice has continued to evolve and to be professionally rewarding. For example, after a peer teaching session in Curriculum and Pedagogy in which we "disturbed" students' practice, our post-class discussion about the episode (what we did and did not do, why, whether it was appropriate and how it impacted teaching and learning) continued via e-mail:

> *Mandi* This process of working through what was in my head at the time is quite cathartic...I think in some instances I had a funny role, not feeling quite in control of what was going on but in a different place to the students. You didn't ever say it, but I think you were both teaching me and teaching with me. Was that what you intended? I'm thinking about the things you can't plan for in a class and how they are (or have to be?) dealt with when they happen. I wanted to plan for each class because it makes me feel comfortable. I wanted to know how I could feel in control of this experience so that I could walk in knowing the beginning, middle and end of what was going to happen. (I know when I am thinking this that this is an unrealistic expectation.) The classes don't work out that way. They are less about planned learning than using the experiences that come out of the plans that the students have for their teaching. I have to trust that I will see and know how to capitalise on these opportunities for learning. That is unsettling. But it's also okay because we do trust each other. I know there is permission to work in different ways and that means being able to take a risk.

> *John* I couldn't agree more. It's developing a confidence to look into and examine what's happening as it happens through being both honest and exposing your own vulnerability so that the "normal" rules of being courteous do not get in the way of genuinely exploring (and feeling) what it means to make sense of a situation and develop new ways of seeing it. You helped me to know when it was working and when to back off (and I assumed you would learn to take the cue from that to do the same) and together we reflected the thinking of both those who were doing the teaching and the range of responses students had to it. It helped release them to be open and honest and to push

beyond what is normally "good enough" in a teaching situation but which is (for us) just too superficial. (Maybe I didn't tell you about how I was doing this because I hadn't realised it quite that way either; the trust also meant many things went unspoken, and in some ways, could have been misinterpreted. There is no doubt though that I learnt to do things in different ways because of the trust that was there). (Berry and Loughran, 2002, p. 17)

This brief exchange highlights the importance of being confident to respond to teachable moments and how through team teaching,[2] confidence grows. For Mandi (at that time) discarding the prescription for what "should" happen in a class was both a challenge and a release while for me, teaching with a valued colleague gave me the confidence to "disturb" practice whilst still receiving feedback and advice about those disturbances in action.

The extract (above) also illustrates how as a consequence of our ongoing collaboration and teaching partnership there was a mutual trust that supported the learning of both our students and ourselves: we were teaching each other about teaching through the process of teaching our students.

Just as we organize Curriculum and Pedagogy so that our students work in pairs (or small teams) so that they might: learn with and from one another; access alternative interpretations of the same events; and plan, teach and inquire into practice together, so too we do the same. This commitment to collaboration is based on the recognition that there is much to learn from others and that such learning is enhanced through making the tacit explicit. And, just as we see that collaboration is important for our students in their learning about teaching, so too we see it as important in our learning of teaching about teaching.

Collaboration creates situations in which it is crucial that ideas, beliefs, views and thoughts about practice be made explicit. In so doing, the underlying features of practice which, under different circumstances may go unnoticed and unquestioned, are presented for analysis, scrutiny and investigation. Collaboration in the classroom, the notion of team teaching, is where the learning about practice becomes very real as, in the same way as our students experience it in their peer teaching, we too are reminded of the feelings and emotions associated with our actions in pedagogic experiences. Therefore through collaboration, we are very conscious of not only how we act but also why; and that is the essence of making the tacit explicit: "Where each of us saw possibilities for learning, we took action and

2 In the way we think about team teaching it means much more than two people sharing "delivery" to a class. It is about interacting together through the way the teaching is done while it is being done, to be both a teacher and a learner and to push and probe the very ideas being developed in the act of teaching. Team teaching is observing one another as well as the class in order to be more able to respond, react and reconstruct teaching and learning episodes in ways that continually focus attention on the issues associated with the particular teaching, learning and the professional knowledge of practice evident at that time.

accepted responsibility for taking that action. This was uncomfortable at times. Teaching with a trusted colleague meant that we felt a little braver to try things that we might not have tried alone. As we recognized potential learning experiences, we tried to tune each other through verbal or non-verbal cues so that we could support each other and the students as we explored what the experience might offer" (Berry and Loughran, 2002, p. 22). As a consequence of our learning through collaboration, we have articulated four general issues important to shaping our pedagogy of teacher education in Curriculum and Pedagogy. We have come to see the value of making explicit for ourselves and our students the importance of:

- seeing into experience through professional critique;
- recognizing different types of teaching decisions;
- recognizing differences between action and intent; and,
- exploring the value of co-teaching.

These four issues are significant in shaping our understanding of, and approach to, practice in Curriculum and Pedagogy and together have helped us see the value in highlighting the importance of teachers seeing practice through their students' eyes. This issue is central to much of the work of self-study of teaching and teacher education practices (see for example the use of backtalk, Russell, 1986, 1997) and is a reminder of the importance of apprehending alternative interpretations of pedagogical episodes.

Seeing our practice through our students' eyes

Of all the pedagogic tasks teachers face, getting inside students' heads is one of the trickiest. It is also one of the most crucial. When we start to see ourselves through students' eyes, we become aware of what Perry (1988) calls the "different worlds" in the same classroom. We learn that students perceive the same actions and experience the same activities in vastly different ways. If we know something about the symbolic meanings that our actions have for students, we are better able to shape our behaviour so that desired effects are achieved. (Brookfield, 1995, p. 92)

Recognition of Perry's (1988) "different worlds" in the same classroom is just as important an issue for students of teaching as it is for teacher educators. If teachers' intentions are to be clear for their students, the space for misinterpretation must be minimized. More so, in teacher education, pedagogic intentions carry additional significance because of the imperatives associated with learning about teaching. It is not difficult then to see the need to make the tacit explicit. In so doing, the likelihood that intentions might be misinterpreted, and their associated practices dismissed by students of teaching, may be diminished.

For teacher educators, perhaps a useful starting point for considering teaching from a student's perspective is to be reminded of, or to experience anew, our own approaches and attitudes to learning in similar situations. For example, how often in seminars, workshops or conference presentations do we bemoan those who: speak down to us?; rush through as much information as is possible in the allocated time?; ask for our opinions only to dismiss them in the next breath?; or, present a mass of complicated/packed powerpoints/overheads? Yet, when we are the presenter we do the same, somehow believing it will be "different this time!" or "different because we are better at it than some others."

For some reason, as learners, we see such practice very differently from the way we come to see it when we are the teacher. Maybe if we approached such situations as being pedagogic our practice would be more in line with an expectation of the interactive relationship of teaching and learning. Bringing the same idea to bear on our teaching about teaching, perceiving *our* practice from *our* students' perspective is essential because: "If actively pursuing an understanding of teaching and learning from a student's perspective is not modeled in teacher education, why would it suddenly materialize as a learning about teaching issue for students of teaching?"

There are many ways of seeing our practice through our students' eyes (see for example, the work of Brookfield, 1995; Bullough and Gitlin, 2001; Dinkleman, 1999; Hoban, 1997; Nicol, 1997; Northfield and Gunstone, 1997; Peterman, 1997). However, fundamental to all is the importance of communicating the *why* of our practice so that students of teaching can make informed decisions about what they need to learn about *their* teaching in order to enhance the learning of *their* students. For such an expectation to be overtly created in teacher education there is an ongoing need for the tacit to be made explicit. The implicit messages and intentions of teaching must be challenged, students of teaching need to know what we think are the intended learning outcomes from our practice and, as teacher educators, we need to be able to articulate not only what we are doing, but why we are doing it and how we are communicating that through our practice.

> Seeing ourselves through students' eyes often leads to our realizing that we have to pay much more attention than we thought was necessary to explaining and justifying our actions. Students can't read our minds. They can't be expected to know what we stand for without our making an explicit and vigorous effort to communicate this. We have to build a continual case for learning, action, and practice, instead of assuming that students see the self-evident value of what we are asking them to do. We have to create windows into our minds so that students can see the workings of our own teaching rationales. Laying bear our pedagogic reasoning helps students understand that our actions are not arbitrary or haphazard. They see that our choices and injunctions spring from

our past experiences as teachers, from our convictions about what we're tyring to accomplish, and from our knowledge of students' backgrounds, expectations, cultures, and concerns. (Brookfield, 1995, p. 108)

The value of seeing our teaching about teaching through our students' eyes has been made abundantly clear in a number of recent self-studies (Brandenburg, 2004; Loughran, 2004b; Senese, 2004; Tudball, 2004; Winter, 2004) and is one way of coming to see how important it is to make the tacit explicit in teaching about teaching.

Overview

In teaching about teaching, making the tacit explicit offers students of teaching opportunities to see into practice so that they can better understand and relate to, the deliberations, questions, issues, concerns and dilemmas that impact the pedagogical reasoning underpinning the practice they experience.

If teaching is to be regarded as more than achieving competence in the delivery of tips, tricks and procedures; if teaching is to be understood as complex, interconnected, dynamic and holistic; and, if teaching about teaching is to make all of this apparent, then teacher educators need to develop ways of making the tacit explicit. In so doing, the professional knowledge of teaching, so crucial to the development and valuing of professional practice, will not only be made clear to students of teaching, it will also begin to be displayed, described, articulated and documented in ways that will enhance the development of a pedagogy of teacher education.

5 A shared language: Conceptualizing knowledge for a pedagogy of teacher education

> When what teacher educators know from the study of their practice is able to be developed, articulated and communicated with meaning for others, then the influence of that might better inform teacher education, generally.
> – Berry (2004a, p. 1308)

A considerable literature exists that describes and portrays the diversity of views and perspectives on the nature of knowledge (Clandinin and Connelly, 2000, 1995; Cochran-Smith and Lytle, 1999, 2004; Elbaz, 1991; Fenstermacher, 1986, 1994; Grimmett and MacKinnon, 1992; Korthagen *et al.*, 2001; Munby *et al.*, 2001; Richardson, 1997; Shulman, 1986, 1987; Whitehead, 1993); some of which was briefly outlined in the previous chapter. Yet, if making sense of teachers' professional knowledge is perplexing, then attempting to translate teaching about teachers' professional knowledge into action in teacher education is an even more daunting task; very little of which exists in the literature.

It is partly as a result of this difficulty that a simple solution to teacher education is so often adopted, thus: "the evidence is that we in teacher education still proceed as if it were simple: 'We tell our students and they go out and teach,' seems to sum it aptly" (Munby *et al.*, 2001, p. 900). Therefore, in proceeding as if it were simple, teacher education tends to exacerbate the difficulties associated with the notion of a theory–practice gap. Fortunately though, one helpful way of responding to this difficulty is through the constructs of episteme and phronesis (Kessels and Korthagen, 2001; Korthagen *et al.*, 2001).

Episteme and phronesis

Episteme is Theory with a Big T. It is expert knowledge of a particular problem derived from scientific understandings. It is propositional and as such, is of a general form applicable to a variety of different situations and formulated in abstract terms. Episteme is cognitive in nature "unaffected by emotion or desires. It is the knowledge that is of major importance, the specific situation and context being only an instance for the application of the knowledge" (Kessels and Korthagen, 2001, p. 21).

Phronesis is theory with a small t, it is practical wisdom; it is knowledge of the particularities of a situation. It is knowledge of the concrete not the abstract. This practical knowledge is perceptual and "uses rules only as summaries and guides... [and requires] enough proper experience. For particulars only become familiar with experience, with a long process of perceiving, assessing situations, judging, choosing courses of action, and being confronted with their consequences. This generates a sort of insight that is altogether different from scientific knowledge" (Kessels and Korthagen, 2001, p. 27).

Kessels and Korthagen's concern with the "inequality between theory and practice" led them to revisit the "classical controversy between Plato's and Aristotle's conceptions of rationality (episteme vs. phronesis)" (p. 21) and, in so doing, allowed them to reconceptualize the perceived theory–practice gap so that it might be bridged. Central to this issue is Korthagen's (2001a) insight that "traditional" teacher education programs appear to be based on three assumptions, all of which "create" a gap between theory and practice. These three assumptions are:

1   Theories help teachers to perform better in their profession.
2   These Theories (with a capital T) must be based on scientific research.
3   Teacher educators should make a choice concerning the Theories to be included in teacher education programs. (Korthagen, 2001a, p. 18)

These three assumptions make it appear as though one form of knowledge (episteme) is more important, more valuable, more "correct" than another (phronesis) and therefore inadvertently skews the manner in which approaches to teaching about teaching are implicitly constructed. However, the reality is that although it is indeed helpful to know the general rules that are at the heart of episteme, it is at least equally important to also know enough of the concrete details of situations and to be experienced in deliberating over such details to know whether the rules may or may not apply in the given case; or whether other rules might be more helpful to the situation.

The theory–practice gap creates an either/or scenario rather than a more holistic view of reality whereby being informed about possible choices is related to appropriate deliberations which themselves are influenced by experience, the context, and the concrete particulars, which requires expertise in its own right. As Kessels and Korthagen explain:

> One of the main problems is that most teacher educators have themselves been steeped in the episteme conception of knowledge. So they have always taken for granted the traditional, epistemic perspective on the relation between theory and practice. This makes it very hard to

understand the full impact of the shift toward phronesis....Let us suppose that the...knowledge that makes the teacher educator an expert is itself mainly perceptual, internal, and subjective. Now, the teacher educator may besides have command of a lot of conceptual, external, and more or less objective knowledge...[but] the pitfall, however, is to consider it [episteme] as more than an instrument for exploration – as the thing itself that we are after, the real thing. The real thing is not conceptual knowledge...it is perceptual knowledge... it is not to make student teachers into collectors of knowledge on teaching. We want them to be good teachers. This also means that there is a second pitfall. It is the idea that the expert's knowledge can be severed from him or her, abstracted from the person, put on a blackboard in front of students, or written in a paper in a purely conceptual form, creating the impression that an insight is the same as the sentences to be read. *We can assure you that it is not the same.* (emphasis added Kessels and Korthagen, 2001, p. 30)

In teaching about teaching, moderating the roles of episteme and phronesis requires expertise. It is not that one is more important than another, both inform good teaching, but it is the manner in which each are called upon and used that dramatically influences the way that each are interpreted by students of teaching, and therefore ultimately accepted, rejected, understood and valued. Knowing of the general may be important in shaping the nature of knowing about, or recognizing a problem; knowing of the particular is crucial in expertly responding to that problem. Teaching about teaching clearly involves expertise in moderating the same situation in teacher educators' practice (i.e. that which students of teaching need to begin to learn to recognize and respond to in their own practice, teacher educators must themselves do in order to model how such knowledge impacts learning about teaching).

An example of the articulation of such expertise is in the work of Jeff Northfield whereby his epistemic knowledge was developed as a result of his learning through an explication of his phronesis such that his knowledge of practice became "named" through the use of summary statements (for a full explanation of this process see Loughran, 2004a). In the manner in which Northfield's summary statements were categorized he created a way of reminding himself of what it was he knew about teaching so that that knowledge informed his practice whilst also offering a way of communicating and sharing that knowledge of practice with others. In so doing, his learning about his professional knowledge of teaching was made accessible, and hopefully became beneficial, to others.

In a similar way, other approaches to recognizing and articulating this expertise have emerged in the literature that offers ways of communicating and sharing it with others. The remainder of this chapter considers some of these forms of articulation. However, the manner in which they are organized for presentation is not meant to suggest that they are more important, or of higher status, than others. Rather the approach to organization and presentation reflects one way of grouping and describing such work.

An immediate difficulty with outlining the following approaches to articulating knowledge of teaching about teaching is that through the linear form of text that comprises a chapter, they may appear solely as examples of episteme. Yet it is through the particulars of the specific situations that phronesis is most apparent and so in constructing an understanding of these forms of articulation, it is important to remember that, just as Northfield's work demonstrates (again, for full explanation see Loughran, 2004a), that phronesis can indeed develop episteme and episteme can itself help to create new ways of seeing into and developing phronesis. It is not so much an either/or situation, it is a response to each better informing the other so that the "what" of knowledge is understood through the "how" of using it (practice informs theory informs practice: theory informs practice informs theory, and to do so, a shared language is necessary; clearly then, articulation matters).

Articulating a knowledge of practice

The need to articulate a knowledge of practice and to access it in ways that are appropriate and helpful to teaching *and* learning about teaching has been recognized for some time. Dewey (1964) called for a greater effort in better understanding the processes of teaching and learning so that it might better inform teacher education (in fact, his initial call for this was in 1904). In addition to this, Calderhead (1988) specifically noted the need for teacher educators and students of teaching to pay more attention to the process of learning to teach. He suggested that teacher educators needed to be aware of the complexity of learning to teach in order to facilitate better learning and to consider more critically the tasks in teacher education that might lead to the development of knowledge. In particular he suggested (among other things) the need for a common language amongst teachers, students of teaching and teacher educators for discussing the professional knowledge of teaching and how it might be used and presented in teacher education programs.

For students of teaching in particular he suggested that: "an awareness of the processes of learning to teach might enable them to analyse their own experiences in professional development, to identify those areas of know-ledge and skill that must be built up, and to recognize the potential of professional learning for their own practice" (Calderhead, 1988, p. 63). Real responses to such requests seem to have been, for too long, hindered by the lack of academic standing afforded teacher educators as researchers of their own, and their students', practice. Despite calls for the teacher educator's voice to be acknowledged and encouraged (Lanier and Little, 1986) the response was muted and the prevailing view was that teacher education continued to replicate that which had gone before (Goodlad, 1990). Despite this, teacher educators were nonetheless still encouraged to develop and share their research of their practice so that their voices might be heard (e.g. Fenstermacher, 1997; Tabachnick and Zeichner, 1991).

Perhaps, one way of interpreting what was happening at this time was that teacher educators' approaches to researching teaching and learning about teaching, although occurring, was not being reported. However, with the emergence of self-study of teacher education practices, acceptance of teacher educators reporting on their own practitioner research led to such practices finally becoming public and therefore more accessible (for a full discussion on the issues surrounding the emergence of practitioner research see Zeichner and Noffke, 2001).

Through the publication of accounts of practitioner inquiry by teachers and teacher educators, conceptualizing what a language of teaching and learning about teaching might encompass is made possible. The following examples are a point in case.

Program principles

This approach to articulating knowledge of teaching about teaching is organized around the idea that particular principles need to be articulated and overtly used to shape not only the way a program might be organized and developed, but also how the teaching within that program might be conceptualized and practiced. The work of Northfield and Gunstone (1997) and Kroll (2004; Kroll *et al.*, 2005) are examples of this approach.

Northfield and Gunstone (1997) described how their set of principles had been discussed, modified, and interpreted over almost two decades of collaboration and reflection on their own practice. These principles are:

1   The student-teacher has needs and prior experiences which must be considered in planning and implementing the teacher preparation program. And, the nature and intensity of these needs should shift throughout the program.
2   The transition to teacher as a learner of teaching is fundamental and difficult and is facilitated by working in collaboration with colleagues.
3   The student-teacher is a learner who actively constructs ideas based on personal experience. These ideas are about: the process of teaching and learning; content (discipline) knowledge; understanding of self; and, social structures within the profession.
4   Teacher education should model the teaching and learning approaches being advocated in the program.
5   Student teachers should see their teacher education program as a worthwhile experience in its own right.
6   Teacher education programs are by definition incomplete. (pp. 50–55)

These principles, as Northfield and Gunstone suggest, are bound up in an understanding of the importance of recognizing and responding to student teachers' needs and concerns, building on their experiences and attempting to bring to the surface ideas about teachers' knowledge in order to help them meet the educational challenges that they will face as professionals. They also acknowledge that their principles are indicative of a pedagogy that is: "easier to argue than implement...[and] that it requires considerable commitment and energy to align practice with principles but [that] no coherent pedagogy of teacher education can be developed without first addressing fundamental questions about teacher knowledge and learning" (p. 56).

In considering the nature of teacher preparation programs, these principles certainly offer one way of immediately challenging the three assumptions that underpin the traditional teacher education program structure described by Korthagen (2001a). However, it is in the manner in which these principles are enacted in practice that perhaps matter most and, that is what Kroll (2004, Kroll *et al.*, 2005) describes through her incorporation of program principles into her teaching about teaching.

In the teacher education program in which Kroll teaches at Mills College (Oakland, California), she strives to ensure that the principles on which the program is based are explicitly used to shape her own teaching and, as such, uses them to inquire into her own practice in order to see how these principles link with what she does and how that influences her students' learning. These six principles are:

1   Teaching is a moral act invoking an ethic of care.
2   Teaching is reflective and requires an inquiry stance.
3   Learning is a developmental/constructivist process.
4   Subject matter matters.
5   There is a need to develop strong collegial bonds.
6   Teaching is a political act.

As a set of foundation principles for a teacher preparation program, Kroll describes how these principles are designed to help students of teaching begin to see more in teaching than what their previous personal experience (as students) might suggest to them about the nature of teaching and learning. In essence, these principles are designed to challenge participants' assumptions of teaching and learning by creating contexts in which such challenges might be enacted and built upon. In so doing, she purposefully attempts to create real ways of developing and implementing practices that will help her students begin to connect understanding with behavior, in line with the process described by Korthagen and Kessels (1999), so that they might begin to "think critically about their own practice in an ongoing developmental manner" (p. 217).

The importance of program principles being translated into practice is significant and, no doubt preferable, for coherent program structure and function. However, other forms of professional knowledge of teaching about teaching also exist whereby personal practice is shaped and formulated without necessarily being referenced to program principles as a foundation for development. For, in many cases, program principles do not explicitly exist as the three assumptions of traditional teacher education programs that Korthagen (2001a) describes tend to set up a sense of dissonance for those who see contradictions for teaching about teaching based on such assumptions. Thus, responding as an individual may be somewhat paradoxical.

Paradox

In her chapter *Seams of Paradoxes in Teaching*, Wilkes (1998) explores the nature of paradox and how she sees it playing out in her own teaching about teaching. She views paradox as a useful vehicle for thinking about teaching for it is not only one way of beginning to unpack the underpinnings of practice, it also helps to create new ways of responding in practice. She notes how paradox is played out through the value of the counterintuitive; being able to respond in a manner that may not feel like it is the right way to act, but it is the effective thing to do for it produces the desired result. Hence, in her teaching about teaching she finds the same often applies: "Often when a student comes to me for help, and they are truly struggling, my intuition tells me to help them by either giving them the answer or telling them where to find it. It is painful for me to listen to them struggle and not give them the information they need. I often have to resist mightily what I want to do, what my gut tells me, and fix the momentary crisis. But I have learned that if I become the source of answers, then I often enable students to stop searching for themselves. So now I employ what, for me, is a counterintuitive practice" (p. 199).

Wilkes discusses in detail three aspects of one of her paradoxes: *Teaching content and manner*, but also raises others such as the paradox of: autonomy and collaboration; silence in the classroom as being most productive and least productive; and, structure and freedom. The point which she continually returns to as she unpacks the notion of paradox is that although a paradox initially appears to be a contradictory assertion, when one digs a little deeper, the paradox opens up new possibilities as multiple levels of meaning emerge. Therefore, that which once appeared contradictory is not really contradictory when it is more fully questioned, examined and therefore understood in practice: "in questioning the *content and manner* of my day-to-day interactions with my own students, I am continually... observing how students act and react and interact and those observations inform my practice in observable ways" (emphasis added, p. 206).

Palmer (1998) also draws on the notion of paradox in articulating his views of practice. He describes paradox as "a way of holding opposites together that creates an electric charge that keeps us awake" (p. 74) and outlines six paradoxes that he is consciously aware of when designing a classroom session. His paradoxes are that his teaching space should:

1 Be bounded and open.
2 Be hospitable and "charged."
3 Invite the voice of the individual and the voice of the group.
4 Honor the "little" stories of the students and the "big" stories of the disciplines and tradition.
5 Support solitude and surround it with the resources of community.
6 Welcome both silence and speech. (p. 74)

Having outlined each of these six paradoxes and explained what each of them mean in practice, Parker goes on to describe in detail how each plays out in his teaching through an extended analysis of a classroom situation. In so doing, what Parker demonstrates is how the generalized knowledge that comprises each paradox sensitizes him to particular problems, issues and tensions within the classroom, but that that alone is not sufficient. He also needs to consciously consider the nature of the situation by unpacking the particulars of each paradox within the context of the teaching and learning interactions. In this way, his teaching is informed and responsive because of his knowledge about, and actions in, practice. Hence, there is no theory–practice gap. There is meaningful teaching and learning. However, this is not to suggest that working with paradox is easy.

> Holding the tension of paradox so that our students can learn at deeper levels is among the most difficult demands of good teaching. How are we supposed to do it?...We will not be able to teach in the power of paradox until we are willing to suffer the tension of opposites, until we understand that such suffering is neither to be avoided nor merely to be survived but must be actively embraced...Without this acceptance, the pain of suffering will always lead us to resolve the tension prematurely... We will ask and answer our own questions in the silence of the classroom (thus creating more silence); we will ride roughshod over the dissenting voice that confounds our learning plan (even though we said we welcomed questions); we will punish the student who writes outside the assignment (no matter how creatively) to bring him or her back in line. We cannot teach our students at the deepest levels when we are unable to bear the suffering that opens into those levels. By holding the tension of opposites, we hold the gateway to inquiry open, inviting students into a territory in which we all can learn. (Palmer, 1998, pp. 83 and 85)

As Palmer suggests, paradox is loaded with tension and, understanding and using tension constructively offers another window into articulating a knowledge of practice. Tension can be particularly helpful in relation to teacher education practices when described and understood in the context of teaching about teaching; being drawn from the very source in which the expertise of bridging the theory–practice gap should be most clearly visible.

If understanding paradox in teaching is helpful, then the translation of that knowledge in and through teaching about teaching must surely offer helpful ways of conceptualizing a pedagogy of teacher education.

Tensions

After an extensive review of the literature on teacher educators' learning about their own practice, Berry (2004a) formulated an articulation of that learning through the construct of tensions which she described as capturing the conflicting purposes and ambiguity of teacher educators' work. Her tensions are:

Telling and growth

- between informing and creating opportunities to reflect and self-direct;
- between acknowledging student teachers' needs and concerns and challenging them to grow.

Confidence and uncertainty

- between making explicit the complexities and messiness of teaching and helping student teachers feel confident to proceed;
- between exposing vulnerability as a teacher educator and maintaining student teachers' confidence in the teacher educator as leader.

Working with and against

- between working toward a particular ideal and jeopardising this ideal by the approach chosen to attain it.

Discomfort and challenge

- between a constructive learning experience and an uncomfortable learning experience.

Acknowledging and building upon experience

- between helping students recognise the 'authority of their experience' and helping them to see that there is more to teaching than simply experience.

Planning and being responsive

- between planning for learning and responding to learning opportunities as they arise in practice. (Berry, 2004a, pp. 1313–1314)

It is not difficult to see the similarity in the themes and implications inherent in Berry's tensions and the paradoxes described by Wilkes and Palmer for they clearly carry a similar message. The message is that in teaching there is no recipe or formula for how best to deal with a given situation. If there was, then episteme alone would indeed be the source of truth for the resolution of all teaching and learning issues. However, through familiarity with the particulars of situations, through appropriate experience in learning to hold on to tensions, by purposefully keeping opposites in balance, a teaching path may be forged, shaped and crafted. And, by working with the relationship of teaching and learning, pedagogy is developed and enhanced.

Berry's tensions suggest that the transformation of this teaching and learning relationship in teacher education clearly requires substantial expertise. There is a need not only to recognize the impact of these tensions on the learning of students of teaching but also to create and moderate them through one's own teaching about teaching so that the tension itself is recognized and responded to as a central source of professional knowledge of practice. Thus the teacher educator needs to balance the tensions in practice while highlighting them in students' learning so that they might experience them for themselves as learners of teaching whilst also seeing them played out in the practice of their teachers of teaching: "the tensions that influence learning about practice...do not exist in isolation from each other....these tensions interact in practice...Instead of interpreting the tensions as situations that evoke despair and frustration, and trying to eliminate them from one's work, teacher educators begin to reframe them as elements that are necessary and pleasurable for the growth and learning that they bring [to themselves, and their students of teaching]" (Berry, 2004a, pp. 1325, 1327).

In teaching about teaching, acknowledging and responding to tensions offers a way of exposing the professional knowledge of teaching so that it can be questioned, critiqued, analyzed and felt in practice. More so, working with tensions to teach about teaching is an indication of the specialist knowledge, skills and practice of the professional teacher educator.

In a similar vein to paradoxes and tensions, another form of articulation of knowledge of practice is described through the use of axioms.

Axioms

Steeped in a constructivist approach to learning, Senese (2002) formulated three axioms that helped him to better understand his own practice. These axioms "each containing overtones of tension and even irony... [are] counterintuitive, and the tension inherent in each rises from the opposing forces at play. Understanding and employing these opposing forces in the proper perspective is key to helping teachers grow professionally and also to helping students grow academically" (pp. 47–48). Again, as with paradoxes and tensions, axioms are another way of capturing the essence of practice *in* practice whilst simultaneously portraying a sense of holism so necessary to managing pedagogy in a fruitful way. Senese's axioms are:

- Go slow to go fast.
- Be tight to be loose.
- Relinquish control in order to gain influence.

Drawing on the work of Wheatley (1992), Senese describes how, through choosing to look more deeply into his practice, that which once may have appeared "shapeless and chaotic" actually contained "patterns." Because he was able to observe his teaching from a distance – of both location and time – he was able to tentatively generalize from his experiences which allowed him to recognize and name the patterns.

In developing ways of naming, Senese found that his knowledge of practice was enhanced as he learnt to: "accept and welcome the contradictory nature of interactions in teaching and learning" (p. 53). Interestingly, like Wilkes, he described the manner in which he came to understand his practice through the idea of not reacting the way he felt he should, but by holding back and thinking about the opposite – thus the articulation of axioms: "when my tongue wants to speak, I have learned to remain silent. When my role...demands action, I wait. When I become impatient I slow down. My intuition has become counterintuitive! Taking this route has freed me to become a better listener, a more perceptive learner, and a fairer coach....I am free to take the balcony view, to embrace the whole and to view the horizon" (p. 54).

The same understanding and intent emerges through Senese's axioms as are apparent in the language of paradoxes and tensions. Each approach to naming communicates important perspectives on practice whilst also capturing crucial aspects of the bigger picture. Thus, naming in this way helps to convey knowledge of practice that, through such articulation, carries much more meaning than the words alone might initially appear to convey.

This knowledge is general in the sense that that from which it is distilled comprises an extensive array of observations and "learnings", but this knowledge is also particular in the way that specific practice is shaped in response to a given situation. Such knowledge is not a blueprint or a recipe for practice, but a guide which, through appropriate reflection, suggests various options, each of which might be interpreted adjusted and adapted to suit the perceived needs of the situation at that time through the expertise of the teacher.

At the heart of paradoxes, tensions and axioms is a common issue; finding an appropriate balance between responding appropriately to one's thoughts and actions in practice. Professional knowledge of practice is tangible through the manner in which this balance is managed as both the general and particular interact to inform and enhance pedagogical outcomes.

Making this complex relationship accessible for others is what an articulation of professional knowledge entails and, for some, that articulation has been a substantial and sustained focus.

Summary statements

As noted earlier, Jeff Northfield, as an experienced educational researcher, teacher educator and high school teacher embarked on a sustained process of learning about practice as he sought to examine and document his knowledge of practice by returning to high school teaching for a year (see Loughran and Northfield, 1996). As a result of his intense, systematic and thoughtful analysis of the data collected throughout his year's teaching, he developed summary statements that portrayed for him, his knowledge of teaching. These summary statements emerged as a result of his recognition of the impact of the differences in intent between his students' and his teacher's views of teaching and learning (see Chapter 2, Tables 2.1 and 2.2). In many ways, these differences also reflect the underpinnings of paradoxes, tensions and axioms as, through a recognition of the opposing perspectives, expectations for action appear to be almost diametrically opposed.

Each of his summary statements was based on a range of episodes, anecdotes or situations that, for him, carried similar underlying purposes that, when considered together, led to common conclusions that were able to be encapsulated in the resultant summary statement. The summary statements then are the generalizations articulated as a result of considering similarities in vivid and real episodes which individually carry particular meaning, but when combined create an understanding of a bigger picture of teaching.

The summary statements were categorized and grouped around common themes to create five overall groupings that together comprised the 24 summary statements distilled from the year's data (Table 5.1).

Although the summary statements in Table 5.1 are drawn from the context of high school teaching, they nonetheless have much to say about knowledge of teaching about teaching. In many ways, that which Kessels and Korthagen (2001) described as "proper experience" is exactly what underpins these summary statements. They carry meaning because of the experiences that led to their formulation. However, it is in seeing beyond the experiences alone that leads to the ability to abstract across each to draw out valuable insights into teaching and learning in general. Thus, both the particular and the general combine to create meaningful knowledge of practice.

For teacher educators, the dual roles of teaching and of teaching about teaching take on new significance when considering the knowledge encompassed by articulations such as summary statements. For example, experiences that shape the statement that "effort and risk taking are critical for learning" need to be created in teacher education contexts in ways that demonstrate

Table 5.1 Summary statements: learning from a teaching experience

---

Nature of learning
1   Quality learning requires learner consent.
2   Learning is done **by** rather than **to** students.
3   Student prior experiences are crucial and often do not fit the learning demands expected.
4   Effort and risk taking are critical for learning.
5   Understanding is rarely experienced, and not expected, by many students.

Creating conditions for learning
6   Teacher change precedes student change.
7   Changes in assessment (beliefs and practice) are essential. Students must see ideas and activities which improve learning being valued.
8   Self-confidence and trust are critical attributes for students.
9   There is a need to have a balance between management demands and maintaining learning opportunities in the classroom.
10 Students can have a significant impact on classroom climate. It only takes a few students to make a big difference.
11 There is a limit to the thinking and learning demands that can be placed on students.
12 There is a need for teachers to respond to contextual factors and make intuitive decisions rather than always following the plan.

Student perspectives on learning
13 Success is gained by the "right answers" to defined tasks.
14 Enjoyment is regarded with suspicion in terms of learning.
15 Lessons with different teachers allow a "fresh start" and give students a chance to see their tasks as being well defined.
16 Students have faith in texts: the tasks are routine and the knowledge is dependable.
17 Students wish to be successful but to be seen as "mediocre" by their peers.

Process of teaching and learning
18 Effective interventions increase the spread of students.
19 Frequent use of particular teaching strategies leads to passive student responses.
20 It is important to increase the repertoire of teaching strategies.
21 In the "dailiness" of schooling there are still rare opportunities for active learning.

Overall reactions
22 Time and careful review are essential for professional development.
23 It is important to have a model and language of learning so that students and teachers can discuss teaching and learning issues.
24 Understanding student responses requires details of student and class context (social structures, expectations of other teachers, etc.).

Source: Loughran and Northfield (1996, p. 124).

exactly that as an outcome of learning about teaching. So, teacher educators' teaching needs to honour the statement through practice, but then unpacking that teaching must also highlight not only that it has been enacted but also *how* it impacted on the teacher and learner (cognitively and affectively) if the knowledge is to carry meaning beyond the statement itself.

For students of teaching, one clear and immediate value of teachers' professional knowledge (such as summary statements) is in helping them to recognize that there is a bigger picture to be constructed from their teaching. Part of teaching about teaching is helping them to see beyond the particulars of experiences so that they do not *just* accumulate experiences, but that through reflection on those experiences, they might begin to see the value in distilling the essence of the learning into a meaningful form that might then inform their practice. But, in the first instance, they must see the same happening in the development and use of professional knowledge of teaching in their teacher educators. Thus, in teacher education, there is a responsibility for all of these facets of knowledge of practice not only to *be* happening, but also to be *seen* to be happening.

The groupings of summary statements in Table 5.1 also help to illustrate how different elements interact to create a big picture view of teaching such that attention to issues that impact teaching and learning are brought into focus in different ways and at different times in order to shape the outcomes of teaching and learning (e.g. creating appropriate conditions, considering alternative perspectives, understanding overall reactions, etc.). The big picture matters in demonstrating through experience that that which may once have appeared shapeless and chaotic actually contains patterns.

Assertions

Another approach to describing knowledge of teaching that, for me, has become particularly valuable in shaping and articulating a knowledge of teaching about teaching is through the use of assertions. Learning from those who have mentored me and those with whom I have collaborated and taught, I have found that slowly, over time, patterns in and of practice have become much more apparent and helpful for practice. These patterns are captured in the notion of assertions, the list of which is continually being refined, adapted and adjusted as new and different experiences impact their meaning.

These assertions have largely been articulated as a result of adopting a self-study stance which has led to the realization of the importance of making teacher educators' knowledge accessible to others through the development of scholarship in teacher education. Detailed explanations of the assertions that follow exist elsewhere (Loughran, 2003) and, as in the previous sections, the list is offered only as an illustration of a form of articulation.

> Assertion 1: Learning about teaching needs to be embedded in personal experience.
> Assertion 2: Start teaching as if you are halfway through the subject.
> Assertion 3: Be confident to be responsive to possibilities in learning experiences.

Assertion 4: An uncomfortable learning experience can be a constructive learning experience – risk-taking matters.

Assertion 5: Articulating personal principles of practice helps in better aligning practice and beliefs.

Assertion 6: Teaching is about relationships.

Assertion 7: Students of teaching enter teacher preparation programs expecting to be told how to teach.

Assertion 8: The needs and concerns of students of teaching shift during teacher preparation and the program should be responsive to these changes.

Assertion 9: The transition from student to teacher is complicated by situations that create cognitive and affective dissonance that need to be acknowledged.

Assertion 10: Quality learning requires learner consent.

Assertion 11: Modeling is crucial – students of teaching learn more from what we do than what we say.

Assertion 12: A shared experience with a valued other provides greater opportunity to reframe situations and confront one's assumptions about practice.

Assertion 13: Challenging "telling as teaching" must occur at a personal level if the rhetoric of teacher education is to be real for participants.

Assertion 14: Teacher education programs should be coherent and holistic.

Assertion 15: Teacher education programs need to acknowledge and value the important differences between teaching and education as disciplines in their own right.

Assertion 16: Teacher preparation is, by definition, incomplete.

Assertion 17: Students of teaching are teachers, learners, and researchers.

Assertion 18: Teacher education requires a commitment to researching teaching and teaching research.

Consider Assertion 10. Having worked closely with Jeff Northfield for a substantial period of time, when he captured in words the ideas that underpin the assertion that "quality learning requires learner consent," it had an immediate impact on my understanding of teaching about teaching. Through this assertion, the idea that teaching (no matter how well that might be done) somehow guarantees learning is anathema.

In teaching, it is too easy to assume that because something has been well delivered, that the intended learning will be a natural consequence. There is ample evidence to suggest (and one's own learning experiences should reinforce) that learners pick and choose what to pay attention to, and that simply paying attention is not the same as learning. Therefore, regardless of how well something is "taught," the learner is still in a position of choosing how to take that teaching on board, what to do with it, and importantly, what and how they will learn from it. Quality teaching may be constructed, but quality learning requires learner consent. And, in any given class, not all choose to learn – much less choose to learn the same things at the same time in the same way.

Clearly then, in constructing pedagogical experiences, there is a need to be reminded of this situation so that an invitation to learning might be created and that the actions, behaviors and teaching procedures used to enhance the pedagogical relationship will be engaging and thus encourage learners to choose to learn. In relating all of this to teaching about teaching, think for a moment about one of the most common situations that students of teaching are confronted by: classroom management.

There exists a plethora of advice and information on classroom management. In the work of Bill Rogers (Rogers, 1990, 1998), one of his central messages for beginning teachers is to maintain a focus on a "disruptive" student's primary behavior and not to be drawn into reacting to the secondary behavior which so often leads to an unnecessary escalation of the problem, trapping the teacher in a not so pleasant encounter of claims, counter claims and a test of wills.

This idea can be well taught in teacher education classes. Role-plays, scenarios, and other teaching procedures might be employed to teach about the information that, on first glimpse, appears to be reasonable and logical. However, many students of teaching, although recognizing and understanding the information, choose not to learn from it because they do not think such a situation will engulf them because they are not going to be "that sort of teacher." Hence, it quickly becomes apparent that despite the best intentions of the teacher educator, learning requires the learner consent.

Having taught about classroom management on many occasions and then observed students of teaching being caught up in difficulties of exactly the type described above, my teacher educator's tacit view that because *it* had been taught *it* had been learned often surfaced. Despite my best intentions and my experiences of pedagogic episodes through which it appeared as though participants had been well taught about classroom management, the learning did not translate in a meaningful way into their practice; so what was the quality of the learning?

Being confronted by the inherent contradiction between one's teaching and students' learning takes on different meaning when viewed through the assertion that "quality learning requires learner consent." It helps one to question the extent to which teaching is responsive to the demands of learning and to push beyond the (apparent) meaningful delivery of the information. Understanding the contradiction is aided through Posner *et al.*'s (1982) suggestion that concepts need to be intelligible, plausible and fruitful; this idea can be seen to impact on both teaching and learning.

In helping students of teaching to learn from the situation, although the idea (theory) of differentiating between primary and secondary behaviors may have been explained and appear intelligible (i.e. it makes sense and can be understood) and plausible (i.e. that it seems reasonable to do), it needs to be used in practice to become fruitful (i.e. to be worth the effort of doing it). However, quality learning requires learner consent offers a reminder that, in this case, something must be happening around (at least) the notion of plausibility. Perhaps in this case, there are two ways of conceptualizing plausibility: plausible in itself and for other teachers' practice, plausible in itself but not needed in "my" practice. Therefore, until students of teaching see the problem as plausible in their own practice, the essence of plausibility will not really be achieved and the necessary testing for fruitfulness will not be to the forefront of their thinking in practice. Thus, quality learning requires learner consent carries important implications for teaching about teaching.

In considering this issue from a teaching about teaching perspective, learner consent hinges on the learner seeing the plausibility of the concept for, and in, their own practice. In so doing, it can be a catalyst for initiating possibilities for testing for fruitfulness. This teaching about teaching situation is very different to one in which teaching is more about conveying the information and ideas alone. In teaching about teaching, quality learning is evident when the information and ideas are enacted in practice as opposed to just being able to be recounted in other, often abstract forms – test papers, assignments.

Quality learning in teaching about teaching requires plausibility to lead to knowing the information and then learning how to act on that information with all the cognitive and affective challenges that might be involved. What encouraging learner consent in teaching about teaching is *not* about is supplying the "correct" response. What it *is* about is creating a real learning need so that students of teaching see *and* feel how to adapt, adjust, and develop ideas and information in their deeds and thoughts of practice so that their own considered responses and actions in situations develop in meaningful and personally informing ways.

The assertion that quality learning requires learner consent, when linked to one's own experiences and episodes of such situations, can become a powerful influence for conceptualizing approaches to teaching about teaching. It is an aspect of professional knowledge that cannot easily be explained for it does not encompass a finite set of knowledge and experience. It is a lens through which to view aspects of pedagogy. Thus, through articulation of the assertion, possibilities exist for making the complexity of teaching more accessible, and therefore considerably more informing to practice for oneself, and hopefully for others. But, it does not govern or direct how practice *must* be enacted, rather it helps to shape thinking about the possibilities for action through the wisdom and autonomy of the professional pedagogue.

Taking these ideas a step further consider the classroom management issue (above) through understandings associated with Assertion 4: "An uncomfortable learning experience can be a constructive learning experience – risk-taking matters." It could well be that one way of encouraging students of teaching to develop their own tests for fruitfulness will require risk-taking. For students of teaching, the discomfort associated with being confronted by a classroom management situation needs to be framed in light of a recognition that their affective response(s) may overshadow the cognitive reasoning necessary to fully carry through on a test of fruitfulness. Thus risk-taking for risk-taking's sake is not the intention, it is risk-taking in order to learn about how one feels and manages the situation so that a better understanding of how to respond in future might be formulated. In so doing, the manner in which context influences professional knowledge of teaching, and its growth, becomes much more apparent and challenges the notion of knowledge as a common and linear causal path. Approaching professional knowledge from this perspective, further highlights the centrality of implications associated with the relationship between different aspects of professional knowledge of teaching for the above discussion clearly leads to issues associated with Assertion 17: "Students of teaching are teachers, learners and researchers."

If students of teaching are encouraged to research their own practice, to better understand what they do and how they do it, they may be more empowered to seek new ways of viewing their practice and therefore of conceptualizing their practice. Their knowledge of practice might therefore become more important in shaping their teaching and of creating a genuine sense of valuing their developing professional knowledge of teaching. It is difficult to see how that would be anything but a most positive outcome from teaching *and* learning about teaching.

Clearly then, the manner in which assertions (and the other forms of articulation of professional knowledge outlined previously) can be used to access knowledge of teaching about teaching means that such knowledge does not exist in isolation but is intimately linked to practice. Thus, such knowledge acts as a guide for informing practice while at the same time encapsulating similar and related experiences through which action might be appropriately shaped. Professional knowledge of practice, from this perspective, may then be viewed as a process of distillation from experiences to find common understandings and views of practice while at the same time using these common understandings to look out in informed ways that might encourage new ways to interpret and respond to the contextual differences inherent in all practice situations – a process of knowledge generation through gathering in, building up and building out.

Overview

This chapter has attempted to demonstrate how the perceived theory–practice gap is not helpful in the work of teacher education. The chapter has argued that teacher educators need to have a shared language of teaching about teaching and that the professional knowledge that such knowledge might comprise needs to be accessible and useable. The use of principles, paradoxes, tensions, axioms, summary statements, and assertions are examples of how such knowledge might be conceptualized and portrayed.

However, in so doing, an immediate difficulty is created whereby "spelling out" each of these forms of articulation can itself be seen as re-creating the very distinction that it is argued is not so helpful to teaching about teaching.

In all cases, I would argue that the form of articulation (principles, paradoxes, tensions, etc.) at the general level may well be characterized as episteme. But, importantly, that such epistemic knowledge is embedded, or better, created through phronesis which itself encourages the sense making that leads to more meaningful articulation. Therefore, one does not carry meaning without the other, that is, in the case of assertions, an assertion itself is not "the knowledge" it is the assertion in concert with the experiences that have shaped the formulation of that assertion that is the articulation of professional knowledge. And, if that knowledge carries genuine meaning for others, it is because others are able to identify with the underlying ideas, concepts and experiences through that form of articulation such that they might feel as though: "that could be my classroom, my experience."

Combined then, the experiences that have shaped the articulations presented in this chapter are tangible examples of how a shared language of teaching about teaching can enhance teacher education practices and demonstrate the richness of the professional knowledge that it sets out to portray.

Boyer (1990) focused attention on what he thought it meant to be a scholar and the nature of scholarship itself. In so doing, he called on academia to develop a more integrated and holistic understanding of teaching and research, its synthesis and application. Shulman (1999), taking Boyer's call further, introduced the notion of scholarship of teaching and suggested that such scholarship depended on at least three key attributes: becoming public; becoming an object of critical review and evaluation by members of that community; and, members of that community beginning to use, build upon, and develop those acts of mind and creation.

Scholarship in teaching about teaching is encouraged through these key attributes being evident in the development of a pedagogy of teacher education. The approaches to articulation outlined in this chapter offer ways of making professional knowledge of practice public and available for critical review. Putting such knowledge into use then lies with the individual teacher educator. However, as the next chapter attempts to demonstrate, using and building upon such professional knowledge is enhanced through considerations of what it means and how it might be reflected and enacted in one's own teaching about teaching. Thus the notion of personal principles of practice emerges and, for individual teacher educators in the way they develop, adapt and articulate such principles personally, may well form the foundations from which to build a pedagogy of teacher education.

6 Principles of practice

In teacher education, what and how we teach are interactive, and we ignore this interaction at our peril. Just as actions are said to speak louder than words, so how we teach may speak more loudly than what we teach.
— Russell (1998, p. 5)

In endeavoring to better understand teaching about teaching it seems inevitable that a concentration on practice must continually resurface, first and foremost, through a focus on our own teaching. As Russell (1998) so aptly pointed out (above), our teaching actions may well attract more of our students' attention than the intended message of our words. Therefore, despite that which we may consider to be our beliefs about practice, saying one thing and doing another, or as Whitehead (1993) described it, being a living contradiction, despite our best intentions, is an ever-present pitfall.

Mitchell (1992) explored the relationship between teachers' teaching behaviors and how they influenced students' approaches to learning. In his study (teaching for enhanced metacognition, see Project for Enhancing Effective Learning (Baird and Mitchell, 1986; Baird and Northfield, 1992; Loughran, 1999) i.e. PEEL), he outlined a number of important teaching behaviors central to students accepting the challenge of making the shift from passive to active learners.

As Mitchell outlined some of these teaching behaviors, his work hinted at the importance of teachers needing to be conscious of their actions and of purposefully attempting to align their beliefs and practices. Mitchell highlighted the value of teachers honestly "seeing" their teaching behaviors and then determining how such behaviors might need to change in order to better reflect the type of learning they were trying to encourage in their students, that is better aligning beliefs and practices.

Being conscious of our teaching behaviours

In teacher education, such a level of consciousness is all the more important as being able to formulate views about that which matters in one's teaching about teaching impacts directly on students of teaching and their developing views of practice (which will of course eventually be played out in their own classes when they are teaching). Mitchell's list of general teaching behaviors (Mitchell, 1992, p. 74) is a helpful way of reflecting upon, and being more conscious of, one's own teaching behaviors. Table 6.1 is an adaptation of Mitchell's general teaching behaviors to a teaching about teaching context and is designed to offer ways of considering changes in behaviors that encourage students to be more active learners of teaching.

Although Table 6.1 is portrayed as a dichotomy, whilst in reality much of our teaching behaviors vary along a continuum, the stark alternatives are helpful in considering how we act as opposed to how we might wish to act in teaching about teaching and is a reminder of how easy it can be for our (taken for granted) teaching behaviors to negate our underlying teaching and learning intentions. Table 6.1 is not intended to list all possible teaching behaviors, merely to illustrate through a concrete example how our teaching behaviors can so easily contradict our teaching beliefs.

In focusing on our teaching behaviors, it is also important to recognize that simply modeling practice through the use of a range of teaching procedures (e.g. concept maps, Venn diagrams, interpretive discussions), or teaching about teaching by using engaging strategies, is in itself not sufficient in teacher education. There is a clear need to continually go deeper and to address the underlying features of teaching and learning. For this to occur,

Table 6.1 Teaching about teaching behaviours: a consideration of changes in behavior to influence learning about teaching

Teacher educator – directed approach	*Students of teaching – focused approach*
Asks closed questions that elicit short predetermined answers.	Asks open questions that require thoughtful, reasoned responses.
Uses minimum wait time, moves quickly from student to student.	Uses extended wait time and encourages students to persevere with their thinking and responses.
Concerned that students know the correct answers, moving on quickly once that has been determined.	Illustrates an interest in students' views and thinking. Listens carefully to responses to appropriately challenge responses regardless of whether they are *right* or *wrong*.
Corrects students' answers and thinking and does not easily accept disagreement or challenge from students.	Withholds judgment and accepts a range of responses. Accepts (and praises) own ideas being questioned or challenged.
Conscious of completing the content of the session, adhering to a fixed routine.	Flexible about timing and approach responding appropriately to students' views and suggestions about how to deal with the topic.
Concentration on what to do rather than why it is worth doing.	Draws attention to purpose and reasons for doing learning tasks.

teacher educators need to work through the very experiences of teaching and learning that they create for, and encounter with, their students of teaching (i.e. through the shared experiences of teaching and learning with students, there is the need to address the dual roles of teaching *and* learning about teaching together). In so doing, there is an ongoing need to articulate one's understandings of practice (purpose, beliefs and intent) in order to access the reasons for teaching actions and, perhaps more importantly, the insights into one's underlying philosophies of teaching and learning about teaching.

Beyond students of teaching needing to know how a teaching procedure works (i.e. coming to know the skills in, and features associated with, using the procedure) they also need to know the complexities of why it works. If a teacher educator expects students of teaching to simply accept the hows and whys of various teaching procedures and strategies because of the authority of their position (Munby and Russell, 1994) then it belies an underlying view of teaching and learning that may well be incongruent with the intention of the teaching procedures. It is therefore important that students of teaching actively question their teacher educators' views, thoughts and actions in conjunction with their own experiences of learning and teaching in order to develop the authority of their own experience (Munby and Russell, 1994). One immediate outcome of such a process is that tacit views of teaching and learning (teacher educator's and students') necessarily become more explicit as the need for a language through which to share understandings of teaching and learning become readily apparent.

The need for articulating principles

Myers (2002) draws attention to the need to challenge the (mis)belief that telling, showing and guiding practice somehow constitutes adequate teacher education. Clearly, confronting telling as teaching is an important aspect of teaching about teaching if pedagogy akin to what van Manen (1991) describes as the *tact of teaching* is to not only be real, but be seen to be real, by our students of teaching. Therefore, the principles of practice that underpin our teaching must be clear and explicit not only to ourselves but also to our students if our beliefs and actions are to be more fully aligned in our teaching about teaching; especially if we expect our practice to influence our students' developing views of, and actions in, their own teaching.

Bullough (1997) outlined eleven principles that he recognized as important in shaping his practice in teacher education. Briefly, they are:

1   Teacher identity is important and teacher education must begin by exploring the teaching self.
2   The exploration of teacher identity necessitates a study of schooling and wider social contexts.

3 An understanding of social philosophy and the aims of education in a democracy are important.
4 Teacher education must challenge beliefs whilst still being supportive and respectful.
5 Articulation of program decisions is important in building a trusting environment.
6 Learners chose whether or not to accept responsibility for learning.
7 There is no one best teaching style or approach to teaching but quality judgments must still be made in developing practice.
8 Individuals make their own meaning of teacher education.
9 Program continuity involves more than just sensible sequencing of content, opportunities for students to create their own sense of continuity is also crucial.
10 A language of learning and applying it with others is part of being a professional.
11 Teaching requires exploring new methods and techniques and purposefully engaging in ongoing data-driven self-evaluation.

He described the purpose of his principles by stating that they arose from:

> my experience and underpin my work which is driven by one fundamental aim: to help prepare teachers who are disposed to be students of teaching, who are morally grounded in the practice of education as the practice of freedom, who are at home with young people, and who possess the skills and knowledge needed to design potentially educative environments characterized by civility, inviting the young to work at the edge of their competence. (Bullough, 1997, p. 21)

Bullough suggested that his eleven principles, although appearing as a list, were not intended to be taken that way as they were intertwined and served as fundamental working assumptions.

Like Bullough, I initially developed principles of practice (Loughran, 1997a) that I have reflected upon and refined in ways that I have found helpful for my own teaching. I do not suggest these principles as the only or right principles, rather they are one way of unpacking an important foundation of that which matters in conceptualizing and shaping practice; they are not a generic checklist. In developing principles of practice I have come to see them as a window into my own pedagogical thoughts and actions. They encourage me to genuinely critique the degree of alignment of my teaching intents and teaching behaviors and have become increasingly valuable in the development of my own learning about teaching through self-study.

These principles (relationship, purpose and modeling) each contain a number of important elements that together comprise the principle itself. They are not presented in a form that is intended to be hierarchical (either across the principles themselves or the elements described within each) although the first principle does stand out for me as being of prime importance as it shapes the nature of those that follow.

> The heart and soul of teaching begins with relationships. Teaching is a relationship. Without building relationships the purpose of teaching is diminished. Other principles of pedagogy are enhanced through relationships. (Loughran, 1997a, p. 58–59)

These principles, I trust, mirror the underlying philosophy that comprises my approach to teaching and I hope they might act as a catalyst for others to consider how they conceptualize their own principles of practice and the value of so doing (an issue considered in more detail in the final part of this chapter).

Teaching is a relationship

> Teaching is a relationship, a way of being with and relating to others, and not merely an expression of having mastered a set of content-related delivery skills. And advising is a matter not just of dispensing information in a timely fashion but of building trust, of talking and problem-solving together. (Bullough and Gitlin, 2001, p. 3)

If teaching and learning are to be closely aligned, if a genuine pedagogical relationship is to exist between teacher and student(s), then an understanding of the needs and concerns of each is important. Clearly, developing relationships in a teaching and learning environment requires developing an understanding of not only the individual, but also the group, for each certainly influences the other. Knowing students as individuals is fundamental to understanding "what works" and what "does not work" in creating motivation, interest and a need to know in the learner.

The way that individuals relate to one another varies with the context of a given situation, therefore, the better the relationship between individuals, the more likely it is that an understanding of the dynamics of the interplay within the group itself might also be apprehended and developed. For the teacher then, developing relationships with individual learners must be in concert with developing relationships with the group. However, the group must also be seen as a group of individual learners. The group is not necessarily a separate, distinct and detached entity with one common set of issues and concerns. Thus the tactful pedagogue (van Manen, 1991) recognizes and responds to the ever-changing nature of the interplay between individuals within the group and works to build positive and meaningful approaches that will be responsive to, and benefit, the changing nature of teaching and learning situations for the group as a whole. Relationships are developed through an awareness of the needs of others and are enhanced when there is a genuine concern to respond appropriately to such needs. In teaching, the concept of caring (Mayeroff, 1971; Noddings, 2001) may be viewed as an entry point for considering some of the features crucial to building meaningful relationships in pedagogical situations and, in teaching about teaching, purposefully displaying a responsiveness to relationships is important and may be done through (at least) each of the following:

The need for sensitivity

Building relationships begins with a genuine concern to listen, to be aware of the changing nature of the teaching and learning context, and to be interested in, and responsive to, the needs of students. Nicol (1997) describes a helpful way of considering how to be sensitive to situations through listening: listening *for* and listening *to*. Listening *for* is what she describes as listening for responses, clues and ideas that help her to determine whether or not her desired teaching goals are being realized. Listening *to* is about paying careful attention to her students' experiences, needs and concerns. The balance between listening *to* and listening *for* comprises a sensitivity that is important in building relationships.

> A focus only on listening *for* makes it difficult to listen *to* students' experiences, to focus on the meaning of the experience from the students' perspective, and to act upon events that are unanticipated. Listening *for* affects what the teacher finds as valuable information. A focus on only listening *to* may make it difficult to interpret students' experiences. Listening *to* means shedding preconceived agendas, being responsive and attending to what students say and do.... The challenge remains for me as I struggle to remain suspended and attentive on a fine balance between accomplishing my own teaching goals and experiencing teaching from prospective teachers' eyes. (Nicol, 1997, p. 112)

Nicol's notion of listening *for* and listening *to* suggests a need to be sensitive to situations. But such sensitivity needs to occur at both the individual and group level, and in so doing it means simultaneously being sensitive to the moment whilst still be conscious of the big picture.

Sensitivity means wisely deciding on what to respond to and how as a result of listening carefully to, and caring about, the manner in which a pedagogical situation unfolds. Allender (2001) describes this as "sensitively adjust[ing] the difficulty of an activity while it is in progress – for the class as a whole, for a particular group, or for an individual.... Teachers have to communicate to students that it is possible to make mistakes ... mistakes are productive and insightful" (p. 9). However, being sensitive does not mean avoiding difficulties or issues in teaching and learning, but approaching them in a thoughtful manner that demonstrates a concern for the learner. In approaching situations sensitively there is a greater likelihood that students of teaching will recognize, through their experiences, that "not all learning is easy, and some learning means moving outside of a comfortable space" (Allender, 2001, p. 9).

Building trust(s)

Mitchell (1992), through his work in the PEEL project, came to see the centrality of trust in encouraging students to change their approach to learning. He noted how important it was for students to trust teachers to support them in their learning and how different forms of trust evolved (and were necessary) when students were confronted by changed expectations of learning.

Trust matters in building relationships and is therefore crucial to teaching about teaching. There is a *trust in teaching* based on an expectation that in a given pedagogical situation, students are willing to learn; it is implicit in their choosing to be involved. In teaching about teaching I need to trust that my learners really do want to grasp the major concepts and ideas under consideration and to grapple with them in ways that will carry meaning in their practice. Therefore, I need to trust that in extending an invitation to learn that participants will come to see it as a collaborative venture shaped by the views, ideas and experiences of all involved. This teaching trust then is predicated on a belief that there are shared responsibilities in teaching and learning; therefore trust in learning (from a learner's perspective) is equally important.

From a learner's perspective, choosing to be involved, accepting an invitation to learn entails trusting that an individual's ideas, thoughts and views can be offered and explored in challenging ways. But, that the challenge is professional not personal. Therefore, there is an important *trust in learning behaviors* through which participants must know that their suggestions, ideas and input will not be ridiculed or devalued by others (teacher and students). Developing such a learning trust is based on caring for others as persons, and carries an expectation within the teaching and learning environment that there will be an overt concern to maintain and develop participants' self-esteem. Learners need to know that they can trust that the teaching and learning environment is a safe place in which they can raise and pursue issues, concerns and the development of understanding. Clearly then, a behavioral norm needs to be established whereby the notion of challenge does not equate with a personal attack on individuals, their thoughts or ideas, but that it is a genuine search for clarification and the development of understanding aimed at enhancing learning.

There is also a trust whereby there is an expectation that problems, concerns or issues that are raised in the teaching and learning environment will be seriously considered; not dealt with in a superficial manner. This *trust in supporting learning* requires the teacher educator to demonstrate a concern for the needs of individuals and is fundamental to students believing that there is value in raising their issues or concerns; trusting that in so doing, their queries will be fairly addressed. Without such a trust, there is little incentive for students to take the risk to speak up and offer alternatives and/or personal perspectives on a given problem, issue, or concern.

Being honest

It seems self-evident that in developing relationships there is a need for honesty. The need to be genuine, to demonstrate an honesty in interactions, is a critical aspect of relationship building. However, in some teaching situations, it may seem difficult to be honest as the level of vulnerability that accompanies the act of honesty can be perceived as carrying too great a risk and threaten one's confidence and/or view of the role of teacher or student. For example, it is not an uncommon situation for teachers when confronted by a challenging intellectual situation, to bluff their way through, pretending to know that which they do not, or to masterfully turn the inquisition back on the students in order to deflect attention from their own uncertainty. Although it is not a situation that one might choose to continually be confronted by, in teaching about teaching there is a very real need to be able to respond to difficult and uncertain situations honestly; to display the vulnerability that is apparent and to ensure that the affective aspects of learning are considered in concert with the cognitive.

Being honest means not only being honest with one's students but also being honest with oneself. Doubtless, many teacher educators have faced the difficult situation of trying to help a student see something in their practice that they (at that time) cannot see for themselves. Clarke (1997) demonstrated such a difficulty in his work with a student of teaching who he was advising during a school practicum experience. In his account of "coaching Mathew," Clarke saw that by *not* helping Mathew see into his own teaching, by avoiding confronting some of the issues that he knew were important to improving Mathew's situation, Mathew was not helped, and consequently continued to flounder. One immediate outcome of Clarke not honestly portraying his view of the situation was that Mathew attempted to rationalize his behavior by placing blame on others rather than looking at himself.

Despite the difficulty of the situation, in a remarkable illustration of the importance of honesty, Clarke listened to Mathew and supported him when he (Mathew) eventually decided to raise his concerns with the class that he was struggling to teach. Clarke was struck by how Mathew's honesty with the class led to a much better relationship between the teacher and his students and, although not all was resolved, a basis for progress and development was established. Mathew's honesty created possibilities for his students to offer their ideas, reactions and advice, and in so doing, Mathew heard that which he was previously unable to hear.

Just as Mathew was honest with his students, so Clarke was honest about himself and his work as a teacher educator – which subsequently led to valuable personal insights into his own pedagogy. Like most things in a relationship, honesty must not only be sought, it must also be displayed.

Despite the fact that being "too honest" (i.e. lacking tact and sensitivity), can be detrimental to relationship building, it should not detract from the importance of honesty in teaching about teaching, or be used as an excuse to diminish its value. Honesty shapes the way in which one might illustrate the pedagogical reasoning central to teaching actions and is crucial to offering our students of teaching insights into the problematic nature of practice. If teacher educators are to challenge the recipe approach to learning about teaching, then students of teaching must see the struggles and issues that their teacher educators face so that their own developing views of practice might be better informed.

Valuing independence

Meaningful pedagogical relationships are not built when one dominates and directs all that occurs in a teaching and learning environment. There is a need for independence to be acknowledged and respected. Independence (and the teacher is a learner too) is important in shaping the extent to which learners might choose to respond to the opportunities presented. The reality is that a learner needs to choose to learn (learning can not be mandated) and if there is a lack of free agency to choose, if the learner's independence is not respected, then learning is likely to be reduced to a superficial process of absorbing knowledge as facts rather than learning though linking, processing, synthesizing and formulating one's own views and understandings.

> A crucial factor associated with the development of independence is the teacher's ability to withhold judgment. Learners are not likely to pursue their own understanding or to reconsider others' views if they have a sense of being judged, or if they are trying to 'guess what is in the teacher's head'. The need to withhold judgment, to be conscious of one's own wait-time and to *want to hear* from others is a key to building relationships that enhance a diversity of learning outcomes. (Loughran, 1997a, p. 60)

For me, the development of relationships is fundamental to teaching and learning because relationships are built and enhanced through being sensitive to students and situations, by building trust, by being honest about teaching intentions and actions, and encouraging learners' independence. These aspects, which together comprise one way of conceptualizing relationships, are equally important from both a teacher's and a learner's perspective.

Purpose

Students of teaching have developed views of teaching through their extended *apprenticeship of observation* (Lortie, 1975). For many, the underlying purpose of much of the teaching they have experienced may never have been made explicit, or they may have interpreted situations very differently to that intended by their teachers. Hence, it is not surprising that for many, the delivery of content (alone) is considered to be the purpose of teaching. Not surprisingly, if teaching is only viewed as being the accumulation of an array of procedures and skills then a technical-rational approach (Schön, 1983) will prevail and the purpose of pedagogy will be seriously diminished.

Purposeful teaching is the use of appropriate methods designed to encourage learning for understanding. For this to be the case, teaching procedures need to be carefully selected because they support and encourage learning of the content/concepts under consideration in a meaningful way. It is therefore clear that teacher educators need to carry and display this sense of purpose as they consider and construct their teaching about teaching experiences. Teacher educators need to ensure that the purpose in their teaching is clear and explicit for themselves and their students and to encourage questioning about purpose to be common place in teaching and learning about teaching.

Inherent in this notion of purpose is the need to distinguish between teaching activities, procedures and strategies. Mitchell and Mitchell (2005) outline the difference between each of these as they consider how the combination of the three offer a view of teaching as developed and coherent. As they explain it, a teacher may use an *activity* to introduce students to a topic by asking them to "construct a concept map of four characters, two themes and two events from Macbeth." The activity is an approach to addressing a given topic and may be applied "as is" to a situation. Though, concept mapping itself is a generic teaching procedure, not a context-specific lesson plan able to be copied and used intact; rather, teachers develop their own content-specific applications of the teaching procedure in their own context and adapt and adjust them to suit their teaching and learning needs. *Teaching procedures* then are tactical in that teachers choose which procedures to use, when, how and why in order to promote different aspects of learning. However, a *strategy* is the development of an overall approach, aim or enactment of a principle such as "build a classroom environment that supports risk-taking" or "share intellectual control" (see principles of teaching for quality learning (Mitchell and Mitchell, 1997) for a detailed explanation).

From a teacher educator's perspective, the centrality of purpose helps to define the skills and knowledge of practice as comprising much more than competency in the technical aspects of practice. It helps to highlight expertise as involving an understanding of teaching as complex, problematic and ever evolving; teaching is not simply an event. Clearly then, from the perspective of students of teaching: accessing their teacher educators' knowledge and understanding through the pedagogy they experience; recognizing why teaching activities are used; what teaching procedures are, how they are adopted and adapted in practice; and, what a strategic approach to teaching and learning really is, is one explicit way of helping them to question and learn about the relationships between teaching and learning and creates real possibilities for them to grasp the value of purpose as a driver of decision making in, and knowledge of, practice.

Through this conceptualization of purpose, the need to encourage engagement and challenge in the learner then cannot be ignored.

Engagement and challenge

As noted above, students of teaching need to be challenged as learners through their pedagogical experiences if they are to do more than just absorb information. There is a need for information to be processed and reconsidered in light of one's existing knowledge so that active and purposeful learning might be encouraged. If this is to be the case, then pedagogy (as described in chapter one), must come to the fore as it is not sufficient to hope that content alone will suffice as a motivator for learning. Purpose in pedagogy carries an expectation that teaching is organized, developed and implemented in ways that will encourage engagement and challenge for participants. It is through linking teaching and learning in this way, with this intent, that an invitation for learners to be active, persistent and motivated might be forthcoming.

The value of engagement and challenge lies in the creation of a need to know. Through a need to know, learners are encouraged to push ideas further, to pursue linking new and existing knowledge and to use their metacognitive skills to develop new avenues of inquiry in the most appropriate ways to satisfy *their* interests, *their* concerns and to develop *their* understanding of the content/concepts under consideration. But it is not just the student for whom engagement and challenge matter:

> Just as learners need to be challenged by their understanding of subject matter, so too it should be that pedagogy has an impact on the teacher. The array of students' responses, the influx of new and challenging ideas and the experience of cognitive dissonance when alternative conceptions are explored should also engage the teacher as a learner. Hence, even though a thorough understanding of certain aspects of particular subject matter knowledge and pedagogical knowledge may reside within a teacher, when the two are combined within an interactive teaching-learning environment, understanding continues to be developed. (Loughran, 1997a, p. 61–62)

The notion of engagement and challenge is important to both teaching *and* learning about teaching. It is instructive for students of teaching to see that their teacher educators are challenged pedagogically and that they are engaged in the process, not simply delivering information in a disconnected fashion.

Gunstone (1995), in reconsidering his understanding of teacher education as a result of his involvement in PEEL (Baird and Mitchell, 1986; Baird and Northfield, 1992) noted: "Often I need to experience a problem to understand it. Others also need to experience problems for themselves. Thinking about learning means thinking about individuals" (p. 288). And it is through realizations such as this that engagement and challenge become personally meaningful to practice.

Engagement and challenge is initiated through the questions and issues that arise when confronted by aspects of content that cause one to puzzle, to see the curious and to delve into the problematic. It could well be argued that the questions and issues that cause a teacher to stop and think about a topic are synonymous with those of a learner (for clearly a teacher is a learner too). Therefore, drawing out these questions and puzzles, using them as a source of genuine inquiry and wondering aloud about the "what ifs", whys" and "how comes" of content and pedagogy are indeed a path to engagement and challenge that demonstrate value and purpose in pedagogy (which includes the associated decisions and actions). Through this process, metcognition has a role to play.

Encouraging metacognition

Why not encourage pre-service teachers to value and analyse their experiences as learners in teacher education classes.... Baird (1992) has argued that teachers need to be metacognitive and become more aware of their practice in classrooms to inform their pedagogical decisions. Pre-service teachers also should be encouraged to be metacognitive and become more aware of how they learn in teacher education courses with the intention of informing their decision-making as they construct their personal pedagogies. (Hoban, 1997, p. 135)

There is little doubt that being metacognitive (questioning one's own learning, or thinking about one's own thinking); becoming more aware of the thoughts and actions that influence the development (or not) of one's own understanding, offers insights into teaching and learning dramatically different to being told what to know and how to think.

Enhancing students' metacognitive skills should be a part of the teaching and learning agenda in teacher education. Consciously questioning one's own learning, building, extending and developing ideas by pursuing the doubts and perplexities inherent in practice is one valuable way of engaging learners in their own learning and of making the purpose of teaching and learning clear.

Just as teacher educators should use their learning through metacognition to enhance their pedagogical approach, so too students of teaching should be encouraged to do the same in their learning about teaching. Students of teaching should be encouraged to speak up in class and ask the questions that they undoubtedly develop (but often publicly suppress) through the teaching and learning episodes they experience. "What is the purpose of this session?" "How does today's session link with what we did yesterday?" "Why are you teaching us using this teaching procedure?" "How does this approach fit in with an overall strategy for learning about teaching?" are all important questions that students of teaching (surely) ask of themselves but perhaps rarely of their teacher educators. If we accept Hoban's challenge (above) and are to actively pursue an agenda of learning about, and through metacognition in teacher education, questions such as these must be asked out loud by our students and not be interpreted as defiant or inappropriate behavior, rather as suitable challenges to, and clarifications of, teacher educators' pedagogy. Asking such questions illustrates purposeful links to learning and can be an avenue for making the tacit nature of teaching explicit; a fundamental purpose in teaching about teaching.

Modeling

> "Do as I say, not as I do" is a notoriously poor formula for getting people to act the way you want them to. Nonetheless, teacher education has largely followed that formula for centuries. Generations of student teachers in America have sat through unnumbered hours of lectures on the virtues of educating children through democratic discussion. Other examples could be cited, much more numerous and varied than anyone would care to review in detail. (Peck and Tucker, 1973, p. 955)

As Peck and Tucker (above) suggest, it is imperative that teacher educators are continually reminded of the need to confront the tyranny of teaching as telling. Teaching should be interactive and challenging as learning does not occur just by listening. It naturally follows then that if learning about teaching is to be meaningful, students of teaching need to be motivated to construct new meaning from the teaching and learning episodes in which they are involved.

The imperative for what Korthagen and Lunenberg (2004) describe as *Teach as you Preach* and the necessity for students of teaching to experience for themselves the nature of learning associated with particular teaching procedures cannot, and should not, be avoided. If students of teaching are to come to appreciate a particular teaching procedure, if they are to know what it feels like to teach using that procedure, and if they are to develop their views about practice with an understanding of teaching strategies in mind, then they need to experience the same as a learner. Just being told, or receiving a teacher educator's wisdom of practice through transmission of the information (i.e. more traditional forms of lecturing) detracts from the real value of students of teaching developing a working knowledge of pedagogy in line with the argument presented in Chapter 1.

Modeling teaching in ways that demonstrates a commitment to students of teaching seeing, feeling, experiencing, reflecting and analyzing teaching practice requires a focus on them experiencing just that and requires teacher educators to teach as they preach.

> However, this does not mean that a model for how to teach is to be placed before student-teachers to mimic; rather it means offering them the opportunity to better understand the pedagogical purpose, to experience some of the likely learning outcomes as a result of the experience (both cognitive and affective), and to allow them to make their own decisions about how they might incorporate that into their own practice. (Loughran, 1997a, p. 62)

Modeling is inherent in all that we do in teacher education. Intended and unintended learning about teaching occurs through our modeling whether we are conscious of our actions or not. With that in mind, modeling then can be conceptualized as teaching in the very ways we encourage our students to teach but to do so with the intention of offering them access to the thoughts of, and knowledge about, such practice by explicating the underlying purpose of that teaching approach. This is in stark contrast to the misconception that modeling is a mock teaching demonstration or a tacit call for students of teaching to "teach like me."

One of the intents of modeling is to offer students of teaching opportunities to not only grasp a deeper understanding of how to use, for example, particular teaching procedures but see the value in developing a working understanding of why to use them. Also, despite the planning and thinking associated with developing an approach to a particular teaching and learning episode, there is always a need to be capable and ready to adapt and change.

Teaching inevitably carries a requirement to be responsive, to recognize and react to the teachable moment. Therefore students of teaching need to see how their teacher educators do this, for us to bring to their attention the instances whereby we have responded to the unplanned or unanticipated. Modeling then matters in teacher education and we need to encourage our students to experiment with, and be responsive to, such situations in their own practice. Knowing why must be linked to knowing how if students' pedagogical knowledge is to be more than a list of propositions, skills, and competences (although these must clearly be developed as well). Thus, modeling is one very real way of helping students of teaching to see and experience responsiveness and flexibility in action and of encouraging them to see that moving beyond the technical is crucial to being a professional pedagogue; an educator, not a trainer.

Reflection

If reflection is to be better understood by students of teaching, if they are to apprehend its nature and value and, if they are to see it as a foundation of learning about teaching, then it stands to reason that reflection must be explicitly modeled for them.

Although there are many interpretations of reflection, two aspects common to most (regardless of the different labels or language used) are related to the ideas of "problem" and of "framing and reframing."

Central to reflection is the need to have something to reflect about. Hence, the problem is important. However, problem recognition should not be viewed as something that carries negative connotations. As Dewey (1933) explained it, "*reflective* thinking, in distinction from other operations to which we apply the name of thought, involves (1) a state of doubt, hesitation, perplexity, mental difficulty, in which thinking originates, and (2) an act of searching, hunting, inquiring, to find material that will resolve the doubt, settle and dispose of the perplexity" [emphasis in the original] (p. 12). Therefore, recognizing that which is a problem in practice is an important starting point for drawing attention to reflective processes.

Framing and reframing (Schön, 1983) are important to reflection for they have to do with coming to see a situation, being able to define it, to describe and account for its features, then to be able to view that situation from different perspectives. Or, using Barnes (1992) explanation, frames are the default settings we carry with us that set up the expectations we have of a situation. Thus, alternative framing (or reframing) is seeing the situation in ways that extend beyond our normal expectations in different ways to our default settings. For example, how a teacher views a teaching episode may be very different to the manner in which students perceive of the same episode. Teachers, being concerned with constructing an appropriate environment, creating opportunities for students to grasp the concepts under consideration and, to do so in an engaging manner, will inevitably be drawn to view the situation through the elements pertaining to their plans and actions. On the other hand, students may be more concerned with completing the task, questioning the value of being involved, determining the ways to manage the situation or finding a path of least resistance. Hence the two perspectives bring into focus very different problems (curious, interesting, and or puzzling enticing moments) and responses because the different perspectives impact very differently on what is seen in the situation, by whom and why.

> Teachers who can only 'frame' in one way what happens in their classes can therefore only see one set of possibilities for teaching....In contrast... the most effective teachers will have other interpretive frames available which will free them to see alternatives and to make informed choices....teachers need to discover that their existing frame for

understanding what happens in their classes is only one of several possible ones, and this, according to Schön, is likely to be achieved only when the teachers themselves reflect critically upon what they do. (Barnes, 1992, p. 17)

In teaching about teaching, being able to illustrate the value of problem recognition and how framing and reframing can influence pedagogical responses focuses attention on the nature of reflection (both in and on practice). Unpacking reflection must then be helpful in developing understandings of teaching and learning for it can help to highlight the value of reflection in experienced teachers' practice (through a teacher educator's ability to personally recognize and respond to problems and to offer alternative perspectives) and, through framing and reframing, illustrate that teaching is indeed problematic and that there is not one right way of thinking or acting.

"Teaching teachers to teach thoughtfully, to consider carefully the consequences of their work, involves creating opportunities for beginning teachers to learn the skills and attitudes required for reflective practice" (Richert, 1992, p. 171). If teacher educators' reflective processes are hidden (even inadvertently) from students of teaching, if the inherent value of reflection to the teachers of teaching is not readily apparent, then it is hard to imagine how teacher education could claim reflection as a foundation stone; despite the number of claims to the contrary.

Risk-taking

Learning about teaching requires a pushing of the boundaries of practice in order to encourage seeing and understanding from a variety of vantage points. When teachers implement teaching procedures with which they are unfamiliar, new ways of seeing and understanding become possible through experiencing the discomfort of being less certain about what is happening. I argue that discomfort is an important attribute for learning, especially so in respect to learning about teaching, as it leads to a heightening of the senses. With the senses heightened, one is more sensitive to the myriad events within a pedagogical situation so that taken-for-granted perspectives of teaching and learning are more likely to be challenged (existing frames are unsettled). Through taking the risk to do something new, something different, something uncertain, one's understanding (both cognitive and affective) of teaching and learning is enhanced through the experience.

Risk-taking though requires a concurrent recognition of the importance of confidence for what may be a risk for one may pose little risk for another. Therefore pushing the boundaries of practice can be dramatically influenced by one's sense of self-confidence and ability to see that the risk is worth taking. Risk-taking in teaching about teaching is important for students of teaching to see modeled, and to experience, as it can create situations commensurate with the intent of W.J.J. Gordon's (1961) synectics whereby making the "familiar strange," and/or, the "strange familiar," is a way of enhancing learning.

> if teacher educators do not take risks in their own practice, if they do not overtly model the need to extend the margins of understanding and experience for their own pedagogy, it makes it difficult for student-teachers to believe that the value of taking risks will be worth the discomfort they will experience in practice. In many ways encouraging risk-taking involves a stepping out in faith, a faith which is based on a trust in believing that, through taking the risk of experiencing both the trials and errors of learning by experimenting with pedagogy in a range of situations, circumstances, subject-content and contexts, an under-standing will emerge. I believe that this is an aspect of learning about teaching that many student-teachers are more than prepared to consider; however, they need to see that their teacher educators will positively support them. (Loughran, 1997a, p. 65)

Principles of practice in action

The principles of practice I have outlined above, for me, are the essence of teaching about teaching. In articulating principles of practice, by trying to hold true to them in teaching about teaching, they help to create conditions for students of teaching to see beyond practice alone as important in shaping how and what they learn about teaching. In developing a pedagogy of teacher education, principles of practice are a foundation for reflection on practice and a catalyst for researching teaching through self-study.

Earlier in the chapter, I suggested that teacher educators should develop their own principles of practice and that in so doing, they might see the value of such an endeavor. In closing this chapter, and this part of the book, I briefly visit the efforts of one teacher educator who began to articulate her principles of practice and how, through that process, she came to see into her teaching about teaching and her students' learning about teaching in new and different ways.

Peterman (1997) participated in a workshop on developing a teaching portfolio and as part of the process was asked to write about her teaching philosophy. Through that process she described the principles that guided her teaching:

> 1 *Promoting good studenting is more important than promoting good students....*Fenstermacher (1986) called for a new genre of research on teaching – one that focused on the student's mindful role in the teaching-learning process and on the moral dimensions of teaching. He introduced the notion of *studenting* to mean what students must do to learn....good studenting involves the students in a critical analysis of what is important to know and how they come to know it.

2 *Knowledge is socially constructed....* Through social interaction and mindful engagement in activity, students construct knowledge, building more complex, abstract schemata representing their understandings of their world.

3 *An ethic of caring guides a good teacher's actions, encouraging good studenting and learning....* The ethic of caring focuses the teacher on the student in a positive, engaging fashion. An ethic of caring requires that the teacher engage in knowing the student – from the student's perspective and without judgment.... It results in affirmations of the student's self, mutual respect, and an open classroom environment in which each individual's knowing and coming to know is valued.... It requires that the teacher know and respect herself in the same way. Therefore, self-knowledge or personal knowledge is as important as practical knowledge. (Peterman, 1997, pp. 156–157)

In light of articulating her philosophy of teaching, or her principles of practice, she reviewed her course, her teaching and her students' approaches to learning to teach. As she began to look more deeply into her practice she saw contradictions between her teaching philosophy and her enacted curriculum. For example, she noted: "My method of classroom assessment rewarded those who learned to be good students in my class – not necessarily those who practiced good studenting. Yes, students socially constructed knowledge. But, the classroom products provided inadequate evidence of my students' constructions. I determined to examine my beliefs and practices more closely..." (p. 157).

Peterman's determination to examine her beliefs and practices more closely prompted her to invite a colleague to observe her teaching and to compare her curriculum-in-action with her teaching philosophy. This led to a major re-evaluation of her approach to assessment and her understanding of how her students were (and were not) approaching learning to teach. She examined her teaching and her syllabi in much more detail and began to critically consider the "real messages" inherent in her course evaluations.

Peterman's account of her efforts to better align her teaching beliefs and practices is far from a self-congratulatory story. It is an open and honest report about what it really feels like to face up to the difficulties and dilemmas associated with attempting to *Teach as you Preach*. Importantly though, despite the difficulties she encountered, her report also highlights the value of teacher educators' articulating principles of practice and choosing to continually pursue an agenda of better aligning teaching purposes and teaching intents. In so doing, she made the problematic nature of teaching explicit to herself and her students. She demonstrated the reality of taking risks in teaching and also experienced the discomfort associated with learning about practice at a more personal level.

Despite the uncertainty she created and lived through, she was nonetheless driven to purposefully continue to seek change because she was, "concerned with the complex ecology in which changes in [her] teaching and [her] students' learning occurred" (p. 162). The learning outcomes she experienced were not always pleasant or affirming, but they were insightful in ways that genuinely impacted her practice. She learnt much about teaching and learning about teaching as she concluded:

> The lived curriculum I have described emerged as a result of interactions among my students and me in a college classroom and in school settings...More than my beliefs, my reflections and personal experiences and those of my students impacted the changes I implemented. I [now] wonder consistently about the contradictions between what I believe and know about teaching and learning and what my students have come to know and believe before arriving in my classroom....My role must be to help them reconstruct their notions of being students, practicing good studenting, and encouraging the same for their own students. (Peterman, 1997, pp. 162–163)

Guilfoyle *et al.* (1997) remind us that in teacher education we need to see beyond the present and into our obligations to unseen children but that in so doing, "living by our principles is neither simple nor easy" (p. 207). Central to the work of teaching and learning about teaching is teacher educators' practice. It seems reasonable then to assert that *if we are to respond appropriately to the learning needs of our students of teaching, if we are to challenge notions of teaching as telling, then our teaching about teaching really matters.*

Whether we intend it to be the case or not, our principles of practice shape our actions. Recognizing and responding to this challenge is at the heart of developing a pedagogy of teacher education.

Part II

Learning about teaching

"Choose a topic, any topic you like, and work out how you'll teach it to a year 7 student," our education lecturer said in a very casual way. "Easy for you maybe!" I thought to myself.

"How are we supposed to do that?" Michelle whispered to me under her breath.

"Why can't they just tell us what to do?" Ali muttered rather desperately.

So this is it. I'm in a teacher education course and the first thing I have to do is prepare *something* to teach for 35 minutes or so to one year 7 kid [first year of high school]. How am I supposed to do that? They haven't taught us anything yet? I'm still waiting for some of the rules about what to do and what not do and stuff like that. What if the kid I get to teach doesn't like me?

Some of my classmates are really worried about what to do and how to do it. I suppose I am a bit too but I'm trying not to show it.

"I think I'll be o.k." I reassured myself, "I can be funny and entertaining and I've certainly got plenty of things to talk about. Maybe I should stick to immunology; I majored in that in my Science degree so I know stacks about it."

I was a bit surprised when we all turned up to teach the year 7 kids. Jenny, Jill, Ian and Jos had prepared notes like scripts of what to say. "What are they going to do, just read their stuff out to the kid?" I asked myself. "I don't want to be that sort of teacher."

So that was it. Not bad really. My kid didn't ask one hard question and although I covered everything much quicker than I expected, he was nice enough and sat there quietly for the 20 minutes or so after I finished just sort of looking around. It was a little uncomfortable at times I suppose, and would probably be a problem in a normal class, but still, I think he liked me and that wasn't a normal class. Yep, if this is teaching I think I'm getting the hang of it; pretty easy really.

"What did your student learn and how do you know he learnt it?" my lecturer asked on our way out of the school.

So that's it. Funny way of assessing our teaching. I think I handled her question pretty well. I told her I had loads of information, didn't need any notes or anything else like that. I was able to just talk about the antibodies, phagocytes, diseases and stuff like that without too much hassle. I also said about how the kid listened politely and asked me some questions; all of which I could answer.

"I hope you've all done the readings on reflection that are in your course booklets." She said as she walked into the room to start our teaching and learning class.

So that's it. Readings. I hope that's not what the rest of the course is about. Maybe they'll give us lots of cool teaching ideas. Yeah, I think that would be good. Some cool teaching ideas. They'd come in handy on the teaching rounds.

(Jason)

The anecdote used to open this part of the book was written using van Manen's (1999) guidelines. In working with high school students, van Manen found that anecdotes offered powerful insights into: "how students experience the interactive dimension of teaching... [and] are strongly suggestive of pedagogical qualities that students admire or criticize in their teachers" (p. 19).

In teacher education, I have found the use of anecdotes to be equally powerful as students of teaching have happily used them to construct, and reflect upon, critical incidents that have influenced their understanding of learning about teaching. Throughout this part of the book, where appropriate, I use anecdotes as a data source to illustrate how some students of teaching have responded to different situations that they have faced in their learning about teaching.

In this part of the book (learning about teaching), the focus shifts from teachers of teaching to the students of teaching and explores how the struggles, difficulties and dilemmas that they are confronted by impact their understanding of the nature of teaching and their learning about teaching. As in Part I (teaching about teaching), an important issue underpinning the ideas that are portrayed is the *dual nature* of learning about teaching: students of teaching must learn about that which is being taught (particular content) while at the same time, learn about teaching through questioning and critiquing the teaching used to teach them.

It is not sufficient for students of teaching to uncritically accept (or reject) the teaching approaches used in their teacher preparation programs. They need to be sensitive to the manner in which the teaching that they experience is conducted and constantly be cognizant of the link between the teaching that they experience and the ways in which it influences their learning. However, doing that is a difficult task, so there is a need for teacher educators to teach about teaching in ways that continually reinforce for their students of teaching, this important focus as they experience teacher education.

Understanding learning about teaching from a student's perspective then is important in shaping a pedagogy of teacher education. And, as the anecdote at the start of this part of the book illustrates, students of teaching enter teacher preparation programs with needs and concerns that need to be addressed if their understanding of teaching is to be developed in ways that will lead them to appreciate the complexity of such work and to expand their teaching horizons beyond the technical. That is where this part of the book begins.

7 Being a student of teaching

I seem to have had five big crises as I learned to teach. After each crisis, my views and attitudes concerning teaching underwent a major overhaul... [the first crisis was at the start of the course]. Back in August I wasn't sure what teaching was going to be all about. I remember my greatest concern was classroom management. What would I do if I couldn't get the kids to pay attention and behave?...I remember not being too worried about making science interesting...I also didn't worry about cool demos...or many of the other issues that we all wanted to cover that week in August. I think the only other issue that worried me was how would I be able to *entertain* the kids for 75 minutes...

– Smith (1997, pp. 98–99)

It has been well documented that prospective teachers enter pre-service teacher preparation programs with strong images of what teaching entails (Lanier and Little, 1986). For the most part, they have had extensive exposure to approaches to teaching and learning that have subconsciously shaped their thinking based on what Lortie (1975) described as the *apprenticeship of observation*. From their student perspective, they have observed teaching for a considerable period of time and have formulated views about what teaching is like and how it is done. It is therefore not difficult to see how their understanding of teaching may well be caught up in a search for the familiar routines and strategies that they experienced as students and how, at one level, their understanding of learning to teach involves simply learning those routines and strategies and applying them in practice. However, what they have not been privy to is the thinking and planning from their teachers' perspective. So, on entering teacher preparation, although their images of teaching might be strong and well formed, they are also confronted by a new set of demands as they begin their journey to the "other side of the desk." Hence, they have concerns and needs that require addressing in order for them to develop broader perspectives on teaching and learning.

Concerns

As illustrated by Smith (above), a common concern for many students of teaching is that of classroom management but, like other issues and concerns that face students of teaching, there will be recognizable shifts as they learn more about themselves, their students and their understanding of teaching and learning as they progress through their teacher preparation program.

Research on learning to teach is a field in which there has been much change as the complexity of the journey has become increasingly acknowledged. As a consequence, critique and development of the field has become more sophisticated over time (see for example, Wideen *et al.*, 1998). However, one enduring aspect of learning to teach is linked to the nature of, and shifts in, concerns of students of teaching as they move through teacher preparation.

Fuller (Fuller, 1969; Fuller and Bown, 1975) proposed a stage theory that described the shifts in concerns that students of teaching experienced as they moved through teacher education based on the results of the *Teacher Concerns Questionnaire*. Analysis of the questionnaire data suggested that students of teaching passed through stages of concerns which were sequential and hierarchical, as they progressed in their learning about teaching. These included (in order) concerns about preteaching, survival, teaching, and pupils.

Preteaching concerns are characterized by students of teaching continuing to identify with the pupils in the classes they observe rather than with the teacher. Thus they are confronted by an initial struggle to make the transition from student to teacher. The second stage is characterized by concerns about survival. In this stage, a more romantic view of teaching – ideal teaching – fades, or is challenged, as they face the reality of simply surviving in the teaching role. The third stage is when issues about their own teaching begin to surface and become the major focus of their attention, shaping much of what they look for and interpret in their teaching context. The last stage is when concerns about their students emerge. In this final stage, students of teaching begin to pay more attention to their pupils' learning as they start to demonstrate concerns for them as individuals, each with issues of their own that need to be recognized and addressed.

Building on this stage model, Hall and Loucks (1977) examined stages of concern in teachers as they implemented innovations in education. Their study concluded that stages of concern applied to teachers generally when implementing change. The use of stage theory thus led to the development of the Concerns Based Adoption Model (CBAM), a seven-stage model of concerns (Table 7.1) based on the notion that learning leads to change and that for change to be successful (i.e. for learning to "take hold"), appropriate support is necessary (Hall and Hord, 1987; Hord, Rutherford, Huling-Austin, and Hall, 1987).

The CBAM model illustrates that generally, concerns associated with coming to grips with understanding and implementing change move from

Table 7.1 Concerns Based Adoption Model (CBAM)

		Stages of concern	Expression of concern
Impact	6	Refocusing	I have some ideas about something that would work even better
	5	Collaboration	How can I relate what I am doing to what others are doing?
	4	Consequence	How is my use affecting learners? How can I refine it to have more impact?
Task	3	Management	I seem to be spending all my time getting materials ready.
Self	2	Personal	How will using it affect me?
	1	Informational	I would like to know more about it.
	0	Awareness	I am not concerned about it.

self to task to impact. Perhaps not surprisingly, Fuller's work maps well onto the CBAM model which unpacks and extends understanding of stages of concerns in detailed, logical, and sequential ways. As one level of concern is met, another emerges as a more detailed understanding of the innovation is sought in order to better comprehend its use in practice.

As Table 7.1 illustrates, the "expressions of concern" offer a most logical account of the type of thinking and questioning that one would expect to ask when addressing a problem or concern associated with learning how to manage an innovation in order to become more expert in its use. Stages of concern have been examined in many and varied learning contexts and have illustrated a number of similarities and differences.

In a longitudinal study into the development of reflective practice in pre-service teachers in a one-year postgraduate diploma in education, Loughran (1996, p. 87) mapped students' concerns in response to three distinct time frames, each of which included university coursework and school teaching (practicum) experiences sequentially throughout the year.

In the first time frame, students' main concerns were about the structure of their teacher education program followed (in dramatically lower frequency) by teaching, self and learning (indications of self- and task-dominated concerns). In the second time frame, teaching emerged as the most common concern with learning also being noted as of more concern than either course or self concerns (a shift from task to impact concerns). In the third time frame, teaching remained as the major concern (although at a lower frequency than in the second time frame) and learning slipped to least concern (suggestive of a move back to task concerns). Analysis of the data suggested that in that particular program, that concerns for pupils' learning did not emerge to the extent that Fuller's stage theory might suggest. Further to this, with the completion of the final school teaching experience, concerns about teaching and learning generally diminished and concerns about self began to recur. Thus, the changing context tended to influence the nature of concerns illustrating a more fluid mix of self, task and impact concerns as different expectations and demands were experienced.

Developmental stage theory offers one perspective on the experiences of learning to teach. Kagan's (1992) extensive review of the literature was supportive of Fuller and Bown's work and many studies in varied contexts have illustrated similar trends whereby shifts in concerns from self to task to impact are noticeable (Furlong and Maynard, 1995). However, others have questioned the adequacy of a model which comprises discrete stages of change in teacher development (see for example, Burn *et al.*, 2000, 2003; Grossman, 1992). Thus, although a developmental model of stage theory may not be universally applicable (i.e. generalizable to all cases in exactly that form), it does highlight the importance of a need for teacher educators and students of teaching to be aware of, and sensitive to, the types of changes in concerns likely to be experienced as learning about teaching progresses.

> Over the past several years, we have seen a movement from relatively rigid, deterministic, hierarchical and traditional stage theories in teaching to more flexible accounts of the developmental process. This more flexible approach suggests that a number of factors affect either the movement from one stage to another or the acquisition of another phase. These factors include biography, experience, context, personality (or stance), and beliefs. These flexible approaches are not deterministic models in which factors – including teachers' decisions – may be altered to add another stage or phase in the teachers' development. For some…these stages or phases become more like sets of developing approaches, perspectives, or ways of thinking. (Richardson and Placier, 2001, p. 912)

Northfield and Gunstone's (1997) program principle (see Chapter 5) that "The student teacher has needs and prior experiences which must be considered in planning and implementing the teacher preparation program. And, the nature and intensity of these needs should shift throughout the program," is a principle that (regardless of whether development stage theory *per se* fully applies) is a timely reminder that learning about teaching must indeed be responsive to participants' perceived needs and concerns if learning is to "take hold." And in so doing, there is a need for flexibility and adaptability in teacher educators' practice as it may well be that "bringing concerns to the fore" rather than "waiting for them" to surface might accelerate possibilities for growth in learning about teaching. In concert with other factors that also play a part in shaping the nature of concerns in individuals' learning about teaching, addressing, rather than avoiding or ignoring concerns is important. Just as raising concerns is an aspect of enhancing learning about teaching, so too is the influence of images and identity.

Images and identity

> "Miss, this is boring!"
>
> Michelle said what everyone else in the class were thinking.
>
> I had planned the lesson with the best intentions. I thought the students would enjoy flicking though magazines and cutting out examples of the Gestalt Principles and creating posters on the poster paper I had brought in for the lesson.
>
> My first Psychology lesson, my first teaching round [school teaching practicum], my first attempt to be a teacher; it was absolutely boring. Even I was struggling to keep my eyes open.
>
> At the end of the class, there were a total of two pictures on the five big sheets of poster paper.
>
> The next class I wrote notes on the board and the kids were happy.
>
> (Sharon)

Like Jason's anecdote that introduced this part of the book, so too Sharon's anecdote carries a message about how her image of teaching is being shaped by her teaching and learning experiences. Both Jason and Sharon's experiences indicate that their needs and concerns impact their understanding of the teacher's role and the nature of teaching itself. Their anecdotes are a reminder of the importance of image and identity and the manner in which each may influence the development of practice.

LaBoskey (1991), in an in-depth study of two students completing the final year of their elementary teacher preparation program noted how, throughout the year, both came to recognize how their prior knowledge and beliefs had limited their development as teachers. Through these case studies, LaBoskey suggested a continuum in growth of students of teaching encompassing shifts from a "common sense thinker" (one who maintains a focus on self and personal experiences) to an "alert novice" and on to a "pedagogical thinker" (whereby the focus is on teaching and pupils rather than oneself). Through this continuum LaBoskey draws attention to the need for teacher education to be responsive to the needs of students of teaching by purposefully challenging and influencing their images of self as teacher.

Bullough has long been an advocate for paying attention to image and identity as crucial to the work of teacher education (Bullough, 1989, 1991, 1994; Bullough and Gitlin, 1995, 2001). He, like many others (see for example, Lortie's (1975) *Apprenticeship of Observation*), has demonstrated how students of teaching enter teacher preparation with images of teaching based on their own experiences as pupils.

Bullough (1991) drew attention to the centrality of identity as he demonstrated how it influenced the development of practice in students of teaching. He noted how those who had a strong image of themselves as teachers were able to grow and develop and thus learn from observing the teachers around them in ways that were not so likely in those who had no clear self-image. Thus, the nature of self-image and issues of identity formation matter if learning about teaching is to "take hold" rather than being seen as superficial contact with a set of pre-organized tasks and procedures – easily forgotten and poorly incorporated into practice.

It could well be argued that students of teaching have been successful in a schooling system in which traditional didactic approaches dominate and that even though they may wish to teach differently themselves, when the day-to-day pressures of teaching are felt, the procedures and teacher behaviors that they have for so long observed will more than likely form the basis of the scripts from which their most common responses will emerge.

Dear Diary,

I had the worst class ever today. Year nine, double Indonesian on a Friday afternoon. The year nines had been on camp so I had no experience of what they were like or capable of! I walked in fairly confident. I had planned this lesson thoroughly as it was my first year nine class and my first ever double. I had created communicative activities: pair work, surveys, everything any beginning teacher would need to engage a bunch of apathetic year nines. I would surely catch their attention and help them see the value of being able to speak another language; as opposed to what I had experienced as a student!

My supervising teacher walked in and the noisy year nines straggled in behind him. I walked to the front of the class and introduced myself.

"Good afternoon year 9. I am Miss Soultan and I will be teaching you for the next few weeks." I said sounding like I'd done it all a hundred times before.

Mr. Cool who reeked of a "couldn't care less attitude" despite needing to have his cap sit "just so" on his head called out, "Are you a real teacher or a student teacher?"

I tried to ignore his question and carried on with some (pathetic) spiel about how we could all learn from each other and how the next few weeks would just fly.

I then launched into my lesson plan. I introduced myself in Indonesian and then asked each student to do the same. I said we would go around the room and hear something about each student. I emphasised that it didn't matter how simple it was, as long as it was said in Indonesian. The first student stood up and hesitantly said, "Nama saya Ben. Saya tinggi."

I could hear some of the boys around him saying how stupid they thought all of this was because they already knew each other but I ignored them as I attempted to reward Ben's effort.

"Very good Ben." I responded.

I was all for positive comments even though I really didn't mean it because I was disappointed with his too simple, "My name is Ben. I'm tall."

I looked along to Josh, the next student. He slowly stood and said, "Nama saya Josh. Saya tinggi."

The class erupted into laughter. Josh was maybe half the size of Ben. My heart was sinking fast as I could feel these year nines slipping away from me.

I battled on, but things got no better. It was hard to get their attention so I waited. I waited a bit longer.

Waiting, waiting, hoping.

I couldn't stand it anymore so I mustered up the angriest face I could and told them all how rude they were and that I would not tolerate calling out and talking over one another.

"Miss, your face is going red," came out of nowhere; but more than likely from under that cap, although they were all starting to look a bit more painful now.

I started sinking ever deeper.

I stormed over to the rubbish bin and threw in the worksheets and surveys I had spent so much time and care preparing then turned and told them all (well maybe I yelled) to begin copying a large slab of writing from their out of date textbook.

I never wanted to be *that* sort of teacher. But there I was doing boring work, punishing them and making them do irrelevant work that would make them like the subject even less.

What have I become? Why did this have to happen to me? (Dana)

Knowing oneself is crucial in coming to understand how one acts in given situations. For Jason (first anecdote), in trying to appear calm and confident and (perhaps) to be liked by his Year 7 student, he avoided "preparing a script" to read out to his student but talked at him nonetheless. Did he recognize this in his own practice? Sharon, after trying to engage her students in an enjoyable and different classroom activity, quickly retreated to more comfortable ground when her first attempt was not as successful as she anticipated. She seemed to be very well aware of how the episode impacted her practice. Dana found herself in a situation that she had not envisaged and she responded in ways that disappointed her and undermined her original teaching purpose. She wanted her students to appreciate a second language and not to experience the type of teaching she had endured as a student. She knew what she did not want to do but it happened anyway.

In one sense, it could well be that each of these situations could be seen as failures. However, in learning about teaching, it is important to help students of teaching see beyond the apparent failure and to uncover that which lies beneath, to step back from the personal involvement in the situation in order to frame it as an opportunity for understanding, learning and growth – despite that being easier said than done.

When Dana asked, "Why did this happen to me?" at a purely cognitive level her actions may be easily explained. However, what she did do, what she wanted to do and what she will do next time are all influenced by how well she knows herself, the image she carries of herself and the professional identity she is gradually developing. Being cognizant of these, being able to use such situations as possibilities for growth and accepting that there are often discrepancies between each requires her to learn how to balance the affective, cognitive, and behavioral responses that combine to form who she is and how she acts. The difficulty though is that learning about how to distill insights from the essence of practice from that mixture of thoughts, feelings and actions requires experiences just like those highlighted in the anecdotes. Such situations, when genuinely apprehended, need to be viewed as possibilities for learning. They offer opportunities to harness dissonance as a powerful catalyst. Students of teaching need opportunities to learn, un-learn and re-learn in order to better know themselves so that they might better understand how and why they teach in the way they teach; especially if they seek to change. Apprehending dissonance offers possibilities for seeing that which might normally be overlooked and is one way of actively seeking out instances of being a living contradiction (Whitehead, 1993).

Thus, in learning about teaching, in order to develop the professional self as teacher, there is a need to acknowledge and better understand the personal self for it seems unlikely that the core of the personal will not impact the core of the professional. More so, one's self image may be well formed and quite resilient. When confronted by contradictory or discon-firming data drawn from actions, behaviors, or attitudes in a given situation, many reasons may be found for doing that which one would prefer not to have done; it is too easy to rationalize rather than reflect on one's behavior. Thus images of oneself may, on the one hand, garner confidence in working with alternative approaches to practice, or on the other, be a barrier to change.

Coming to know oneself therefore matters in learning about teaching. If, as Segall (2002) suggests, prospective teachers need to become students of their own education then the manner in which self-image and professional identity are shaped and influenced by beliefs must be encouraged so that it can be addressed at a personal level. Otherwise, tacit, unquestioned, taken-for-granted images of teachers and teaching that have dominated students' observation of practice as students may well unintentionally prevail.

> as students, [we] get so worked up about wanting lesson plans and wanting techniques and strategies and stuff. We've seen what teaching is like. We've had 16 years of it...Now we want to know how to do it. [We say to ourselves,] "How am I going to control a class of 32 kids and make them learn what I'm asked to make them learn?" So I think we are working with the model of teaching that, at some level, we're not really actively thinking about. We're working with this model of teachers that we have had in the past... (Segall, 2002, p. 158)

In the case of the five crises that Smith (that opened this chapter) experienced, he found himself confronted by situations that were contradictory. What he thought he needed to know and be able to do in one instance was negated in the next. In each crisis, what he thought he believed was different to what he saw he was doing. Because in these situations he apprehended the difference between his beliefs and practices and felt the sense of dissonance, he was able to grow personally and professionally.

Beliefs

In reviewing the construct of beliefs, Pajares (1992) offers insights and explanations that demonstrate how powerful beliefs are in shaping who we are. He asserts that: "beliefs are the best indicators of the decisions individuals make throughout their lives... [and] the beliefs that teachers hold influence their perceptions and judgments, which, in turn, affect their behaviour in the classroom [therefore,] understanding belief structures of teachers and teacher candidates is essential to improving their professional preparation and teaching practices" (p. 307).

Pajares' review addresses the daunting task of distinguishing between beliefs and knowledge and raises interesting and important issues about how assumptions, feelings and actions influence each. He draws particular attention to the manner in which the cognitive tools one uses to solve problems are inextricably bound up with beliefs, and how beliefs then influence the manner in which a problem may be defined (framed and reframed). Importantly, he highlights the role of the affective domain which, I would argue, has a defining influence in learning about teaching but is too frequently overlooked in teacher education.

> The affective components of beliefs... facilitate their storage in long-term memory and become gestalts that are efficiently represented and retrieved and acquire a signature feeling. This signature feeling serves three functions: It facilitates recall by improving access to memory files due to the coloration of the feeling, it acts as the glue that holds elements of memory together for long periods (perhaps indefinitely), and it serves a constructive and reconstructive memory function by filling in incomplete memory gaps during recall and/or filtering information that conflicts with the signature feeling. Ultimately, this information-processing model of belief prominence depends on the affective/episodic/emotional nature of beliefs... (Pajares, 1992, pp. 321–322)

In relation to pre-service teachers' beliefs, Pajares goes on to restate that which many others have noted before, that beliefs about teaching are "well established by the time students get to college... [and] include ideas about what it takes to be an effective teacher and how students ought to behave, and, though usually *unarticulated and simplified*, they are brought into teacher preparation programs" (emphasis added, p. 322).

An important aspect of the influence of Lortie's (1975) *Apprenticeship of Observation* is that although beliefs may well have developed over a considerable period of time from observing teaching, that does not mean that they are always compatible with the educational hopes of teacher educators, nor does it mean that they are necessarily compatible with the educational hopes of individual students of teaching. The point that many beliefs may be unarticulated and simplified is an important issue for learning about teaching and so, apprehending situations through which articulation and possible dissonance might be highlighted is crucial. However, dealing with such dissonance in constructive and meaningful ways requires skill and expertise on the teacher educator's behalf. Of itself, that expertise is a subtle reminder of the value of responding appropriately to the assertion that *An uncomfortable learning experience can be a constructive learning experience*. It takes on special meaning when considering the nature of beliefs and the manner in which discrepancies between beliefs and practices might be confronted.

Further to this, the context for learning about teaching based on the development of beliefs through the apprenticeship of observation carries an important message for teacher education. Pajares describes the difference between students entering other academic disciplines and those entering teacher preparation: "When most students enter their academic disciplines, they are unlikely to have well-developed theories and preconceptions about their field of study...the confidence of strangers in the validity of their thinking as usual is first shaken by finding their surroundings quite different than expected. Medical students must enter operating theaters and emergency rooms; law students encounter courtrooms and law offices. These places are new to students, what goes on in them is alien, and understanding must be constructed nearly from scratch" (p. 323). This is in stark contrast to students of teaching who are "insiders."

When students of teaching enter teacher preparation, the context has a certain familiarity. When they re-enter schools and classrooms, they are "insiders." Their familiarity with classrooms, schools, the profession, the images of teaching, the identities they meet – and are reminded of from their past – all combine to create a sense of confirmation about the job at hand. The strong images and episodes of these places are filtered through the familiar images of their past.

As insiders in a familiar world, a greater effort is required to question conceptions. Much of what "could be" new is too easily subsumed into the taken for granted. Challenging existing beliefs (especially those that are unarticulated) must surely be a difficult task, especially so given that their familiarity with so many situations and contexts creates frames through which making the familiar strange will be increasingly difficult; as opposed to graduates in other fields who no doubt work hard to make the strange familiar.

Pajares' review is a strong reminder of the influence of beliefs on the way in which students of teaching learn about teaching. A consideration of how their beliefs might impact the way in which they filter, construct, adjust, adapt and adopt approaches to creating and using professional knowledge of practice in learning to teach is important for teaching about teaching. Pajares' synthesis of sixteen findings about beliefs are therefore most pertinent to teacher education, a brief summary of these follows:

1 Beliefs are formed early and tend to self-perpetuate and persevere despite contradictions.
2 Belief systems are acquired through a process of cultural transmission.
3 Belief systems help individuals define and understand the world and themselves.
4 Knowledge and beliefs are inextricably linked and new phenomena are interpreted through the affective, evaluative and episodic nature of beliefs.
5 Belief structures filter information processing; screening, redefining, distorting and reshaping subsequent thinking.
6 Epistemological beliefs play a key role in knowledge interpretation and cognitive monitoring.
7 Beliefs are prioritized according to their connections or relationship to other beliefs or other cognitive and affective structures.
8 Belief substructures, such as educational beliefs, must be understood in terms of their connections not only to each other but also to other, perhaps more central, beliefs in the system.
9 Some beliefs are more incontrovertible than others.
10 The earlier a belief is incorporated into a belief structure, the more difficult it is to alter.
11 Belief change during adulthood is rare, the most common cause being a conversion from one authority to another or a gestalt shift.
12 Beliefs play a critical role in defining behaviour and organizing knowledge and information.
13 Beliefs strongly influence perception and can be an unreliable guide to the nature of reality.
14 Individuals' beliefs, strongly affect their behaviour.
15 Beliefs must be inferred, and this inference must take into account the congruence among individuals' belief statements, the intentionality to behave in a predisposed manner, and the behaviour related to the belief in question.
16 Beliefs about teaching are well established by the time a student gets to college. (Pajares, 1992, pp. 325–326)

With a recognition that beliefs and knowledge are so closely tied to one another, students of teaching need opportunities through which they might begin to purposefully confront, define, redefine and realign their practices and beliefs for, at the heart of the development of their professional knowledge, is a need for articulation. However, if such a process is to be helpful in informing oneself about oneself, then teacher educators need to be reminded of the implicit advice on learning described through the axiom: Go *slow to go fast*.

Understanding self

As the previous sections illustrate, coming to understand oneself is enmeshed in a complex web comprising (at least) experiences, episodes, images, knowledge, culture, identity, contexts, and beliefs. In learning about teaching, coming to see oneself may be encouraged through "trying on" different identities and attempting to draw from them the similarities, differences, expectations, and prospects that encompasses as the possibilities created offer new ways of seeing and feeling the thoughts and actions that are associated with different identities. Trying on different identities may not always be something that is preplanned, sometimes it may just happen. But being sensitive to such situations is an important starting point for understanding that which may be revealed.

For students of teaching, some of the things they feel they need to do to "fit in" may well be contrary to that which they would prefer to do. However, in so doing, they may begin to feel what alternative identities are like and, as a result can learn more about themselves. For example, Sharon's anecdote suggests that she felt herself trying on a different identity, even though she did not mean that to be the case. Yet, in acting the way she did, in being confronted by a situation that she had not anticipated, she recognized something more about herself.

Under different circumstances, some students of teaching consciously do things differently in order to fit in. They therefore find themselves briefly living out a different identity.

Playing a role

I am a relatively calm and relaxed sort of person although some of my supervising teachers have interpreted it differently. On my last teaching round [school placement], my supervising teacher gave me a bit of grief for not making the students put their hands up to ask questions and other stuff like that that he said made the class too noisy.

"You're really too friendly and quite ineffectual!" Mr. Do-What-I-Say said to me after one lesson.

It just seemed to me that all these old cranky teachers I've had as supervisors expect me to run the class just like them. You know what that means: no fun for the kids, always do what you're told, don't ask any real questions, and never think for yourself. Just get on with playing the same old game and do what you're told.

You can imagine how I felt when I turned up at Highview Grammar for my last teaching round.

My supervising teacher, "Mr. I've been here since Noah was a boy," barely even looked up over his pile of corrections when I was introduced to him and everywhere I turned I saw kids being rounded up like sheep, being chased into their classroom pens and doing what they were told, "Bah, Bah, Bah, three bags full sir!"

"Five weeks of this. It's a sentence not a placement!" I thought to myself, "How am I ever going to cope?"

I decided that attack was the best form of defence so I made up my mind to be like the others here and avoid Nightmare on Highview Grammar.

I justified it in my mind easily enough because this was the [teaching] round I was to be assessed on, and so I knew I'd have to be seen to be teaching like all the others to be marked as "competent to teach."

In my first lesson, after a bit of noise and calling out I slammed my book down on the desk and said, "O.K., that's it, I've had it with you guys. This is not good enough."

Thank goodness the sound of my voice didn't really reflect the shaking in my boots. In fact I surprised myself as to how authoritative I sounded. "You'll all stay back at lunch-time. You've wasted enough of my time, now I'll waste some of yours."

Almost immediately I was swamped with:

"Oh no."

"Why?"

"I've got football training."

"I have drama practice."

"You didn't warn us."

"I'll miss my spot in the tuckshop queue." And so the plaintiff cries spewed forth.

I carried on regardless despite quietly questioning why I would want to give up some of my precious lunch-time too.

"I won't say it again. Let this be a lesson to you all!" I heard myself saying.

"Where did that one come from?" I asked myself.

By now even my supervisor was paying attention.

"I bet he thinks I'm doing a great job." I thought as a terrible feeling of hypocrisy started welling up inside of me. "I suppose this is what they mean when they talk about teaching as acting."

When the bell went for the start of lunch, I looked at them all wondering if I'd be squashed in the stampede for the door.

Fortunately none of them gave even a hint of moving.

"O.K., here goes," I said to myself. "Now, when everyone has finished their work we'll think about leaving. But only after I've seen everyone's completed passages." I sounded amazingly confident as I dug my grave even deeper. D.R.I.P. Cranky teacher below. I could see the headstone now.

As I wondered around checking their work I kept a stern face.

"They might be doing what they're told but I feel like a fake." I thought, "At least the supervisor will love me. I bet this is just maintaining the status-quo."

As the last kid left, my supervisor looked across the room at me.

"This has made me late for a meeting so I'll see you later." He said rather gruffly, certainly not inviting a follow-up conversation.

Straight after lunch I had the same class again.

They came in and to my surprise, everything ran like a charm. They didn't seem to be too concerned about the way I had carried on last lesson. In fact, they were quite a pleasure to teach. It was a good lesson. I actually enjoyed it.

After class, as I slumped down in the chair in front of my desk in the staff room. My supervising teacher came over to me.

He looked down and I looked up.

I was taken aback by the gentle smile that slowly spread across his face. "Well, that was an interesting couple of lessons with year 9." He said, "They can be a bit rowdy at times, but you know, they aren't malicious. Give them a bit of rope and you'll find they'll respond really well. You can afford to let a bit more of yourself come through. Kids don't carry a grudge. How you carry on one lesson won't be held against you for the rest of your life. Relax a little. Be yourself."

That started the best teaching round I had all year. I learnt so much with that year 9 class, and Mr. Hayes was such a good supervisor. I did lots of things I never really thought I could or would do and I think I really started to feel like the teacher I want to be. (Elena)

Learning about teaching is a very personal experience. Helping students of teaching to capitalize on that learning is an essential aspect of teacher education. In so doing, there is a clear need to *create conditions for learning* through which real possibilities for growth exist so that development in learning about teaching might be grasped in ways appropriate to individuals and, that are responsive to their needs within their given teaching and learning context. In conceptualizing such situations, the relationship between aspects that shape learning about oneself become all the more important as aligning beliefs and practices takes on added significance in the search for who one is as a teacher and what that teacher hopes to be.

Korthagen (2004), in pursuing a better understanding of that which makes a good teacher proposed the "onion model" as one way of understanding different levels of self and considering how they impact the development of the individual. His model comprises six levels (6 being the inner most level of the onion and 1 being the outer layer) each of which offer different perspectives on how teachers function:

1   Environment
2   Behavior

3   Competences
4   Beliefs
5   Professional identity
6   Mission

The first two levels (Environment and Behavior) are those which tend to attract the most attention from students of teaching. These levels are most readily observable and are aspects which tend to raise the most immediate and obvious problems in their developing understanding of practice. The next level, competences, is influential on the nature of behaviors. However, as Korthagen explains, competences offer potential for behavior but should not be confused with a given behavior itself.

These first three levels illustrate an important feature of the onion model. As these levels "line up" a sense of harmony in being is created which can radiate in both directions – from the inside out and from the outside in. Just as the environment can influence a teacher's behavior, so too behavior can influence the nature of the environment. Behaviors that are triggered often enough can lead to a level of competence that increases the likelihood that such behavior might be used in different situations, that is in learning about practice in one situation there is greater possibility that such learning might be informative in others.

The previous part of this chapter made clear the complex nature of level 4 (beliefs), and Korthagen explains in great detail the importance of this level in shaping possibilities for the development of competences and associated behaviors. He then goes on to outline how notions of identity (level 5) are crucial in shaping "who a teacher is" but draws attention to the fact that change in identity is a slow and painful process. The final level (mission) is what Korthagen describes as that which is "deep inside us and causes us to do what we do," it is the level at which the deeply felt personal values that are the essence of a person's existence reside.

The value of the onion model is in consideration of the process of change (in this case, change through learning about teaching) and how the alignment of all levels leads to a coherent whole so that discrepancies between the environment and self, or self and the environment, might be better understood and addressed. Thus the onion model can be very helpful for students of teaching as they search to learn to be better teachers. Further to this, the onion model helps to situate where a concern may exist, that is at what level a concern is felt and, as concerns can be the driving force for learning about teaching, better understanding what a concern is linked to (level) can be a most influential way of achieving successful resolution.

Korthagen also offers possibilities for interventions that are more responsive to the level at which a concern exists and suggests that in appropriately aligning both, learning about oneself and one's teaching is likely to be much more meaningful. However, for teacher education to pursue this approach, he also warns that teacher educators themselves need to be in touch with their mission. Korthagen considers this to be a prerequisite for highlighting the same for students of teaching.

I close this chapter with the voices of two students of teaching that each illustrate in different ways the importance of Korthagen's onion model, first in terms of the practice of teacher educators, and then in the practice of students of teaching. The first anecdote is related to the way in which a teacher educator's practice was not in harmony with the expectations of the environment and the resultant incongruity was strikingly apparent to his students of teaching. However, despite the incongruity, there was still something in the experience to be learnt for it certainly shaped the author's own understanding of the impact of *not* aligning practices and beliefs.

A lesson on policy

The tutorial room was quiet. Only the professor's voice broke the silence. I had to say something. I disagreed with what he was saying. I spoke up. That's what I thought we were supposed to be learning to do. To be actively engaged in our learning. To question our understanding. We're certainly expected to be doing that with our students in school.

'I don't think that policy has to be about change!' I said, and I gave some examples to support my point of view. With that, others in the class also started to contribute.

'This is what the definition is! Reputed researchers agree!' was his rather forceful response.

Faced with that, what else could I say? He was the expert. He would take it as a personal insult if I again raised issues, so I kept my mouth shut. As the rest of the monologue surged forth, the class returned to its earlier silence. I opened my note book and wrote furiously, 'I disagree, I disagree.'

We had just been talking about including people in discussions, accepting others' point of view, inclusion, understanding. I don't think that classrooms should be lecture theatres. Teaching is not a one-way process. (Loughran, 1997b, pp. 5–6)

The next anecdote illustrates how a student of teaching who was working toward a particular way of being as a teacher took a risk to try to encourage students' responses. In so doing, the rewards that accompanied working to use teaching behaviors that were in accord with his beliefs enhanced his learning about teaching and empowered him to further pursue developing a student-centred learning environment in his classes.

Wait time

My first class. Palms sweating, breathing shallow, tie too tight, pulse too fast. I guess I was kind of nervous. I had fully prepared the whole lesson in intricate detail, and even rehearsed certain key sections. I shuffled my books, watching them enter the room noisily, with attitude to burn. They sat down. Eventually, I swallowed.

"Good morning 10B! My name is Mr. Burns, I'm a teacher from Monash University. Today we are..." and into the lesson I launched. Cool as a cucumber and smooth as a strawberry smoothie. I wrote on the board in big letters. 'What Makes A Film?'

Having bonded with the students on an incredibly deep and substantial level in the first three minutes of the class, I swiftly and confidently turned to face the class. With a big smile and the most open of expressions I could muster, I threw out my first question.

"Can anyone tell me some elements of film making?"

I paused for the expected barrage of excited responses. I waited and waited. Anyone? Longer and longer. Help? It felt like an hour. A week. A year. Would the wait be worth it? A...yes? Finally from the back of the class! "Um...scripts, sir?"

"Thank you!" I said, hopefully without too much desperation. The trickle of answers gradually became a waterfall. I was finally safe, splashing gleefully in the puddles of their intuitive responses, the dam of silence broken. (Loughran, 2002, p. 37)

Overview

This chapter was designed to highlight how the nature of concerns influence understandings of learning about teaching and how considered responses to concerns is an issue for students of teaching and teacher educators alike. In exploring the nature of concerns and the manner in which they develop and shift throughout the course of a teacher preparation program, the need to better understand oneself inevitably emerges. For students of teaching there is a need to "come to know oneself", and in so doing, to use such knowledge to help shape the development of the professional self through a recognition of, and response to, the behaviors, competences, beliefs, identity and mission that influence the manner in which the self functions in, and influences the nature of, a teaching and learning environment.

The use of anecdotes throughout this chapter has been designed to offer the student voice and to highlight how, if teacher education is to truly be an educative experience, an insider's perspective on learning about teaching needs to be actively pursued. The links between learning about teaching and teaching about teaching are ever present and are an integral part of conceptualizing how each interact to influence the development of a pedagogy of teacher education. Thus the occasional links to ways of portraying and articulating a knowledge of teacher education practices throughout the chapter.

I close now with one final anecdote that illustrates this parallel and how important it not to take for granted that which is, and is not, happening in a pedagogic experience because *The transition to teacher as a learner of teaching is fundamental and difficult.*

It was just one student

This would be it. The day that my efforts would shine through. This class would show how to develop quality learning. Today was it.

I had put so much time and effort into developing this investigative task for my Year 7 Accelerated Learning Program Mathematics class, I didn't want anything to go wrong.

Things seemed to be going well. I wandered around the room helping the groups that needed help and ensuring the class stayed on task.

Hands were up and with each question I gently redirected their efforts so that they solved their problems together, found out what to do, how to do it and why, without me telling them the "answers."

Then Mel put up her hand.

With my heart thumping in my chest so loud I thought the entire class would hear it I walked over to her.

Of all my students, Mel was the one who never wanted to think for herself, she just wanted to know what to do to get it right.

"Miss, what's the answer to this question?"

This was it. What would I say? How could I promote investigative learning skills in my class with a question like that?

I took a deep breath and slowly went through the key concepts of the question with her.

By the end of the discussion I felt confident had I had helped her enough to get on with the work without actually telling her the answer.

"Phew!" I thought, "That was hard work. It's not easy to do this. No wonder so many teachers just tell kids the answers."

That night at home, whilst I was reading over their work, I came across Mel's paper.

I began reading.

"All right so far." I said to myself, "Still o.k. Yep, not bad. I think she's got the hang of this." I thought as my relief broke out in a smile.

As I turned the page my eyes were drawn to the last question.

"Explain how you got the above answer." Written below was Mel's honest response:

In class I asked the teacher how to do that question and she told me to do it that way. That's how I got my answer.

My heart sank.

"Were all my students doing this?" I asked myself. "Had all my efforts to promote investigative learning gone to waste? Is this really how I teach?"

With the best interests of my own well being I decided to "forget" this little episode when it came to my final assignment at university into student centred learning. After all, it was just one student. Right? (Bethany)

It was just one student. I wonder how often the insights offered by one student are pushed to one side because they do not fit the picture of ourselves that we wish to see? Learning and teaching about teaching is a risky business. There is a need to risk seeing what may too often be overlooked, not seen, or even purposely ignored. What learners of teaching see is important regardless of whether the learner is a student or a teacher of teaching. Hence there is an ever-present need to be reminded of the importance of responding to both *the voice of the individual and the voice of the group*.

8 From student to teacher: The place of effective reflective practice

The prospect of becoming a real teacher is both exciting and scary. The question in the forefront of my mind this year has been, "Will I really be ready to teach at the end of this year?"

(Sylvia)

Chapter 7 explored a number of important aspects of being a student of teaching that influence the nature of learning about teaching. When considered together, these aspects combine to highlight another feature of learning to teach that encompasses a crucial phase in understanding the learning about teaching experience: the shift from being a student to being a teacher.

The transition from student to teacher involves a realization that some changes are quite personal (e.g. coming to know oneself) while others are more generalizable (e.g. initially identifying more strongly with students than teachers; concerns about subject matter knowledge). These changes influence understandings of such things as responsibility, experience and professional autonomy and impact (in sometimes unexpected ways) views of that which was seemingly familiar from a student's perspective when re-considered from a teacher's perspective. At the same time, it is important that the existing knowledge and experience from a student's perspective be viewed as complementary and informing to the developing knowledge and experience as a teacher. The transition is not a time in which one set of understandings (student's) should be replaced with another (teacher's), but a time in which the student perspective is valued and appropriately responded to as new understandings of the world of teachers and teaching expand and develop.

In order to explore this interaction between being a student and a teacher simultaneously, a précised version of Sylvia's (author of the quote at the start of this chapter) end-of-year reflective paper is presented which leads to a consideration of the place of reflection in learning about teaching.

Becoming a real teacher

This paper documents some of the major elements of my journey from university student to graduate teacher... [and has] come about as a result of my attempts to apply what I have learned in the university classroom to my own teaching... It is my hope that the accounts I have chosen will give you a window through which to view my understanding of my development as a pre-service teacher.

My supervisor

As it turned out, my supervisor at the school was incredibly helpful. His teaching style was one that I admired greatly, as he was completely dedicated and committed to helping others learn, no matter what. One of the most helpful things was his willingness and encouragement of me to experiment in my teaching practice. His openness to discussion about ways I could improve on my teaching practice was incredibly beneficial. I owe him a lot in the development of my own style.... [However,] he had developed a [music] program [that worried me because]...I found it difficult initially to adapt my knowledge [of music] to the program that was in place. While I am open to these [program] styles I found it difficult to adapt my classical [music] thinking to styles that I normally wouldn't teach [jazz and pop].

Episode one

"I was working so much harder than the students were!" (Journal entry)

I felt well prepared for this class....I was sure that the questions I was asking were easy to understand and answer. However, I was pushing constantly to get a response. There seemed to be an incredible resistance to participation.

"I really tried to share the questioning around, but it was centered on a group of three students." (Journal entry)

This was my first awakening to the influences of peer pressure and it was difficult....What I had intended to be a large group discussion had become a teacher performance. The students weren't going to challenge me on this as long as I didn't make them do any work.

Episode two

The reflections following my first class led me to make changes in the second class. I decided that small group work would help break down peer pressure and it did. The groups settled quickly and actually responded very well to the material I presented. They had picked up quite a bit more than I expected in the last class. However, there was still that one group who wouldn't participate and the thought that I wasn't reaching the needs of the whole class left me unsettled. These students didn't present a management issue for me as long as I didn't challenge them to do any work....I felt it was a large part of my job to try and get through to them, but I didn't know how.

Sandy [student pseudonym] made me aware of the fine line between giving a student the freedom to learn in their own way at their own pace, and that of giving too much freedom. In the time I was there [school practicum] I didn't feel that I solved this issue.

I knew before I taught this class that the students had not received a lot of exposure to classical music, but I really hadn't accounted for their reactions to what I would play them....I wasn't expecting the sorts of answers [I received] at all. I had envisioned them responding with relative maturity to the task. I had also thought that they would automatically be able to link it back to the previous lesson. I discovered that I had assumed too much.

I knew that my supervisor had to deal with similar management and teaching issues when he was teaching this class, but I still felt myself battling to try and do it perfectly every time. I kept feeling frustrated with myself at the issues that seemed to arise every lesson. I was in constant tension, wondering if a real teacher would have these difficulties (surely the four-year education degree had given me the tools, so why was I having so much trouble applying them?). I also felt the pressure to be accepted by the students. I hadn't been accepted through the [type of] material I was presenting, so I think I gave in a lot more to other management issues, simply because I wanted their approval.

Episode three

The feelings of inadequacy came to a head...my fears in this class stemmed from wanting to have the "correct" content. I was worried that the students would think the things I had planned for them to do were stupid and irrelevant. I was worried that even though I only finished school 5 years ago, that I was out of touch with where they were at. I had trouble planning the lesson for this class and trouble teaching it with conviction. My supervisor had suggested a compositional lesson, so I thought that this was a sure winner. What I hadn't accounted for was my own thoughts and style in teaching. It appeared easier to replicate someone else's. Creating and taking responsibility for my own style was a completely foreign concept and I wasn't sure I was good enough. I went in unsettled.

"I was out of control today and I stepped over some boundaries that I shouldn't have. I feel like I lost complete control. I had no strategies to deal with this. I have no idea what boundaries to put up without being overly strict. I did things today that I thought I would never do or never say. I want the acceptance of the class too much and in too many ways. I have to change things if I'm going to be an effective teacher. I need to ask for advice more – I have no idea how to deal with these situations." (Journal entry)

One of the most disappointing things...was that I felt I had been really unkind, when I didn't have to be. After reflecting on the lesson I could see that there were quite a few times when I could have changed tack to decrease the tension and try to get the students to participate. However, in the heat of the moment I just didn't have the working knowledge to put all the theory into practice.

In retrospect

As time has passed since these classes I have been able to reflect and realise that there are so many positive insights to come out of experiences like this.

Firstly I realised that discussion with others can be a helpful way of dealing with mistakes. Hearing other teachers in the staff room say how much they struggled with [difficult students] as well made me realise that others go through similar experiences too. The notion of the staff in a school working as a team now takes on greater significance. I also began to recognise some painful, but nonetheless helpful truths about my teaching....I believe that my lack of set rules was affected by my desire to be liked by the students and will hopefully be something [that I get better at] over time.

I also learned that developing clear questions is important in keeping students' interest and getting their participation during classroom discussion. In contrast I learned that being flexible in my response to student questioning is incredibly important, but also believe that this will be a result of time and confidence.

In addition I learned that I need to believe my ideas are valid and that what I teach is ok. Listening to and trying other teachers' ideas is good, but it will work best when I adapt these to my own style. Finally I learned that I am passionate about student engagement! The frustrations I felt at students who wouldn't participate is a sign that I care about these students getting every opportunity they can. I just have to learn to do this in a way that is positive.

Building on learning

While this paper has tended to focus on the negative aspects of my teaching, I found that the reflection had helped me to grow. During the rest of my time on [teaching] rounds I could see this happening... However, I hope it is the sort of growth that continues in the future.

The final class was probably the most rewarding class I have taught....I had intended to spend one period teaching theory and the other allowing the students to go on with prac. I was a bit nervous about the prac, since I had done very little to set up this class and my supervisor was away. However, in the previous classes I'd taken I had focused on rehearsal and performance technique. So I thought I could focus on this area again if needs be.

"When I entered this class (period 5 and 6) on Friday, I was pretty determined to teach at least one period of the 'theory' I had previously prepared. As the students entered the room I was confronted with comments like, "aw miss, we're not going to do theory again, we did that on Wednesday." In my head I was planning a way to convince them that theory would be a good thing to do. However, as each of the students straggled in I started to think it wasn't going to work. Sure I could enforce theory, and yes I had spent hours on a lesson that I may never use again, but I just didn't think it was worth the battle. I decided that the best thing to do would be to allow them to set up for prac. As they got prepared I sat back and let them go…I was amazed that they knew so much about the equipment; they even started to show me new ways of doing things. The period was a success, they left very happy with what they had done and I left with a feeling that somehow they had learned something that no lecture could ever teach – making music is a lot of fun!" (Journal entry)

I don't think I would have had the confidence to throw away a lesson like that if I had not had the experience with the year nines. This class was crucial in helping me regain my confidence as a beginning teacher.

In conclusion

I finish this paper on the last day of [my time at] university.…The biggest lesson I have learned is that learning is an ongoing process for both the teacher and the student [and I have been both]. I've heard this said in many lectures and tutorial rooms before, but living it was a completely different experience.

This paper certainly hasn't given me a clear set of answers to apply to any situation in schools, but the process…has given me a greater awareness of my own teaching skills and also given me a hope that with careful reflection and also much guidance from others, I too can conduct quality teaching…in time. (Sylvia, end of year reflective paper)

Sylvia illustrates how, in her transition from student to teacher, she comes to see different problems that are influential in shaping her understanding of her role as a teacher. One in particular, which was also raised by Jason and Elena (see Chapter 7), is the need to be liked by the students. This problem may be played out in different ways by different students of teaching,[1] but is commonly manifested through the need to be "in touch" with students which creates tensions when coming to understand, accept

---

1 The difference perhaps most apparent between those students of teaching who have entered teacher preparation at the completion of high school and are therefore beginning teachers in their early 20s in comparison to mature age and/or second career students of teaching. Yet, although the sense of being "in touch" *per se* may be different (due to age considerations), the tension between responsibility and authority is generally still apparent.

and enact the responsibilities that accompany authority. As Sylvia demonstrated, in coming to recognize this particular problem, she also began to see how her developing understanding influenced her thinking about teaching. In so doing, she learnt to manage the tension and see things in, and about, her teaching that she was previously unable to see.

It could well be argued that Sylvia has demonstrated that her learning about teaching has been enhanced through reconsidering her experiences and seeing them in different ways. She has adopted a reflective stance characterized by framing and reframing (Schön, 1983) that has helped her to learn through her experiences and, importantly, positively impact her practice. Her reflection on practice, by being grounded in her own experiences, has led her to apply *her* reflection on *her* experiences to her *own* practice and so is enacting effective reflective practice (Loughran, 2002).

Effective reflective practice: Moving beyond the abstract

Reflective practice is a term that carries diverse meaning (Grimmett and Erickson, 1988; Richardson, 1992). For some, it simply means thinking about 'something', whilst for others it is a well defined and crafted practice that carries very specific meaning and associated action. Along this continuum there are many interesting interpretations but one element of reflection that is common to many is the notion of a 'problem' (a puzzling, curious or perplexing situation). What that 'problem' is, the way it is framed and (hopefully) reframed, is an important aspect of understanding the nature of reflection and the value of reflective practice. It is also a crucial (but sometimes too easily overlooked) aspect in learning about teaching. (Loughran, 2002, p. 33)

Reflection has become the cornerstone of many teacher education programs. However, what reflection is, the way it is used, taught and (sadly) assessed,[2] is as varied as the programs themselves. For students of teaching, just as learning to teach may present difficulties in moving beyond the technical, so too the same applies to learning to be reflective, thus the notion of effective reflective practice and the immediate reminder that *Teaching is reflective and requires an inquiry stance.*

A central feature of enacting change is bound up in the ability to see the problem. If the problem is not seen as an issue requiring attention, then there is little need or impetus to do anything about it. In learning about

---

2 I never cease to be amazed when confronted by situations in which reflection is assessed. To allocate a grade or to in some way formally assess students of teaching on their reflective processes, in my view, undermines the very essence of encouraging reflection for, like most things that carry the expectations of assessment, quickly becomes part of the "game" of doing that which will be rewarded by grades thus trivializing reflection and its value in learning about teaching.

teaching there is a clear need for students of teaching to see *their* own problems in order to choose how to act on them and, this is dramatically different from reflecting on the problems of others or reflecting on the problems that might be pointed out by a (school) supervising teacher or teacher educator. Thus, there is an important teaching about teaching issue inherent in helping students of teaching to develop effective reflective practice and it hinges on the ability to help them see that which they might not be ready to see at that time. Empowering students of teaching to search for, and respond to, their *own* problems can be encouraged through the use of anecdotes. Hopefully, those anecdotes that have been used so far in this book have already illustrated this point. However, to build on it further, consider the following anecdote and how it highlights an interesting issue that is perhaps more easily stated than genuinely understood in practice and how it is brought to life through an apparently simple episode because the student of teaching sees it himself in his own practice.

What you hear in silence

This was the first time I taught this particular year 10 class. The topic was melody writing and I was more than prepared for the lesson with every word scripted and carefully emblazoned on the pages in front of me in my lesson plan.

"O.K., melody writing is a fairy simple concept." I started, "As long as you follow the seven rules."

"Rule number one is..." and so I started blurting out the rules as the class frantically raced to write them down in their note books.

"And rule number seven, are you with me now James?" my confidence growing with every word as I pushed them to keep up, "You must *always* end on the tonic."

It was as easy as that!

I knew that now all they had to do was follow the rules and they would all be melody writers extraordinaire.

"And for homework tonight I want you to follow those rules and write your own melody. Any questions?" I asked as I scanned the room quite pleased with my delivery.

The silence beckoned so I asked again, "O.K., quite simple really. Any questions?"

Not a sound.

"Great, they all understand." I thought to myself in a congratulatory tone.

The bell sounded right on cue and as the students filed out of the room I started to pack up my things to follow them out.

I was pleased with today's lesson and was quietly rewarding myself on a job well done as I strode to the door.

"Did you understand any of that?" Ben asked Jeff as they spilled out into the corridor.

"Nup, not one bit." Jeff said.

"Me either." (Brad)

Dewey's (1933) work has been the basis of many of the approaches to, and incorporation of, reflection in teaching and teacher education. The enduring message of Dewey's conceptualization of reflection is that it: "is a holistic way of meeting and responding to problems, a way of being as a teacher. Reflective action is also a process that involves more than logical and rational problem-solving processes. Reflection involves intuition, emotion, and passion and is not something that can be neatly packaged as a set of techniques for teachers" (Zeichner and Liston, 1996, p. 9).

In outlining his views on reflection, Dewey suggested three attitudes that he considered important in predisposing an individual to reflect: open-mindedness, responsibility and wholeheartedness.

Open-mindedness is demonstrated through the ability to consider problems in new and different ways, to actively listen to others, to be sensitive to alternative views and to be able to hear and take account of views contrary to one's own. Responsibility is the need to know why; to examine the intellectual underpinnings so that why something is worth believing is fully realized. Whole-heartedness "is displayed when one is thoroughly involved in a subject or cause. It is being enticed and engaged in thinking. It is associated with experiencing a flood of ideas and thoughts. Interest is maintained and ideas are sought in ways which an enthusiasm and desire for knowing is enacted" (Loughran, 1996, p. 5).

Building on purposefully highlighting the development of these attitudes in learning about teaching, effective reflective practice emphasizes the importance of reflection for action so that, in the process, deeper understandings of practice might be developed. For that to be the case, effective reflective practice responds to the assumptions that:

- a problem is unlikely to be acted on if it is not viewed as a problem;
- rationalization may masquerade as reflection;
- experience alone does not lead to learning – reflection on experience is essential;
- other ways of seeing problems must be developed;
- articulation matters;
- developing professional knowledge is an important outcome of reflection. (Loughran, 2002)

Effective reflective practice may be highlighted in learning about teaching in many ways, not least of which is through Berry's (2004a) tension of *telling and growth*. For the teacher educator, this tension is bound up in moderating between the desire to want to tell students what they should see and/or know as opposed to creating possibilities for them to see and/or seek for themselves. For students of teaching, this tension is felt through the desire to find a "recipe" for learning about teaching in contrast to accepting greater responsibility for their own learning about teaching. This tension illustrates how many of the teaching about teaching issues are mirrored in issues pertaining to learning about teaching. In this case, it draws attention to the reality that it seems much easier to tell than to help others see and grow and, unfortunately, in formal teaching and learning environments, the former is most commonly experienced to the detriment of the latter. Consequently, the teacher education environment must be *the* place where the latter is the norm if it is to gain a foothold and be seen as a valuable learning experience. In so doing, eventually, the incongruity of teachers' and students' views of teaching and learning (as per the Northfield experience see Chapter 2, Tables 2.1 and 2.2) might then be more meaningfully addressed.

Brandenburg (2004) demonstrates one way of generating real possibilities for achieving such a goal through her use of roundtables in teacher education classes. She places great emphasis on the notion of co-learners and co-creators of knowledge through the use of the ALACT model (Korthagen, 1988). In this way, she establishes practices and creates an environment that: "allows for, and encourages learner risk-taking and, within these spaces, systematic reflective practice based on experience enables the complexities of learning about teaching to be teased apart" (p. 179).

Brandenburg's roundtables are an overt encouragement of the development of effective reflective practice as she helps her students of teaching to extract, evaluate and articulate the essence of *their* learning from *their* experiences of teaching and to share *their* developing knowledge in meaningful ways. The process involves careful consideration of both *seeing* and *action* in order to enhance learning through experience. In so doing, knowledge creation is viewed as a normal expectation of learning about teaching, and that is in accord with the notion of effective reflective practice. Consider the following case in point that illustrates how Berry's (2004a) tension is played out in both teaching *and* learning about teaching and, hopefully, illustrates how a consideration of effective reflective practice impacts both:

> A common post-practicum teaching approach is for teacher educators to 'extract' the learning from student-teachers' experiences so that it can be presented back to them in ways that might be helpful and offer insights that they had not previously recognised. However, if the focus is genuinely on the student-teacher as learner, then it is their ability to analyse and make meaning from experience that matters most – as opposed to when the teacher educator filters, develops and shares the knowledge with the student-teachers....the knowledge developed may well be the same, but the process in developing the knowledge is very different. Who is doing the learning really matters and is directly related to where the effective reflective practice occurs...So consider again the traditional teaching round de-brief. Student-teachers are often asked to share their practicum experiences in small groups and it is not unusual that they find this to be an interesting and engaging experience. [But,] what comes from such tasks beyond some form of support for knowing that others face the same challenges and dilemmas, or that acknowledgment that the transition from student to teacher is difficult

and that some common issues can be tackled and so on. However, if these small groups are asked to develop assertions about their practice as a result of this sharing, the outcomes can be qualitatively different to that of the support and acknowledgment outcomes noted above. This difference is extended even more when student-teachers document and share these assertions with their peers...Although the knowledge developed through this process may not necessarily be new or different for many teacher educators [Table 8.1], it [is] new and meaningful for the student-teachers...because of the ownership derived from the direct link to their experiences. In so doing, their effective reflective practice is evident in the manner in which their possibilities for future action are enhanced because of the new perspectives they now conceive of – their taken-for-granted assumptions about particular situations were challenged and so their 'normal' and/or 'developing' practice could not so easily be rationalised... [Table 8.1] represents an important transition in thinking by student-teachers as their effective reflective practice is embedded in what might be described as a beginning point in the development of professional knowledge about the practice setting... Through the notion of effective reflective practice, it is possible to consider teacher knowledge through particular concrete examples. Just as the student-teachers (in the part above) were beginning to articulate their learning, effective reflective practice can be viewed as that which encapsulates a knowledge of the practice setting gained through reflection on practice, such that the way it is documented carries meaning, and offers insights into wisdom-in-practice. (Loughran, 2002, pp. 38–39)

As Table 8.1 aptly demonstrates, the development of assertions about practice derived from one's own practice can of course be seen as simply

Table 8.1 Assertions about practice: articulating learning about professional knowledge

- The medium of instruction influences the success (or failure) of the lesson.
- The students have a management script, you have to de-program before you re-program.
- Sometimes you teach in ways you don't like because it helps you cope.
- Teaching in a way that works isn't always a way that you'd like to be teaching.
- Too much enthusiasm (student and teacher) may lead to other problems.
- Students and teachers can have different ideas of what is fun and exciting.
- Students have more control over what works in the classroom than the teacher.
- Students have to make connections between their school work and their existing knowledge for the tasks to be meaningful.
- Clear expectations and guidelines are important for students to know how to act/learn.
- The success of teaching strategies is dependent on students' skills – they may or may not have these skills.

Source: Loughran (2002, p. 39).

confirming "existing knowledge." However, the importance of such knowledge being developed by individual students of teaching through reflection on their own experiences is what matters. More so, as they develop such assertions in small groups, the need for articulation in a manner that carries genuine meaning is paramount, thus effective reflective practice carries with it an expectation of a language for sharing knowledge of practice. This process (as per the approach outlined above) is similar in many ways to the approach to developing summary statements as described by Northfield (see Chapter 5, Table 5.1) and therefore is another reminder of the importance of the constructs of, and relationship between, episteme and phronesis.

Learning through phronesis and episteme

Learning about teaching needs to make clear that the "traditional" boundaries between theory and practice are not distinct and immovable and that what boundaries exist vary dramatically with who is setting them and for what purpose they are being set. Another way of considering this issue is through the idea that there is a gentle ebb and flow that characterizes the influence of one on the other and, that the learning borne of the relationship is influential in the development of practice. Episteme and phronesis therefore become useful constructs for recognizing and responding to such learning.

Russell (2002) offers interesting insights into the purposeful linking of theory and practice through his examination of the faculty liaison role which developed through questioning the place of experience in learning to teach. In an initial radical restructure of the teacher education program in which he taught:

> significant new features included an early extended practicum experience (fourteen weeks) accompanied by two field-based professional studies courses...the major assignment for secondary candidates...is an action research project carried out in the final weeks of the early extended practicum....Beginning the program in schools (after a week long orientation period at the university) with support from Associate Teachers and a Faculty Liaison was a powerful way of demonstrating how one learns from experience. Most teacher candidates seem to have little or no sense of what it means to learn from experience, yet this learning goes to the heart of the constructivist reforms that many argue are needed in our schools and in our teacher education programs. (Russell, 2002, p. 76)

Through this radical change (early extended school practicum), well-entrenched views of learning to teach were immediately confronted eventually leading to it being dropped in favor of much more preparation time at university before students of teaching could be trusted to safely embark on school experience. This challenge to the place of experience in learning to teach was informative.

In teacher education it is typically argued that students of teaching need to be prepared before being sent out to schools to teach. Interestingly, what the results of the early extended school practicum demonstrated was that much of the traditional preparation argument was a misnomer. Rather than preparing students of teaching for school experience, traditional preparation tended to inadvertently establish a theory–practice divide. Russell characterized this through contrasting views of the nature of learning to teach (transmission comprising barriers to be overcome vs. interpretation comprising frames for professional learning).

The transmission view of learning to teach is: "When others tell me how to teach and I watch experienced teachers, then my learning is automatic and I easily become a good teacher. Teaching experience generates a steady progression to *mastery* that is largely unaffected by the students who pass through classes" (emphasis in original, Russell, 2002, p. 85). While the interpretation view of learning to teach is: "Good teaching requires constant effort to bring my actions in line with my goals for my students' learning and my own professional learning. Teaching is an inherently unstable activity that requires building and maintaining a unique and *dynamic relationship* with each new group of students" (emphasis in original, Russell, 2002, p. 85).

Russell concluded that with the early extended practicum, students of teaching tended to adopt an *Interpretation* approach to learning to teach. When the early extended practicum was changed and greater university preparation time was reinstated (and the reasons for so doing were many, not least of which included administrative and organizational issues that were difficult to overcome), students of teaching more readily adopted a *Transmission* approach to learning to teach. As he noted, "while experience is powerful, learning from experience is far from automatic" (p. 84), thus the move toward an Interpretation approach to learning to teach should not be mistaken as learning through osmosis. What it is though is the interaction of experience with: reflecting; hypothesizing; testing; processing; synthesizing; generalizing; and, abstracting from practice to practice so that there is a process of building of one's professional knowledge of teaching. In so doing a symbiotic relationship exists whereby, phronesis informing episteme informing phronesis is enhanced.

Korthagen (2001c) similarly argues the importance of bridging the theory–practice gap in learning about teaching by also invoking the language of professional learning. He offers the pertinent reminder that there is an essential need to recognize and respond to the ways in which students of teaching construct their views of teaching and learning so that new experiences designed to challenge these preconceptions might be created.

There is little reason for students of teaching to change their views just because they are told something, change must come from within, there needs to be a desire to change and that desire is part of what Korthagen suggests comprises professional learning. He proposes three principles which form a firm foundation for building professional learning:

1   A teacher's professional learning will be more effective when directed by an internal need in the learner.
2   A teacher's professional learning will be more effective when rooted in the learner's own experiences.
3   A teacher's professional learning will be more effective when the learner reflects in detail on his or her experiences. (Korthagen, 2001c, p. 71)

The importance of these principles is evident in the recognition that professional learning is not developed through simply gaining more knowledge, rather professional learning is enhanced by one becoming more perceptive to the complexities, possibilities and nuances of teaching contexts. Thus, developing awareness of situations is a knowledge building exercise of a type based in phronesis and shared as episteme (e.g. assertions, tensions, paradoxes, etc. as outlined in Chapter 5). And, students of teaching need opportunities to do just that in the way they approach their teaching experiences; learn from their teaching experiences and abstract to other teaching experiences so that the value of phronesis is evident in developing an understanding of the particular, but that applicability across contexts might be carried through episteme. In this way, they might see their own developing knowledge of practice as a meaningful and valuable aspect of their professional learning applicable in, and informing to, teaching and learning contexts.

Overview

This chapter has been organized in such a way as to place the experiences of students of teaching at the centre of learning to teach and to be a reminder that experience of learning is fundamental to developing deeper understandings of teaching. In so doing, the rhetoric of the need to "listen to students' voices" needs to be matched by real world actions of doing just that. Hence, the use of anecdotes to offer insight into the issues and concerns that influence approaches to learning about teaching that tend to be crowded out (or perhaps not even sought in the first place) when considering professional knowledge of teaching.

The place of reflection takes on greater significance when considered in concert with experience and jointly offers genuine ways of helping students of teaching to value their developing knowledge of practice such that not only what they know, but also how they know it, and the manner in which it can impact their understanding of teaching and learning across pedagogic contexts may be viewed as significant to the development of professional learning.

9 Student-teacher as researcher: Recognizing and valuing the development of professional knowledge

I hate to open with a cliché but I think this year has been one huge, steep learning curve for me. I think I have learnt so much this year, and, at the risk of sounding corny, so much about myself. So doing this 'research project' into my teaching is probably a good way to get my thoughts down on paper...Even when I'm not officially researching my teaching I think that I'm still researching it on one level. Like most teachers (hopefully!), I'm always trying to think of the best way to present content to the students and assess what they have learnt. After I've presented it I then analyse the lesson. What worked? What didn't? How can I improve on what I did? How will I do it differently next time?

(Heather)

Scriven (in Cooley *et al.*, 1997) asserted that educational research had largely failed to deliver in terms of meeting a duty to identify educational best practice and to improve it. He put forward a number of interesting arguments to support his claim and then posed a couple of provocative questions: "Is it a lingering belief that single cases do not make science? Could it be – an ignoble motive this – that we dislike having practitioners rather than professors be the experts?" then he ended with: "there needs to be a shift from the theory-based approach to an expert-practitioner-based approach...the real experts in teaching, learning, and administration are, on present evidence, not academics" (p. 21).

The argument that teaching should include a research responsibility has persisted for a considerable period of time but the rhetoric has rarely been translated into practice so that the conditions of teachers' work might also encourage their development as researchers. Stenhouse (1975) was a strong advocate of teachers as researchers arguing:

it is difficult to see how teaching can be improved or how curricular proposals can be evaluated without self monitoring on the part of teachers. A research tradition which is accessible to teachers and which feeds teaching must be created if education is to be significantly improved. (Stenhouse, 1975, p. 165)

In recent times there has been growing interest and support for teacher research, an important impetus for this development evident in the "new knowledge" and understanding that teachers can contribute to education (Cochran-Smith and Lytle, 1999; He *et al.*, 2000; Loughran *et al.*, 2002; Lytle and Cochran-Smith, 1991; Mitchell and Mitchell, 1997; Senese, 2004; Zeichner and Noffke, 2001). This new knowledge resulting from teacher research is in part due to the nature of the research questions, approaches and reports of such inquiry being qualitatively different to traditional educational research because of the privileged position teachers, as experts of practice, occupy.

Teacher research, it could be argued, is related to the growth in understanding and applicability of Schön's (1983) ideas of practitioner reflection, and the notion of the "authority of experience" (Munby and Russell, 1994) offers further encouragement to teachers to research their own practice because, through the authority of experience, teachers' confidence and trust in their knowledge of teaching and learning is further developed. There is also a realization that there is no educational change without teacher change and by focusing on personal practice and experience, teachers may undertake genuine enquiry that can lead to a better understanding of the complexities of teaching and learning.

Because the authority of experience encourages teachers to place more faith in their own experience and knowledge in meeting the demands of teaching it further encourages a teacher-focused understanding of the nature of the problems inherent in teaching. Thus teachers are both generators and users of knowledge and, in many ways, the teacher research movement has created a strong agenda for the development of knowledge of educational research and practice that would not be possible without their explicit interest and involvement.

In considering teacher research, Richardson (1994) distinguished between two forms of research on practice: formal research and practical inquiry. She argued that: "Both forms... may be conducted by the practitioner, and at times, practical inquiry may be turned into formal research... one could suggest, then, that practical inquiry may be foundational to formal research that will be truly useful in improving practice" (pp. 7, 8). One aspect of Richardson's perspective about knowledge creation in this case is perhaps based on the realization that participant research has unique features which influence not only "what" such knowledge is, but also how it is "understood" by others. Therefore, teacher research could well be regarded as a distinct genre; there has been some debate on this issue (Baumann, 1996; Northfield, 1996, 1997; Wong, 1995). In addition to the arguments about teacher research, there is one issue that matters way beyond the academic standing of the work and that is the nature of the professional learning that occurs when practitioners gain the confidence and skills to reflect on, and reframe, their experiences. Thus, a commitment to conducting teacher research may be viewed as an indication that a professional is willing to accept that their experience is the major source of improvement in their practice and an important place from which development and growth might be nurtured. Encouraging teacher research then appears as a meaningful option for all those committed to the improvement of professional practice while also being an important strategy for teachers' professional development.

In a similar way to the manner in which these arguments (above) play out in education generally, so too a *student-teacher as researcher* stance can be argued for teacher education. Just as Scriven (Cooley *et al.*, 1997) questioned assumptions about the implications of a possible line of demarcation between professors and teachers, so too in teacher education there is a need for taken-for-granted assumptions to be questioned. It is surely the case that students of teaching ask qualitatively different questions about their own practice than might their professors.

Students of teaching live a different reality in learning to teach than do their professors who observe their students' situations, and so, students of teaching are rightly the experts in relation to understanding *their* context, *their* position and the expectations *they* feel, face and create for themselves and/or have imposed on them by others. In adopting a student-teacher as researcher stance, students of teaching might realize new and meaningful ways of becoming more informed about the manner in which their own learning about teaching is shaped and may therefore become better informed about their own professional learning.

Collaboration in learning about teaching

> This process of attempting to make our joint knowledge increasingly public, helped lay to rest some of the self-doubt and uncertainty that surrounded our discussions and sense of professional identity as valued members of a knowledge community. (Bulfin, 2003, p. 33)

Bulfin (2003) as a beginning teacher highlighted how, for he and his peers, researching practice (and reporting on it) was enhanced through collaboration. When students of teaching meet to discuss their knowledge and understanding of teaching and learning they share, and identify with, one another's concerns and readily respond to each other's ideas. In sharing their experiences and teaching approaches they gain confidence and trust in each other and risk introducing episodes that demonstrate their own difficulties and "failures." In so doing, they also create situations through which, together, they can freely brainstorm reasons for limited progress in their classes without the sense of judgment that often accompanies working with more experienced others (e.g. supervising teachers and teacher educators).

In discussing with one another – their particular issues, concerns and situations – students of teaching begin to generalize about their practice and test these generalizations with others in similar positions. With appropriate support, they may well begin to develop tentative theories in ways similar to that which Richardson (1994) was perhaps suggesting in terms of practical enquiry. However, as students of teaching have access to the detail and complexity of the classroom that, from their perspective, is growing and changing dramatically as their learning from experience influences what they know, how they know and what it might mean for their own practice, their developing knowledge inevitably carries particular and idiosyncratic features rooted in the beginning teaching experience.

> Reframing beginning teachers...as knowledge producers has important implications for continuing professional learning. Knowledge production processes, including engaging in reflective practice, pursuing research, theorising one's lived experience, as well as an honest participation in 'authentic conversation' and professional dialogue – all have the potential to 'open up the classroom door' (cf. Loughran and Northfield, 1996). Thinking about this metaphorical and physical 'opening' of the classroom provides a way of examining and rethinking a variety of issues, such as the isolation and separation that are often a part of teaching. This sense of isolation, or of having to 'go it alone', was often a concern expressed by my colleagues and me. There are many reasons why this is the case – many of them related to the pressurised nature of teachers' work, the lack of opportunities for 'teacher talk', and 'sink or swim' induction programs....Repositioning teachers as legitimate professionals involves more than overcoming the isolation that presently characterises practice. Giving teachers time to work together in intellectual and practical ways can also assist in opening classroom doors by eschewing deficit or reductionist descriptions of what teachers 'should know and be able to do'. Essentially, this means allowing teachers control of their own work, and giving them the support they need to achieve high standards and powerful learning for their students....Research conducted in a particular practice setting is more likely to be taken up in that same practice setting. Opening the classroom to research by teachers... [offers]...new ways of seeing the familiar and of conceiving possibilities for self-initiated collective change. (Bulfin, 2003, p. 37)

Students of teaching are in an ideal position to generate knowledge and insights into learning about teaching and its impact on their own understanding about teaching and learning in ways different to that of more experienced, or distanced, others. Thus, the knowledge they are able to generate speaks very differently to other students of teaching than that which might be seen as advice or knowledge derived from a more extensive experiential base from a school or university supervisor/teacher. And, it is through this realization that the value of episteme and phronesis as a way of conceptualizing the generation and use of knowledge recurs as a lens through which to better view and understand learning about teaching. For the student of teaching, episteme as propositional knowledge does not necessarily carry the feelings, experiences, decision-making possibilities and strength of learning that might be realized when phronesis is an explicit and valued focus. Consider, for example, the following anecdote as one way of beginning to see into the subtle mix of the cognitive and affective in learning about teaching that students of teaching experience:

Enveloped in an impending shadow of doom I realized I had 7D next lesson. "I'm sure they're not really human." I thought to myself as I reflected on our previous music class in which Beethoven's Fifth Symphony was reduced to farce. It was all too fresh in my mind.

I could feel the pounding in my chest which spread through my body like a fever engulfing me head to toe as I tried desperately to control my breathing. "Everything's O.K, you'll be right, everything's O.K." I kept repeating to myself as I walked down the corridor to face them.

"It'll be O.K." I reminded myself again as I unlocked the classroom door, "I've put in the work. I'll win them over today." The class straggled in full of energy and attitude to burn.

"Good morning 7D." I started desperately trying to speak over their noise.

"I'll call the roll. Maybe that will settle them down." I thought to myself.

As I moved down the list of names I thought it would be a miracle if I got through this class alive. They were still very chatty so rather than trying to explain the lesson I just launched straight into it playing Jagged Edge's "Let's Get Married."

The song went for nearly four minutes and something amazing happened.

There was complete silence.

Twenty-six pairs of eyes peered at me. There were looks of confusion, or perhaps shock, awaiting some sort of explanation, seeking direction.

"Following up on your responses about the music you enjoy listening to." I started, "I thought it a good idea to look at some of these songs."

Silence remained but their facial expressions turned from puzzlement to interest. Was I dreaming? Did I have their full attention?

"OK, what's the driving force of the song we've just heard?" I asked.

"Rhythm!" Johnny called out enthusiastically from the back of the room.

Yes, yes! I was filled with a welcome feeling of triumph as students started critiquing the music with intelligent answers as they freely offered their opinions.

Their excitement and interest built a foundation for a fantastic class discussion on the elements of music. The key was that what they were learning had some worth because they could relate to it. The same ideas I had for understanding Beethoven's Fifth were being played out (pardon the pun) through their music.

I couldn't believe it, it actually worked.

I finally had them.

Through the discussion I finally understood what a sense of mutual respect and trust really felt like. They were my class at last! (Clare)

As Clare's anecdote suggests, seeing into one's own experience can be affirming as good ideas, and clearer understandings of classroom events can encourage students of teaching to gain satisfaction through sharing new insights and realizing that their concerns and interests are shared by others. More than this though, they may also begin to pay more careful attention to their assumptions as there is often a need to reframe existing ideas and issues through which significant personal learning may then occur as a consequence of seeing a concern from another perspective. Such reframing is enhanced through interaction with colleagues who might also be prompted to question their taken-for-granted assumptions. Thus, the "new knowledge" about classrooms and teaching that develops can be stimulating for all involved as a sense of greater control, and understanding about practice leads to new possibilities which, in turn, engenders valuable professional learning for students of teaching in ways not so possible if it were episteme alone.

Communicating learning about teaching

An important reason for students of teaching to engage in a research process is associated with the need for new understandings of practice to be communicated with others so that such learning moves beyond individual reflection and creates an expectation for professional dialogue, critique and inquiry. In a professional community there is value in clarifying or sharing new insights and in developing and adjusting practice in response to evidence. Thus having an audience for research helps to keep the search for new understandings on the teaching agenda. And, in preparing sessions for peers or writing papers, students of teaching create new opportunities for enhancing their understanding of their classrooms, and of teaching and learning in ways that go beyond simply sharing experiences. However, conducting and reporting on research can be a difficult and confusing task for students of teaching and that is one reason why appropriate support is necessary; support that should be a common feature of teacher education.

As detailed in Loughran (2004c), the research topics conducted over a four-year period by students of teaching at Monash University demonstrate a strong focus on teaching procedures and strategies (approximately 70%). Thus, the overwhelming concern of those students of teaching was related to the development of their own practice; further accentuating the importance of phronesis in learning about teaching. As their reports illustrated, support, as a feature of teacher education, is necessary because students of teaching:

- Begin with comprehensive big picture aspirations and find it difficult to narrow their focus to a manageable question/project. As their studies generally centre on classroom concerns which represent tensions, dilemmas and difficulties they often search for ways of improving their teaching through initiating new and unfamiliar teaching approaches and procedures, thus drawing attention to a complex array of inter-related issues and concerns. They therefore focus on the complexity and uniqueness of their own classrooms and the way many factors interact in these settings makes narrowing a research focus difficult.
- Are conscious that their studies of their classrooms impact their expectations of generalizability of findings and are initially concerned that their work is too idiosyncratic or particular to be of value to others. This has implications for the development of a useable and meaningful literature that speaks to students of teaching. There is a clear need for literature that forms a coherent research base for and by students of teaching that offers them access to the knowledge of practice that matters to them and creates an expectation that research itself is a normal aspect of professional practice.
- It is common for students of teaching to base much of their learning about teaching on a critical incident. Such incidents are significant for them and may well be the initial catalyst for articulation of a basic concern (as per Claire's anecdote above, in which "relevance" of content matter could well be described as the underlying concern). Importantly, constructing such incidents as anecdotes may serve to communicate the nature of the particular concern to others so that they know "what it means" through linking it with their own experiences. Anecdotes may then be viewed as an invitation for others to become involved with the issue and helps to illustrate ways of articulating issues in ways that go beyond problem stating and encourage problem setting such that action is initiated.
- Are primarily concerned with teaching. Therefore new findings from their research are continually interwoven with their ongoing teaching practice experiences. Inevitably then, they feel a need to act immediately on new possibilities and adjust their teaching in response to that which they learn through their research as it unfolds. Thus their research focus alters as adjustments are made and new insights and possibilities emerge that may not have been so important to the initial project. So not only their research shifts and changes during the process but their teaching focus, understanding, aims and purposes may also shift in response to these developments.
- Almost always includes designing and implementing new approaches – classroom interventions that are intended to achieve change. However,

these are not always successful, especially when first tried, but these failures may lead to valuable insights and to ways of avoiding such failures in the future. However, a consequence of this situation is that they have to deal with the consequences of their interventions as part of their daily teaching routine. And, negative consequences may affect the manner in which they are assessed or evaluated, therefore research can be a high risk activity that can significantly affect their development as a teacher.

- Have limited possibilities or outlets to publish their findings, thus much of their work exists only as a "university assignment." However, when they are encouraged to describe their learning and their new understandings, the response from others (peers, experienced teachers and teacher educators) can be very positive (see for example, Bulfin, 2003; Russell and Bullock, 1999). Such accounts increase our understanding of teaching and learning about teaching as they offer insights that can really be achieved only from their student of teaching perspective.

Support for a student-teacher as researcher stance in teacher education matters for all of the above reasons, but it also matters because of the clash of research views that many experience. Their undergraduate studies often portray research as only being positivistic with a focus on objectivity, generalizability, research instruments and researcher expertise. Therefore, when they embark on a research project they find themselves in the difficult situation of being confronted by an (often singular) expectation of what research is while at the same time recognizing that such an approach is not necessarily possible, applicable or relevant to that which they might want to do in terms of their own research questions, needs and concerns. Added to this is the accompanying perception of what a research report should like. Therefore, portraying their research in an appropriate form adds another dimension to the contradictions that they feel is embedded in the research task. This is perhaps best explained through the preface a student of teaching wrote to her research project.

Preface: What is valuable research?

I struggled enormously with this question when attempting to determine my research topic. What was important to me was not going to necessarily be important to everyone else. I have never been confronted with the task of researching an area of my teaching, in an environment unfamiliar to me. I will admit feelings of apprehension and fear at the thought of implementing research in a class full of strangers, with a [school teacher] supervisor breathing fire down my neck and *myself under enormous pressure* to do well. I thought long and hard about my topic and thought I would benefit immensely from researching an aspect of my teaching that I perceived as weak. However, I had a preconceived notion of what research should be i.e., graphs, surveys, interviews and theories. To me, research was using data to develop an answer to the specific question. Nevertheless, I am an Arts graduate and my area of research took shape in journal writing, teacher feedback, self-evaluation and student reaction. I found it easier to get my head around this form of data as opposed to a scientific approach. (emphasis in original, Leila)

Understanding practice by researching practice

A student-teacher as researcher stance requires trusting that students of teaching are able to learn from their own experiences and that teacher educators' expertise is not necessarily bound up in just "passing on" their experience to their neophytes but in helping their learners to see, and respond to, the teaching and learning opportunities they experience; all the more so when teacher educators purposefully create such pedagogic episodes for their learners.

Long ago Dewey (1929) drew attention to the importance of teachers investigating their own pedagogical problems. He noted that "teachers as investigators" were important not only for the development of knowledge about schooling but also for the development of good teaching. And the development of good teaching (for both students of teaching and teacher educators) must be a central purpose of teacher education.

Central to good teaching in teacher education is that it does not ignore the development of effective approaches to conveying information but goes beyond it by embracing teaching for understanding whereby the significance of the knowledge, ideas and actions inherent in the process excite, expand and enhance learning. Just as those who have revisited this notion of the development of good teaching through teacher research have made clear (Duckworth, 1991; Kincheloe, 2003), so too in teacher education, the development (and expectation) of good teaching is more likely through researching practice.

> By making teacher research a central point of the conversation about good teaching we can extend the value of the concept....A more textured reflection of one's teaching involves a teacher's self-understanding of his or her practices, especially the ambiguities, contradictions and tensions implicit in them....This is the basis of education change, of critical pedagogy, of a democratic workplace (Elliott, 1989; Torney-Purta, 1985). Teacher education which neglects these aspects of teacher research misses the point – it misses the distinct demands of the teaching workplace, the implications of democracy for educational theory, the ambiguity of practitioner ways of knowing....teacher education which confronts this three dimensional relationship cannot be simplistically technocratic, it cannot help but connect theory and practice, by necessity it must view teachers as self-directed agents, sophisticated thinkers, active researchers in a never-static, ambiguous context....A recurrent theme here is teacher education's history of ineffective incorporation of research into professional education programs. (Kincheloe, 2003, pp. 39–40)

Acceptance of a student-teacher as researcher stance in teacher education is a powerful way of impacting the predominant teacher education practice of teaching as telling. A student-teacher as researcher stance also creates new and more meaningful ways for students of teaching to examine educational research as the purpose of such work and its links to *their* practice is better realized and valued. At the same time, a growing understanding of the diversity of approaches to conducting and portraying research also creates diverse possibilities for bridging the theory–practice gap as links between phronesis and episteme lead to new ways of conceptualizing and articulating professional knowledge and learning.

Overview

This chapter has suggested that teacher education needs to embrace a student-teacher as researcher stance. In so doing, there are a number of issues that need to be acknowledged and responded to from both a teacher educator and a student of teaching perspective.

The fundamental nature of teacher education changes when a student-teacher as researcher stance is accepted as a positive way of influencing the development of teaching and learning about teaching. To place this argument in context, it is important to see how such research is conducted and reported. Therefore, the following chapter offers one example of a student-teacher as researcher project. The report that comprises Chapter 10 illustrates how the range of issues raised through this chapter are played out in practice and also highlights the way in which insights into learning about teaching emerge and are grasped differently when a student of teaching is trusted to be what Kincheloe (p. 40) described as a "self-directed agent, sophisticated thinker and active researcher in the never-static, ambiguous context" of the world of teaching.

10 Learning through experience: Students of teaching researching their own practice

> teacher education struggles with the contradiction in practice between imposing (perhaps unintentionally) solutions on student teachers and assisting them to develop their own responses to their own situation themselves.... Finding ways to help student teachers see in their own teaching what they may not be sufficiently experienced or ready to see for themselves can lead to teacher educators telling student teachers what they should know and do – [Clandinin's (1995)] sacred story.... [But] how might student teachers be encouraged to learn about their own practice and not approach it as another imposed task? One possibility is through the development of [the] student teacher as researcher ...
>
> (Loughran, 2004c, p. 213)

The student-teacher as researcher project that comprises this chapter is illustrative of the way in which such research is often conducted and reported. The topic of the report is indicative of the large majority of projects that students of teaching tend to develop and makes clear how, with a focus on practice, the researcher soon begins to frame and reframe problematic situations. In so doing, much of the learning about practice that emerges is driven by the student-teacher researcher's own issues and concerns and is responsive to that which they are ready to attend to at that time. Thus it can well be argued, that the development of good teaching (i.e. teaching for understanding) is enhanced as change is driven by the individual's desire to better understand that which, at first glimpse, may well have appeared much more simple and straightforward. The student-teacher as researcher therefore comes to better see the complex nature of teaching and learning and the diversity of ways in which various aspects of teaching and learning impact practice as the pedagogic situations in which they are personally involved, develop, evolve and change over time.

By adopting a student-teacher as researcher stance in teacher education, students of teaching become more sensitive to, and better informed about practice as they learn through their experiences of, and responses in, their particular pedagogic contexts. By extension, it does not seem too much to expect that teacher education should carry a responsibility for developing such a perspective for in so doing, the subtleties of practice might be better opened up for exploration and learning. Through adopting a student-teacher as researcher approach in teacher education, students of teaching may be encouraged to grow beyond the technical and into the independent, autonomous and sophisticated professional pedagogues primed to teach for understanding.

The student-teacher as researcher report that comprises this chapter is not meant to be a model for how such work might be conducted and reported. Rather, it is an example of the way in which a student of teaching came to understand her practice as a result of researching it in a manner that was appropriate to her needs. Although the paper has been lightly edited for publication, the chapter is nonetheless a genuine representation of the type of research and reporting typical of the work of student-teachers as researchers. I trust it demonstrates well how trusting students of teaching to direct their own professional learning (with appropriate support) is an important aspect of developing a pedagogy of teacher education.

Student-teacher as researcher: Vicki's project

First school teaching experience: Miss Davenport's year 7 French class, Surrey high school

"Correct. Thank you, Eugene."

"Now I want everybody to imagine you are in Paris. You can close your eyes if you'd like. What can you see? What does it feel like? What does it smell like? What are the people like?"

"My dad says that all Frogs are arrogant bast..."

"Thank you, Eugene, for that insight, but we might leave that one there. OK, getting back to Paris. It doesn't matter if you haven't been there. Just imagine and think about the things you have seen and heard about the city. Alright, you are walking down the Champs-Elysees. Who can tell me what that is? Um,... ahh,... oh alright, Eugene?"

"It's a big, huge street a bit like Collins Street."

"Yes. That pretty much sums it up. Good. Does anyone else know what is at the end of this street? Anyone? No? Anyone want to take a stab? Come on, give it a go."

"Eugene has his hand up, Miss."

"So nobody is game to have a try? Okay, I'll give you some clues."

"But Miss! I know the answer! It's the Arc de Triomphe!"

"Eugene, you mustn't call out. Put your hand up next time."

"But I did!"

"Oops, silly me. I must have been looking beyond the front row. Alright, who can tell me of any other famous French landmarks? This time we might get someone else to answer. Um, how about up the back. The girl with the blonde ponytail? Sorry, your name has slipped my mind. Have you got any ideas? Yes? No?"

"Miss, her name's Svetlana. She's on exchange from Russia and she doesn't speak English."

"Okay, Eugene. Fire away buddy."

After struggling through class after class at Surrey High School, doing battle with Eugene the Formidable and his silent subjects, I realized something had to be done. While I did make some attempt to rectify things and to prevent every class from being utterly dominated by the one student, before I knew it, my time there was up. Five weeks had passed and the bony little hand in the front row was still flying high.

Twelve weeks later, heading off for my second school teaching experience, I entered through the gates of St. Mary's Girls' School; a different kettle of fish altogether, thought I. Walking past a small group of well-groomed young ladies discussing the disgraceful drug problem apparent in our capital city and the part they could play in its eradication, I could not help recalling the waft of mid-pubertal armpits mingled with smoke escaping from the boy's toilets at Surrey High School. Wolf-whistles and snarls were replaced by polite greetings and instead of war cries of "Fight, Fight, Fight," I entered the building to the sound of a choir of angels (oops, I mean school girls). As I stepped over the threshold and into my first classroom, I took a deep breath and soaked in the sweet scent of learning. This is what it is all about, thought I as I tossed all my classroom management techniques aside and prepared to push the boundaries of knowledge, to tackle the big questions and to challenge traditional notions of classroom learning. I could just see them all standing on their desks at the end of my time here exhorting me, "Oh captain, my captain."

What? A tad carried away? A tad unreal in my expectations you think? Well, we'll see about that.

Second school teaching experience: Miss Davenport's year 7 English class, St. Mary's girls' school

"All right girls. After listening to that song, what would you say was the overall message? Yes, Siobhan?"

"Did you know that Michael Jackson has spent $90 million on plastic surgery?"

"Really? Well, that's interesting, but has anyone got anything to say about the message of his song?"

"I reckon he's an idiot because in the song he's saying, 'It don't matter if you're black or white' but he's spent all this money on changing himself to become white! What a tosser!"

"Good point, Siobhan. Does anyone else have an opinion on this? Do you think he's a hypocrite? Tasha?"

"Yes."

"So... do you want to add anything more?"

"Not really. I think what Siobhan thinks."

"Okay. Does anybody want to stick up for Michael Jackson? Does anyone think he may have suffered a lot from racism when he was younger?"

"Yeah, but why is he singing one thing and saying another? He's just a loser who doesn't...."

"Righto, thanks Siobhan. It might be good to let somebody else have a go now. Have you got anything to add about Michael Jackson and his song lyrics, Lucy?"

"Um.... not really."

All of a sudden the sound track in my head began to fade, the lights began to dim and the director called "Cut." They were not following the script at all. Siobhan had taken centre-stage and the others had unwittingly become her sidekicks – either that or they had just forgotten their lines. It was an awfully familiar scene. The setting may have been different, but don't be fooled as I was! Underneath the facade, St. Mary's was really just another Surrey. Or perhaps I was simply learning more about human nature and the way that students operate in big groups. Whatever the case, the problem was clearly a common one and the issue had to be pursued. My self-evaluation after one particular lesson included this excerpt:

> While most people were contributing at one point or another, I did become aware of some girls who seemed tuned out and who were not contributing at all. I think this is something I need to consider and to pursue. I find it hard when I ask a question and the same hands keep popping up. I don't feel I want to ignore these hands, but at the same time I do not want others to be able to just sit back and depend on the dominant ones.

There it was! A research project staring me in the face. How does a teacher encourage and invoke whole-class participation? This was the question that would underpin and guide much of my teaching over the next 5 weeks.

So, my plan of attack? Go with the flow. Play it by ear. Sound a touch lackadaisical? It may do, but in my opinion this is the best way to do it. While some planning and forethought is essential, there needs to be room for movement. The best research is conducted in response to what goes on from class to class. To plan it all beforehand is to completely miss the point. Spontaneity is an important element of research as teachers should be monitoring students' learning all the time, assessing whether things are working or not, and reacting accordingly in every class they conduct.

With this in mind, I lay low for the first week or so, not only using my teaching periods but also sacrificing my precious spares to extend my antennae wheresoever I could. Observing, taking notes, building profiles, gaining trust, planting microphones and bugging pencil cases. Well, I did spend some time getting to know the students, seeing how the classes were accustomed to working, and trying to identify the "roles" they each played in class. Before long I knew where my challenges lay; classes 9B and 7V. However, I knew I could take them on.

Within my first lessons with these two classes it was clear what was going on. The girls had the routine down pat. Teacher asks question. Student answers. Teacher asks another question. Same student answers. Teacher asks further questions and encourages others to answer. No response. Teacher panics and resorts to lone raised hand. Same student answers. As a student-teacher, I was putty in their hands for I didn't have a memory bank full of their names to lean on. This left the door wide open for the quieter students to lay low and rely on others, while the few chirpy ones had a field day. One of my self-evaluations reveals the situation.

> I struggled a bit not knowing names and consequently the answers tended to come from the same girls all the time.

Try as I did to use the roll and get a range of responses, this strategy became the active enemy of the all-important "flow" factor. My mind worked over-time. Okay, how should I phrase this question? Who answered the previous question? That girl there hasn't said anything yet, or hang on, maybe she has. Where is the roll? Alright, let's take a stab. Umm, "Genevieve." All this effort only to be met with "She's not here today, Miss," or, "What was the question again?" How could I be annoyed at them? I also needed reminding about the question.

The roll technique failing me, I resorted to the "round the class, row by row" method. As could have been anticipated, the results reflected the name. The class rapidly came to resemble a "not so well-oiled" machine, any signs of life and spontaneity obliterated completely. Not only was this a problem but so too was the fact that students basically only had to listen and participate when their "turn" came around. The remainder of the time could be productively spent sticking the latest pop-star pin-up in their dairies or pondering whether that cute guy from St. Michael's Boys' with the "wicked" smile would be at the station after school. There was no suspense, no surprise factor. Everything became very predictable and boring. So, there was no way around it. The class list was up on the toilet door that night and before long the names had stuck...in my mum and dad's minds. Then, not long after that I knew them too and could put a face to each of them. From this moment on the world was my oyster.

Knowing the students' names was definitely a step in the right direction. No longer were my questions random arrows. With a name preceding each one, my questions were now shot forth in confidence, hitting the targets with force. No longer could the girls hide under the shelter of my ignorance. None knew when they would be called upon to answer. Concentration levels were high. Not only did knowing names help in getting the whole class participating to a greater degree, but it was also an important part of building a rapport with the students and gaining their confidence. My knowledge of names in itself encouraged some students to contribute more often in class. Perhaps they sensed my genuine interest in them and saw that this "outsider" was not such a suspicious character after all. In any case, some students who had initially been silent were offering comments and responses. This was noted with approval from the throne of judgement at the back of the room. My supervising teacher did, however, seize upon the window of opportunity constituting her feedback session to make a suggestion for further improvement. "Your use of names is pleasing to the ear," said she, "but think about position. Position is the key. There must be an element of surprise for the listeners." These words of wisdom were taken on board and applied in the following lesson. "In what ways has Mary changed since the beginning of the book?" ....(and wait for it, here it comes)... "Chelsea?" Chelsea sprang out of her mental inertia into a flurry of waffled garble not remotely related to the question. Her cheeks sent out bright red warning signals to the rest of the class.

"No longer can we rest easy waiting for our name to be called. The name comes later now so we actually have to listen to every question in case our name is called. Such suspense." The realisation struck them with horror. Suddenly, however, the pendulum swung, striking me with even greater horror. My classroom had become a place of fear. The concentration levels may have been higher but these girls were not paying attention because the subject matter was enthralling or because they had a passion for learning. They were doing it merely to save face. In my quest for whole-class participation I had lost the vision. I had lost sight of the bigger picture. My research project had become all-consuming and begun to devour quality teaching and learning.

Seeking to verify my impressions, I designed a questionnaire for my students to respond to (see Appendix 1). After administering it in class I scurried back to the staffroom and assumed my place in my allocated corner. I was anxious to delve into the depths of their minds. While I am not convinced that I accessed the depths as such, there were some interesting responses.

One interesting factor related to the interpretation of "participation" and "contribution." While most students defined these concepts in terms of verbal acts, there were a couple who challenged this notion, suggesting that although they were fairly quiet and did not talk much, they listened, thought about the questions raised and responded in other ways (such as writing). This was a good point to raise and it broadened my outlook on the whole research project.

I was also interested to know the girls' perceptions of the situation in class. Did they feel that certain class members dominated the teacher's attention? Did they feel that they were given ample opportunity to "have their say" in class? The responses to these questions varied. There was a pattern though. Most students in the Year 7 class seemed to be oblivious to any student domination, whereas the Year 9 class was very aware of it.

To some degree this reflected an oversight on my behalf. Year 7 students need much more explanation and preparation leading up to a task and I feel I did not make the purpose of the questionnaire all that clear for them. This was one girl's response. "I don't think anything could motivate me [to participate in class] more. I have really enjoyed Miss Davenport's class, her classes are great fun, interesting and I have gained a lot." Apart from boosting my self-esteem, this response showed me that I had not made the purpose of the questionnaire all that clear. It implied that some of them thought the questionnaire was some sort of tool used by the university to assess my performance. Consequently I felt I could not rely too heavily on these responses.

On the other hand, the responses received from the Year 9 students seemed to be pretty honest and perceptive. A number of them recognized that certain students often dominated and some even offered reasons for this state of affairs. One put her lack of participation down to: "simply being a moody teenager so my attitude really changes," some felt they would contribute more if they had some sort of grounding in the topic prior to the teaching and others suggested the activities needed to be "more exciting."

The next thing to determine was the effect that my "involvement" techniques were having on the atmosphere of the classroom. Was my classroom a chamber of fear? To partially determine this I asked the question, "How do you feel when the teacher asks you to answer a question when you don't have your hand up?" The response was telling. Thirteen students (out of thirty-eight) circled "annoying" or "nervous." These figures are significant. Not only were some students quaking in their boots, but some were harboring bitterness and resentment.

In addition to the negative feeling being generated (particularly in my Year 9 class), the flow of my lessons was still affected. While I was basically getting whole-class participation, my lessons were still lacking something–that all-elusive spontaneity! Oh yes, I was in control all right, but did I really want this? My lessons had become static and regulated. Suddenly it struck me. That old, familiar phrase; favourite in the Education Faculty: "Student-centred learning." It continued to ring in my ears as I realized the teacher-centred nature of my teaching at that moment in time. Sure they were answering questions, but I was completely controlling the process. The old saying "children should speak only when spoken to" had become a shocking reality in my classroom. Ah, yes. There was much work to be done.

Back in the lab (a.k.a. the staffroom) I donned the spectacles and set the cogs into action mode. While all previous efforts had not been completely wasted, a fresh approach was definitely needed. Where was the injection of life to come from? I looked longingly across at my supervisor, deeply searching her face for inspiration. However, there was nothing forthcoming. I scanned my text books. Again, there was nothing. No, there were no easy answers. Some serious reflection and brainstorming must be done and it was I who had to do it. Suddenly, a brainwave rose up from the ocean of notions.

Well actually, some of the students wrote something akin to it in their questionnaire responses. "I would be motivated to participate more if the classes were more fun." Okay, so maybe it doesn't sound so revolutionary when it is put like that, but there was definitely something in it and I would ride this wave in to shore. Though I had been putting effort into making my classes different and interesting, the structured question and response routine was proving to be a hindrance. Perhaps this whole thing could be transformed into some sort of game.

Introducing fun

In my Year 9 French class at that time we were working on making arrangements via the telephone. This was conducive to interactive activities and definitely "game" material, so I went ahead with my planning.

The game that evolved was in the form of a "whole-class phone conversation." The class was divided in two and placed opposite each other. Setting up the room differently was effective because it helped to convince the students that this was indeed a game and it also meant that the quiet ones could not hide behind others and escape my line of vision. One team was given the name "Brigitte" and the responsibility of inviting the other team, "Pierre," on an excursion somewhere. Between them they had to negotiate when and where, and so on. Each person in the team had to offer a line in the conversation and could only sit down when they had done so. This encouraged everybody (not just the traditionally dominant students) to get in early and say something (as did the desire not to be left without anything to say). To maintain the concentration of those who contributed early I established the rule that anybody who spoke any English would have to stand up again and contribute a second time. I also told them that they would have to concentrate and remember where they came in the conversation because the aim was to perform the conversation a number of times, getting quicker and more fluent each time. Each go would be timed.

They all liked this idea. There was a competitive element to it but they would all be working as a team and not against each other. The fact that they did not want to let one another down was good incentive to contribute. The class in which we did this was fantastic. The whole class was participating enthusiastically and all my objectives in terms of the language and the learning were met. C'etait magnifique!! (Sorry. I'm getting carried away with the recollection of it all).

It was a roaring success. However, I was lucky in terms of the subject matter I was teaching. I had to remind myself that while this would be a nifty little activity to stick up my sleeve for later use, it would not be like this all the time. The question now was "how do I introduce some of these principles to the regular classroom set-up? Could it be done?"

Another wave began to surge forth. Perhaps the regular class discussion could be adapted into a game. I could implement a system whereby each student had a certain number of turns to respond. There could be points involved. The blood began to flow through my veins at a rapid rate. Could this be a solution?

In effect, I would be achieving the same level of participation from students as previously but now the onus would be on them, and once again, it was a game! Surely this would fool them. Wouldn't it?

Crash! The wave was a dumper! Reason and reality soon began to rain on my parade. Despite the guise of a game, the idea was not much different from what I had been doing before and it would not be solving my problems. Allocating turns and points for responses would once again hinder the spontaneity and the natural flow of things. Discussion would remain too structured and the addition of a personal competitive element may not be helpful for those reluctant to speak at the best of times. It could simply serve to widen the gap between students, instead of bridging it. So, abandoning this idea, it was back to the drawing board.

Wait time

Another Education Faculty catch phrase began to stir, emerging from the recesses of my mind. "Wait time." Perhaps I had simply not been allowing enough time for girls to respond. If I waited a little longer after posing a question maybe the old faithfuls would be joined by some new hands. With this in mind, I entered my next classes. "Okay girls, who can recall what we were talking about last lesson?" As expected, the girls followed the familiar routine. The same hands rose and the same buttocks slid low on their chairs. Refusing to bow to pressure, however, I simply waited. Index fingers poked the air with extra vigor but still I waited. A look of perplexity passed from face to face. Their routine was being threatened. Still I waited, until suddenly from the back row I received vindication. "Yes, Georgia!" I uttered, with perhaps just a little too much enthusiasm. As progress was being made, I persisted along this line and my self-evaluation after this lesson reflected the success I felt.

> I found that with extra "wait" time after questions, more hands came up as they had more opportunity to think. This was really good because it gave those who perhaps are a bit slower at thinking the chance to have their say. While I initially felt that the "wait time" was a bit awkward and slowed down the pace a bit, I feel it was worth it.

So, the "wait time" was a winner, yet I felt there was more. Waiting longer did bring out a few more responses, but there were still several students for whom this was not the answer. I had not yet got to the nitty-gritty of the problem and was feeling my need to do so. Instead of continuing to go with the flow, it was time to dictate the flow to a greater degree. I began to ask myself, "what is at the root of some girls' lack of participation?" It was more than simple boredom. My informal assessment of the classroom atmosphere backed up my ego on this matter. Whatever it was, I needed to get at it and to work from there.

Throwing my misgivings to the wind, therefore, I buried myself in the questionnaires once more, analyzing the validity of the reasons given for the lack of participation of some girls. Sifting through the responses, one simply refused to slip through the colander. A line leapt from the page and sent my thoughts into a whirlwind. "The class is too big and intimidating." Of course! Simple wasn't it?! I knew the feeling myself. It can be hard to pipe up in front of a big group, particularly for those with low self-esteem. How others perceive you is such a big issue during the early years at secondary school, too. What a break-through! The obvious path of action? Break down these big groups.

Group work

Soon enough my line of thought developed into a line of action. My next classes were designed to incorporate pair work. By reducing the audience size, my hope was that students would be more comfortable and confident to openly speak their mind. To extend this even further I opted to reject the advice of my supervising teacher (all in the name of research) and allow the students to choose their own partners for the tasks at hand because I felt they would be more relaxed interacting with their friends. In addition to this, I felt that the element of choice was important for students in terms of giving them ownership over their learning and for motivating them.

Encouraging students to make decisions develops their skills as an independent learner. The introduction of pair work signaled the end of dependence. No longer could certain ones sit back and rely on others to do the work. As with the "whole-class" phone call, each student was now part of a team and had an obligation to her partner to "put in." Getting students to work together in pairs also gave me the opportunity to wander round the room and ask them how they were going. There was one girl in particular who had been a bit distant and disengaged in my classes with whom I really made an effort at this time. I felt it was rewarding for both of us. While she may have been a little uncomfortable with the one-to-one attention, after I had spoken with her and showed interest in her, I sensed a difference in her attitude and her output. This reinforced my earlier reflections. The importance of showing all students that they count and that their contributions are valued continued to impress itself upon me. As I wandered around the classroom, I also became aware of some loopholes in the system.

Most girls were on task but faintly mingled with the dulcet tones consti- tuting "la langue d'amour" were noises of another kind. "Are you serious? I saw him kissing her best friend at the social on Friday," Hmm. Something told me somebody was not on task. Slowly, but surely, I stalked my prey. However, sensing the approach of the predator, they leapt into action. One step ahead of me, they came up with a question to put me off the scent. Of course they were on task. What had I been thinking? Ah, yes. I let them think they had fooled me, but little did they (and the several other culprits) know. Next time things would not be so easy. The words of advice from my supervisor had indeed been ones of wisdom, "I wouldn't advise that you allow them to choose their partners." She had allowed me to learn through experimentation, though, and for that I am ever grateful (well, until the end of my teaching round anyway).

While choosing partners led to a productive lesson for some girls, there were too many who felt their time was better spent gossiping and planning their weekend. The task did involve making arrangements with a friend but I intended this to be hypothetical (and conducted in French).

While I had witnessed first hand the negative consequences of giving the girls too much choice, I was finding the concept of putting the students into pairs myself a little hard to swallow. It seemed to go against all the Educational buzz words. "Ownership," "choice," "student-centred learning," "shared control." Once again this method was too teacher-centred. The control was completely with me.

Though her lips were sealed, the remainder of my supervisor's face said, "What is the problem with that? These trendy young teachers and their new-fangled ideas!" However, a classic textbook response was ready on demand. "Students are more likely to engage in quality learning if they have some choice and control in the matter." My lecturers would be proud. The key, therefore, was to devise a system whereby pairs would be formed without any dictatorship on my behalf. Of course the old numbering system could be used but this was a bit boring and routine.

As I thought of other systems I had seen in classrooms, one came to the fore. A teacher I had observed on a previous teaching round had combined the forming of partnerships with learning. The perfect combination! There was so much scope for this in the teaching of a foreign language too. In the following class I had girls roaming around the room calling out French words and phrases trying to find their match. Anybody walking past may have called it chaos, but I called it fun, interactive quality learning, and through it all pairs were formed without any teacher manipulation. There could be no blame laid. The level of productivity in this class was fantastic. Everyone was contributing and seemed to be on task. From that lesson onward this pairing strategy became a regular part of my teaching, and each time I got them to practice something different. One of my self-evaluations indicates my partiality to this technique.

> The pairing strategy is working brilliantly because students work with someone different all the time and often with someone who they do not feel comfortable in mucking around with. The slacker students often find themselves paired with conscientious ones and are therefore lifted to their level because they feel they are responsible for playing their part

and not letting down their partner. The pairing is a good way to ensure full participation (provided the activity really requires dual contribution). As well as all this, the actual pairing method helps to reinforce some small aspect of the French language.

After experiencing such success with pair work in both of my classes I decided to raise the bar and follow the natural progression. Would students work this well in small groups? There was only one way to find out. After going through the same interactive process to form small groups they were off and away. I wandered around the room with baited breath. Would the good habits they had formed during their pair work hold out under added pressure? I was excited. I was hopeful. I was expectant. I was... disappointed.

Much to my surprise, many of the students were reverting to their old ways. The same old voices rose above the rest while the same buttocks slunk in their chairs and the same pens doodled in diaries. Some girls seemed to think that having more than two working together was licence to just "chill" because after all, "too many cooks spoil the broth." As I pondered the next step, my mind began to drift, and the lights began to fade. I could feel a flashback coming on.

Flashback: My old school days

"I really think that Scout is the one who..."

"I don't think the question relates to Scout, Vicki. Let's discuss the role of Atticus."

"Yeah, good idea, Tracy."

So the two of them steamed ahead, Tracy dictating while Jenny took notes. Any suggestion that they were on the wrong track was poo-hooed disdainfully. Well, of course! What Tracy says goes. Every now and again I would put my two bob's worth in but soon enough I realized that it wasn't worth the effort. I hadn't even wanted to be in this group in the first place. Usually I loved groupwork. My friends and I worked well together. We each knew our "roles" and played them with gusto.

That was it! The unfolding of the flashback featuring me as the learner had revealed a possible key. My own extensive experience with group work told me that it works best when everybody has a role to play. While students in some groups had simply fallen into roles which ensured even contributions, others were struggling. Certain students were taking on multiple roles and leaving others with nothing to do. I took this on board and decided that next time it might be more effective to allocate group roles for each student. Depending on the actual task somebody could be monitoring the contribution of each student; ensuring that everybody had an equal opportunity to speak, somebody could be the scribe, somebody could be the group spokesperson and somebody else could be the one to make sure everybody was on task. These roles could vary from task to task, but these are just some of the roles that I devised.

Both my Year 7 class and Year 9 class responded well to this, as was evident by the improved classroom atmosphere and the buzz of productivity. Each student experienced a sense of importance and enjoyed having a role to play. Nobody felt redundant and everybody took turns at playing different roles. Though it may sound childish, sometimes younger students need this kind of guidance. As they get older and more used to the idea it will not be necessary to do this for them because they may well start doing it themselves.

As I wandered around the room, everybody was on task and taking their roles seriously. The classes that I conducted in this way were probably the most productive and, most importantly, the whole class was participating. To spoil the fairytale ending, I must point out that some groups did not work as well as others but it was all a learning process for them and for me. The groups were rotated and shuffled regularly, which meant that they were all able to experience different group dynamics and to find out who they worked best with. To their surprise, it was not always their friends (as I discovered through speaking privately with a number of them).

Conclusion

Before I knew it, my days at St. Mary's Girls' School were at an end. Fighting back the tears, I closed the staffroom door behind me and walked to my car with a slow, ponderous gait. Driving out of the car park, something caught my eye. I turned to see a hand waving goodbye. It was Olivia. Her hand was one which had gradually become more familiar to me over the last couple of weeks. She was now a regular contributor to class activities. Her final salute was symbolic of something greater. "Keep that hand a-waving, Olivia," I thought to myself. I smiled and waved back.

Through experimentation and persistence, I had found some useful and effective ways of getting whole-class participation. I may not have found all the answers, but this was certainly the beginning of a lifelong journey.

Appendix 1: Student questionnaire

1   How would you rate your contribution/participation in class?

Low   Moderate   High

2   Explain what you mean by your answer to question 1.

3   Do you feel you are given ample opportunity to have your say in class?

Yes   No

4 Do you ever feel that you are ignored by the teacher?

Yes   No

5 Do you feel that certain class members dominate the teacher's attention?

Yes   No

6 If you circled Yes for question 5, what would you suggest could be done about it?

7 Do you feel comfortable about asking questions in class?

Yes   No

8 If you circled NO for question 7, why do you think this is the case?

9 How do you feel when the teacher asks you to answer a question when you don't have your hand up?

Confident   Comfortable   Neutral   Annoyed   Nervous

10 What would motivate you to participate/contribute more often in class?

Overview

This student-teacher as researcher project offers interesting insights into learning about teaching. The project illustrates a developing understanding of the complex nature of teacher–student interactions and the manner in which such interactions can influence students' learning. It also suggests that some of the issues that may well have been conveyed as episteme in her teacher education classes at university (e.g. higher order questioning, wait time and learning theory) were more meaningful and applicable in practice when she explored them through experience as phronesis. Thus, in this particular case, the student of teaching actively constructed understandings of practice that, at one level could be seen as generalized pedagogical principles, while at a personal level impacted her practice in ways that encouraged her to learn about and experiment with these ideas to develop her own way of responding to the needs of her students in her classes. She was developing her style of teaching within a framework of understanding that was being articulated through researching her practice.

Vicki's project also highlights how her pedagogical growth has moved beyond the technical as she has begun to theorize and refine her practice in response to her developing views about teaching and learning. It could well be argued that her report demonstrates a serious exploration of implementing a *quality learning requires learner consent* approach to teaching, thus her approach has been both strategic (paying careful attention to the big picture of teaching and learning she is concerned about) and procedural (experimenting, developing and trialing new and different teaching techniques and procedures). Importantly, all of this occurred in response to her pedagogical needs and concerns which is in stark contrast to the search for a "recipe" for successful teaching, or teaching in ways that are necessary in order to please others (e.g. school supervisors and/or teacher educators).

Finally, hidden away but noticeable from time to time in little snippets are clues to the world of students of teaching and how they feel as learners in the world of teaching. "I scurried back to the staffroom and assumed my place in my allocated corner" or, "Though her lips were sealed, the remainder of my supervisor's face said, What is the problem with that? These trendy young teachers and their new-fangled ideas!" and, "Students are more likely to engage in quality learning if they have some choice and control in the matter. My lecturers would be proud;" all hint at some form of judgment about being a student of teaching that, in itself, clearly has the ability to shape the risks a student of teaching might be prepared to take in learning about teaching.

In Vicki's case, her research project had perhaps helped to concentrate her attention more on what she was doing than what she may have felt she was "expected to be doing", thus alleviating some of the barriers to the development of practice that many students of teaching experience. However, there is also the need for caution and to be reminded that in some cases a "research project can become all-consuming"; and that would also be an unfortunate outcome.

The message that I trust this chapter conveys is that there is great value in teacher educators supporting students of teaching to pursue their own agenda for growth and development in their learning about teaching and learning. As learning about teaching involves both the cognitive and affective, students of teaching need opportunities to feel what it is like to act in different ways in their classes. They need opportunities to experiment with their practice in situations in which judgment and assessment are minimized in order to encourage risk-taking so that strong personal learning might be experienced. They need to be able to explore their own reactions and behaviors, to begin to learn how to learn about what they do, how they do it and why. In so doing, they might begin to generalize about their practice and to theorize about teaching and learning in ways that might directly and explicitly impact their pedagogy. A student-teacher as researcher stance is one way of opening up such possibilities in supporting the development of professional pedagogues.

As I read over [my project again], I see how the dilemmas discussed in this paper are typical of teaching, and, to some extent, my research therefore reveals nothing new. Having discovered this for myself, however, it is like a new revelation to me and stirs within me a stronger determination to address these age-old problems. (Conclusion to student teacher as researcher project; James)

Just as the teacher educator as researcher literature (see Loughran *et al.* (2004), *International Handbook of Self-study of Teaching and Teacher Education Practices*) has supported and encouraged the development of understanding of issues, concerns, and interests about teacher educators' practice, so too it is time that teacher education encouraged and supported a similar synthesis of literature by students of teaching, primarily for students of teaching. Valuing such work should be evident through a pedagogy of teacher education.

11 Teacher education as a beginning not an end

> it is clear that learning to teach involves more than the mastery of a limited set of competences. It is a complex process. It is also a lengthy process, extending, for most teachers, well after their initial training. The multi-dimensional nature of learning to teach has often not been fully recognized in the design of initial teacher education courses, which are often tightly constrained in terms of both time and human resources.
>
> (Calderhead and Shorrock, 1997, p. 194)

Although it may well be recognized that teacher education is a beginning for teachers' professional learning rather than an end unto itself, the reality is that this point is often overshadowed by an array of demands that compete for time and space in the teacher education curriculum. Even though *teacher education is by definition incomplete* (Northfield and Gunstone, 1997), the perceived needs of others (e.g. schools, policy-makers, education systems) combined with these demands create expectations that are not necessarily able to be fully realized. Further to this, in trying to respond to such needs and demands, practices may be employed that actually detract from the very purpose and value of teacher education. Therefore, when considering what teacher education should be able to do, it is helpful to be reminded that "excellent teaching may be among the most difficult of human accomplishments. Like any other expressions of excellence, its achievement is enhanced through the study of its practice; and in good measure this is what we conceive teacher education to be.... [it is about] explor[ing] ways of creating the conditions needed for beginning teachers to become students of their own thinking and practice, not just student teachers" (Bullough and Gitlin, 2001, p. 11). For this to be the case, teacher education needs to foster genuine ongoing professional learning.

Professional learning

Calderhead and Shorrock (1997) describe five different types of learning processes and experiences that students of teaching are confronted by in their teacher education programs (knowledge accumulation, performance learning, practical problem-solving, learning about relationships and processes of assimilation). In considering what each of these entails, it is clear that completion of teacher preparation does not equate with the end of professional learning. These five areas (and no doubt others) continue to impact teachers' professional development and growth as broader understandings and responses to situations lead to ongoing refinement of their professional learning and knowledge.

Hoban (2002) argued that professional learning required a shift from a view of teaching as the development of expertise to teaching as the development of scholarship. Hoban's view of scholarship is in accord with Shulman's (1999) conception of scholarship in which explicating and making public understandings of practice leads to enhanced understandings of teaching and learning: "We can never fully remove the uncertainty from teaching... But as a profession, we can grow much wiser about how to anticipate and deal with uncertainty" (Shulman, 1999, p. 15). Developing scholarship entails becoming much wiser about how to anticipate and deal with the uncertainty of practice and sharing such wisdom in professionally meaningful ways with others. It is about encouraging individuals to have confidence and trust in their professional judgments in relation to the manner in which they respond to the uncertainty of practice.

When teacher educators demonstrate for their students of teaching how they anticipate and deal with uncertainty in their own practice and, when they make explicit how they respond to the contradictions and constraints of their own program structures, they demonstrate scholarship. In so doing, they also offer a window of opportunity for students of teaching to consider the value of adopting a similar position in terms of their own professional learning.

Following extensive investigation, Hoban concluded that, in teacher education, a key factor that influenced understandings of professional learning was bound up in the very structure of teacher education programs (Hoban, 2002, 2004, 2005). He was disturbed by the disjointed and disparate nature of programs and the manner in which competing interests tended to detract from possibilities for coherence in teaching and learning about teaching. As a consequence, he conceptualized a four-dimensional framework that he considered crucial to engendering program coherence and fostering professional learning. His four dimensions comprised: conceptual links across the university-based curriculum; theory–practice links between schools and universities; social–cultural links between participants in the program; and, personal links in shaping the identity of a teacher educator.

In describing each, Hoban (2004) asked teacher educators to consider a question that encapsulated the essence of that dimension. He asked: "What are the links across the university-based curriculum and why are subjects organized the way they are?; What links are there for pre-service students between theory and practice in schools and university?; What efforts are made to encourage social interaction between academics, student teachers and teachers to break down their cultural barriers so that they have more of a shared vision about teacher education in their relevant settings?; and, How do teacher educators and teachers who supervise students on practicum perceive themselves and what is their conception of teaching?" (pp. 127–129). He also stressed the point that these dimensions were not mutually exclusive, but one in particular stood out to him as most important:

> the most important is the social–cultural dimension because this over-lays the other three. It is the social and cultural connections among teacher educators, student teachers and teachers that impact on how they each shape their identity, and on how well key ideas or themes are shared to get connections between university and school experiences. Additionally it is the social interaction between the participants that enables a program design to be dynamic and change according to relevant cultural or political needs. Relationships and communication among participants are the heart of a coherent teacher education program. (Hoban, 2004, pp. 129–130)

Clearly professional learning requires social interaction and, in learning about teaching, such interactions need to be purposefully encouraged. As has been well noted in studies of teachers' professional learning, critical conversations (Bell and Gilbert, 1996; Bodone, Gudjónsdóttir, and Dalmau, 2004; Dalmau and Gudjónsdóttir, 2002; Williams, Prestage, and Bedward, 2001) and mentoring (Bullough, Young, and Draper, 2004; Calderhead and Shorrock, 1997; Tickle, 1994) are consistently to the fore. So too, as Hoban suggests, they are crucial in teacher education.

It is not difficult then to see how Hoban's views link with the importance of teacher education as a start, not an end, in teachers' professional learning and how the development of critical conversations and the nurturing of mentorship through social–cultural dimensions stands out as an area that should be of concern for teacher educators and students of teaching alike. Clearly, critical conversations and mentoring need to be infused in teacher education practices so that an expectation to further both is inherent in teaching as a profession. Thus, teacher education becomes a serious beginning point for ongoing professional learning.

Developing critical conversations

> If appearing less than perfect calls our competence into question, we are hardly likely to spring enthusiastically into conversations with colleagues about how we have learned from experiments and mistakes. So, for critical conversation to have any chance of happening, participants must feel safe in declaring imperfection. (Brookfield, 1995, pp. 142–143)

Despite the many successes students of teaching experience, they tend to continually re-live those pedagogic episodes that were not quite so positive or did not go "according to plan." It is not uncommon for students of teaching to quickly gloss over those teaching and learning episodes that "went well" and to dwell on those that were not quite so successful; despite the fact that the successes tend to dramatically outweigh the failures. It is important that both sets of experiences are considered of equal merit when reflecting on practice as each creates opportunities for valuable learning about teaching.

This tendency to concentrate more on the not-so-successful experiences comes to the surface quickly when students of teaching talk about their critical incidents. For example, the situation described by Judy (below) is typical of the type of anecdote written about a school teaching experience – no doubt also partly initiated by the intense emotional aspects of the episode that bring it to the front of the mind so quickly. However, in the absence of critical conversation, Judy may find her reflections on the situation to be less than enlightening. In sharing such a critical incident with peers, without the appropriate support and guidance, the discussion may not progress beyond a sense of guilt or blame. But, through critical conversation important issues for learning about teaching may be highlighted that extend thinking beyond the personal alone.

The visit

It's period six, last lesson of the day, that dreaded period six. "Why does it have to be with 9C?" I ask myself. What's more, my method lecturer from university has come to watch me teach.

"It's no big deal." I tell myself. "But who do I think I'm fooling? Not me, not my school supervisor, and certainly not the students."

The butterflies are almost choking me as they rush to escape from my body through the parched opening that was once my mouth. I make a joke to start the lesson. "Oh yes, start with a joke!" I thought. "That will ease the tension at the opening of the class." Not surprisingly, it sank; taking my confidence with it.

I feel somehow locked in silent combat. The students can sense my apprehension and are continually looking around at one another as if judging how the presence of the "university visitor" in the room is affecting me. "She's being assessed." I can see them thinking.

"Will we play along with it or make her life miserable?" is the look on all of their faces.

They seem to be subtly undermining the lesson and getting a response from my questions feels like pulling teeth.

I fight the urge to leap onto a table and shout, "It's not always like this! If only you were here yesterday. It's not like this at all."

Then, with five minutes until the end of the class, it happens. I stand there dumbfounded not knowing what to do.

The activity I had planned hasn't worked and I'm too strung out to revise it in these final, deadly, five minutes.

I can hear the hands on the clock at the back of the room groaning as they slowly move. I seem to be caught in a time warp as the second hand echoes in my ears, "Tick, bang, boom; you dill! Tick, bang, boom; say something! Tick, bang, boom..."

I open my mouth but nothing comes out. Then, from nowhere, I hear myself saying, "I'm very disappointed in you 9C."

"What am I saying?" I try to tell myself to stop but the words keep coming. In fact they keep coming out until the bell rings finally putting us all out of our misery.

As I leave the classroom I just want to cry. The only person I'm really disappointed in is myself. (Judy)

Judy certainly lived through an uncomfortable experience. The events that unfolded in the last five minutes of the class captured her attention drawing her thoughts away from her actions in the rest of the lesson. Although there may be much in that last five minutes to ponder, dwelling on it may well be counter-productive. However, there is much in the situation as a whole that Judy's anecdote opens up for critical conversation and much with which other students of teaching would immediately identify. In teaching and learning about teaching, it is important to remember that *an uncomfortable learning experience can be a constructive learning experience* – with the focus on the learning.

Critical conversations can highlight aspects of teaching and learning experiences that, in Judy's case, may be unable to be readily apprehended at the time because of the emotion tied to the event. A teacher educator, in initiating non-judgmental review of the situation, may catalyze critical conversation by asking Judy to ponder what it was about the class activity that caused her to think that it had not been successful; or, how her supervisor, method lecturer and/or students viewed the last five minutes. Judy might also be asked how she behaved when she was nervous – did her feelings come through or was there a difference between her inner and outer persona?; or, What did she do at the start of the next lesson – why? It would be interesting for her to consider how this particular experience influenced her thinking about her developing teacher identity; or to describe how she would have preferred to have reacted in that last five minutes. She might also be asked to describe how she sought, and reacted to, feedback on her teaching – what cues did she look for in her students' actions/responses to her teaching and their learning? Any of these questions may well be the invitation to a critical conversation that could help Judy learn more from the situation than the last five minutes alone might suggest.

Brookfield (1995) reminds us that critical incidents are important because of the way they open up "new possibilities for our practice and new ways to analyze and respond to problems. Colleagues can open up unfamiliar avenues for inquiry, and they can give us advice on how they deal with the problems we're facing" (p. 141). In learning about teaching, ensuring there is a critical edge to conversations about practice is paramount. But the critical edge is not about teacher educators "dishing out" more advice, or telling students of teaching how to act differently, or pointing out where they went wrong and what the "real" problem might be. Critical conversations depend on the manner in which students of teaching are brought to see these things for themselves; to ask their own questions of the situation and to be encouraged to frame and reframe episodes in ways that broaden their understandings so that they might confront their own contradictions in practice. And, this is important for both successful and not-so-successful teaching and learning experiences.

There is a need for teacher educators to help students of teaching to also pay attention to their pedagogic successes. It is important beyond the confidence building that it can engender, but also to ensure that they begin to abstract from the particular to the general. Instead of students of teaching seeing good teaching experiences as distinct and separate events, there is a need to help them see into their pedagogical reasoning and actions and begin to consider how that thinking might influence their teaching in other situations. There is a need to encourage them *not* to see successes in isolation (i.e. not to "save that activity" for the next time they teach that topic), but to look toward the features of the teaching and learning that were fundamental to that particular success and abstract that learning to other aspects of practice. Margaret's anecdote (below) is an example of the possibilities inherent in learning from successful pedagogic experiences.

Making it relevant

"Can we just watch a bit more?" Jobe called out from the back of the room.

"Yeah, can we?" Mitch added to the plea.

"Sorry, we don't have time. We will probably be able to watch some more next lesson." I said with a contented smile slowly breaking out.

I had just been showing my Year 9 English class the opening garage fight scene from Baz Luhrman's *William Shakespeare's Romeo and Juliet*. Their eyes had been glued to the screen, transfixed by the colour, movement, music, cars and guns.

I was delighted by their enthusiasm but had to move on. We needed to discuss the cinematic techniques used in the scene not just keep watching for fun.

This was their first attempt at analysing a scene, and I was hoping they had understood and taken on board the task I had set for them. I hesitantly turned to Michael for a first response. He didn't normally offer his ideas in class so I felt it was important to hear what he wanted to say as he had his hand up and looked so eager.

"In the 'Give more Fuel to your Fire' sign, the fuel is like the words the Capulets and Montagues are saying to each other, and the fire is the feud between the families." Michael said with a rather authoritative tone.

I think I caught my jaw just before it hit the ground; but maybe not. Anyway, I don't think they saw what I felt. All of a sudden there was fantastic response after fantastic response about the symbolism, lighting, costumes, music, setting and genre. I wrote furiously on the whiteboard trying to keep up with their responses.

"Was this really Year 9 English?" I thought to myself. These boys were willingly offering ideas about cinematic techniques they had observed during a ten minute scene from a film.

It was at this point that I realised I had them. Two and half weeks into exploring one of the greatest love stories of all time, this class full of adolescent boys were genuinely enjoying the work and understanding the play. (Margaret)

Margaret may well have thought that teaching *Romeo and Juliet* to Year 9 boys would be "hard work." However, in questioning the reasons for such a view, considering carefully how to respond to the possible difficulties and then working to tie the content and the learning together through making both relevant to the students created a very good pedagogic experience for all.

In reconsidering this experience through critical conversation, it is important that Margaret look beyond the episode as an event and into the manner in which the students were engaged in the learning – and why. It would also be important for her to consider what she learnt from the experience and to abstract that to her understanding of practice more generally. Without so doing, there is the danger that this episode might simply be archived as an activity, limited to this particular content, diminishing the possibilities for learning about practice that may be possible by reconsidering notions of linking and relevance and ways of creating a "need to know" with her students. All of this may easily be overlooked thus inhibiting her growth as a student of teaching if such successes are not also the subject of critical conversation. Successful teaching experiences need to be part of the conversation if they are to be critical for growth in understanding practice.

PEEL (Baird and Mitchell, 1986; Baird and Northfield, 1992) is a good example of a teaching and learning project that offers strong evidence of the value of critical conversations about practice. It demonstrates how, through critical conversations, teachers' initial focus on gathering teaching procedures and activities to try out in their classrooms shifts to analyzing the nature of the teaching and learning. Through critical conversations, PEEL teachers have consistently demonstrated growth beyond teaching as comprising activities and procedures to framing their pedagogy so that better aligning teaching and learning becomes a central purpose of practice. In teacher education, it is important to be reminded that students of teaching need similar opportunities. They need to see and feel how critical conversations and support can positively impact their understandings of teaching and learning. Mentoring is a concrete way of encouraging, and building on, such conversations.

Mentoring

> teacher education needs to be thought of as an ongoing community affair, one that employs public strategies and brings *with* it the responsibility to reach out to others who share the quest to become effective teachers and to *work with* them and others to strengthen and improve our schools. (emphasis in original, Bullough and Gitlin, 2001, p. 17)

Mentoring is a way of helping students of teaching to study their practice (and thinking about practice) with others so that alternative perspectives and possibilities might become apparent and can be acted upon. Mentoring is about creating ways of building on critical conversations so that the actions that follow might lead to concrete learning outcomes whereby the valuing of experimentation, risk-taking and learning through experience might foster the notion that learning about teaching is a *community affair*. Mentoring is important in demonstrating community appreciation of the fact that studying practice requires a personal commitment to public sharing so that professional critique might lead to enhanced knowledge building for all involved.

Teacher educators and teachers carry out important mentoring roles in teacher education and, through interacting with mentors, students of teaching may be offered rich opportunities for learning with others. Calderhead and Shorrock (1997), in their extensive study into the experiences of students of teaching, noted that: "The relationship between student and mentor was an important feature in determining how effectively the student learned from the experience. Being able to confide in the mentor was felt to be important by several students" (p. 177).

Mentoring requires trust and trust develops through a relationship in which mutual acceptance is to the fore. Through mutual acceptance, agreement and disagreement can be viewed positively. Growth in understanding of practice occurs through doing that which one wants to do and is comfortable with, and from doing that which one might be uncomfortable with, but needs (or is expected) to do. It is in these more uncomfortable moments that trust and mutual acceptance matter so that maintaining a focus on learning about practice, as opposed to individual preferences (likes and dislikes), prevails. And that is more likely to be the case if mentoring is concerned to foster learning through the "authority of experience" rather than assuming compliance through the "authority of position."

Calderhead and Shorrock (1997) suggested that, in teacher education, mentoring influenced learning about teaching in six ways. The first influence is mentoring *by example* and is in accord with providing a model for students of teaching to observe, critique, use as a source of actions and solutions and generally to compare and contrast views and practices of teaching. The second influence is mentoring *by coaching* which involves supplying ongoing support, careful observation and thoughtful follow-up in developing and refining skills and practices in teaching.

The third is mentoring through *practice-focused discussion* which helps students of teaching to clarify interpretations of their own practice and to focus attention on their goals, purposes and intents as they compare and contrast what they do, what they think they do and what they aspire to do.

The fourth is mentoring through *structuring the context* which is an interesting aspect of learning about teaching as students of teaching are often confronted by a particular "set-up" in the context in which they find themselves. "The mentor therefore has a strong indirect influence on the practices that the student teacher can feasibly adopt, or which will 'work' in the given context" (Calderhead and Shorrock, 1997, p. 200).

The fifth, and perhaps most commonly recognized, is mentoring through *emotional support*. This influence is crucial as students of teaching are frequently confronted by "uncertainty and self-doubt" and clearly require support and encouragement as they push to extend their competence and ability in coming to understand the complex nature of teaching and learning.

The final influence is mentoring through *devised learning experiences* which are evident through the construction of learning about teaching tasks that are created for students of teaching so that they might experience particular situations or practices in order to be "sensitized" to them in the teaching and learning environment.

Each of these influences is clearly shaped by the work of teacher educators through the manner in which they interact with their students of teaching. Mentoring cannot be taken for granted nor can it be assumed to be understood by all participants. By recognizing and responding to Calderhead and Shorrock's influences, teacher educators (university and school-based) are afforded opportunities to create, shape and unpack learning experiences with their students of teaching so that richer understandings of practice might be recognized and developed. Thus, mentoring in teaching about teaching needs to be actively embraced, not passively absorbed.

Students of teaching need, and seek, professional critique of their practice and they learn best from such feedback and advice when, in a supportive environment, their mentors are trusted, respectful and genuine teachers of teaching. Feiman-Nemser (2001) encapsulated the difficulties mentors often face in performing their role when she noted their concern to moderate between the danger of imposing their own style on students of teaching as opposed to being too laissez faire. Finding a balance between the two extremes is important. Consequently, in helping students of teaching to confront their problems of practice and to use their own teaching as a site for learning about teaching requires good mentoring. Teacher educators therefore carry a prime responsibility in initiating good mentoring if quality learning about teaching is to be an outcome of teacher education. And, in so doing, they may well establish the importance of mentoring as a critical aspect of career-long professional practice.

Overview

This chapter has attempted to offer ways of considering the purpose of teacher education and, therefore, what it realistically is able to do. In essence, teacher education is about preparation for a teaching career and some of the crucial aspects of such preparation must include establishing practices and expectations that should be central to the profession itself: responsibility for, and active development of, professional learning through critical conversations and mentoring. Therefore, when considering what teacher education programs might "look like," it may well be that an important starting point is not the structure or model that will best prepare students for the reality of teaching, but to look to an articulation of the principles that, when enacted through the practice of teacher educators and students of teaching, creates an agenda for career-long development and growth. McIntyre (1988), when considering this issue in respect to designing a teacher education curriculum concluded that:

> first... [students of teaching] have their own extensive repertoires and their own agendas; and that we as teacher educators, if we are realistic, need to accept that we can only help them in their efforts, not define the enterprise in which they are engaged. Second...even if we did believe that we had 'the answers', reliable knowledge about how best to teach, student-teachers would not accept it but would want to test it for themselves in various ways; we can probably exert more influence by encouraging this process of testing than by pretending it is not necessary. And third, we can have some confidence that if we do not put student-teachers into situations which overwhelm or seriously threaten them, we have good reason to believe that they will explore the problems of teaching with a high degree of objectivity about their own performances and rationality in their investigations. (McIntyre, 1988, pp. 104–105)

Teacher education is a beginning, not an end. Teacher educators need to be confident to challenge and support students of teaching in their professional learning by shifting the focus from the curriculum to the learner and embedding learning in experience (Loughran, 2001), as opposed to searching for the "correct program structure" while having little influence on participants' (teacher educators and students of teaching) actual practice.

12 Conclusion: Enacting a pedagogy of teacher education

> educators need to be thoughtful about their work, which means that they must question assumptions, consider multiple perspectives, avoid judgments, recognize complexity, and be primarily concerned with the needs of their students.
>
> (LaBoskey, 1997, p. 161)

The pedagogic imperatives that LaBoskey describes (above) need to be evident in the practice of teacher educators so that teaching about teaching might foster meaningful learning about teaching. One compelling reason for so doing is that "In school classrooms, pedagogy tends to be invisible and taken for granted – students become accustomed to working with teachers in similar ways, year after year. In teacher education classrooms, pedagogy suddenly becomes highly visible" (Russell, 2004, p. 1209). Therefore, if the well entrenched, taken-for-granted aspects of teaching resulting from years of an *apprenticeship of observation* (Lortie, 1975) are to be seriously examined with students of teaching, then the "highly visible" teaching in teacher education must make clear all of that which has hitherto been unseen and unappreciated. To do so is obviously a demanding task and helps to account for the growing momentum for the articulation and development of a pedagogy of teacher education.

The way in which a pedagogy of teacher education has been conceptualized in this book is not as a set of specific rules and procedures for what to do, when and how. Rather, the suggestion is that by drawing on the wealth of information about teaching, learning and teacher education, foundations for practice may be developed that will be responsive to the issues, needs and concerns of participants in ways that might make the unseen clear, the taken for granted questioned and the complex engaging. With such a purpose at the heart of a pedagogy of teacher education, real alternatives to the "tyranny of talk" may be developed that might allow teaching for understanding to be better realized both in teacher education and in schools.

A big picture view of the foundations of a pedagogy of teacher education is portrayed through the interdependent worlds of *teaching about teaching* and *learning about teaching*. By combining these two worlds in a big picture, the knowledge, concepts, ideas and practices of each can better interact, and therefore influence, the shaping of a pedagogy of teacher education which, of itself, must be dynamic, flexible and responsive to the needs, concerns, issues and practices of participants (both students and teachers of teaching).

At the centre of a pedagogy of teacher education is the difficulty of continually responding to the alternative perspectives of being both a teacher and a learner. However, if through a pedagogy of teacher education these dual perspectives are overtly valued and consciously acted upon, then there is a greater likelihood that teaching and learning will be understood as changeable, complex and vital, rather than static, unsophisticated and simple. In so doing, professional learning carries particular meaning for enhanced understanding of teaching and learning in and through different contexts thus challenging the view that expertise is solely the attainment of mastery.

Seeking to better understand one's own practices is a natural starting point for better understanding teaching about teaching and its impact on learning about teaching. The knowledge developed through such learning may initially be informing, applicable and useful to one's own practice, but when it creates the need to better articulate and communicate such learning with, and for, others, a developing pedagogy of teacher education is evident. And, for teacher educators, such learning may be realized through instigating inquiries based on a self-study of teacher education practices methodology (S-STEP, Hamilton *et al.*, 1998).

Self-study of teacher education practices

The questions, problems, tensions and dilemmas that so often cause one to ponder the problematic nature of practice are common starting points for self-study inquiries. For example, when teacher educators create challenging situations for students of teaching to be confronted by their existing practices in order to begin to conceptualize the way they might shape their future practice, they are immediately drawn into the problematic. In constructing appropriate pedagogic situations, there is always the uncertainty of that which might comprise a suitable follow-up experience as students of teaching inevitably respond differently to the same situation. Self-study is a way of purposefully examining this relationship between teaching and learning so that alternative perspectives on the intentions and outcomes might be better realized. Through self-study, a teacher educator may then become better informed about not only the nature of learning from a given pedagogic situation but also the possibilities for developing appropriate alternatives for future experiences.

An important point about self-study which is particularly relevant to the development of a pedagogy of teacher education is the nature of the learning resulting from the interaction of the self with the experience. Senese (in, Austin and Senese, 2004) explains this well when considering the similarities and differences between action research and self-study. He notes that

Action research still maintains a distance between the teacher researcher and the study.... When I reframe my research as self-study, I enter through another door, the door of the self. Self-study is much more challenging for me because it requires that I put myself, my beliefs, my assumptions, and my ideologies about teaching (as well as my practice) under scrutiny.... Action research, like self-study, does put teachers' practices under the microscope and thus may make teachers feel vulnerable. After all, presenting one's classroom practices to colleagues (or strangers) for their scrutiny can be intimidating and threatening.... On the other hand... [self-study] demands a profound curiosity about who the individual is as a teacher. The impact lies in the belief that how one teaches and what one teaches is a product of who one is and what one believes to be true. (pp. 1235–1236)

Senese captures well a key aspect of self-study that is so important to developing a pedagogy of teacher education. Being part of the experience is crucial to the development of understanding teaching and learning about teaching as something more than a cognitive process. Clearly then, if there were distance between the teaching and the learning, the researcher and the researched, the self and the experience, the resultant influence on practice would be significantly different. Being a part of the experience matters in a pedagogy of teacher education because it is about enacting practices that are sensitive and responsive to the cognitive *and* affective needs, issues and concerns in teaching and learning about teaching. It is also why Korthagen's (2001c) reminder to the teacher education community of the value and place of phronesis (demonstrated in the Realistic Teacher Education program) has been so important in shaping understandings of what knowledge of a pedagogy of teacher education might not only *look* like, but *feel* like.

Hamilton (2004) reminds us of why the work of teacher education is so difficult and therefore why the development of a pedagogy of teacher education requires both personal and collective knowledge construction.

Teachers attempt to empower their students, teacher educators attempt to empower their students to empower their students (Pinnegar, 2003). From this perspective, teacher educators are the more capable Others preparing their students to be more capable Others for their students in the public school settings. Teaching and learning in relation is a powerful perspective to consider when exploring knowledge and the knowledge bases for teaching [/teacher education]. (Hamilton, 2004, pp. 400–401)

One final point on the relationship between self-study and a pedagogy of teacher education is drawn from the work of Korthagen and Lunenberg (2004). They noted that:

The difference between traditional research and self-study research has most of all to do with the usefulness of research for practice. Traditional research seemed to focus more on the question of how isolated variables in teaching and learning relate to each other, but generally tells little about the question of what this should mean for the often different and complex situations teacher educators have to deal with. As Hagger and McIntyre (2000) remind us, at the core of expert practice is the need to make subtle judgments in unique situations. (p. 434)

These issues raised by Hamilton and Korthagen and Lunenberg combine in powerful ways to make clear why a pedagogy of teacher education is so important to realizing quality in teaching and learning about teaching.

Developing a pedagogy of teacher education

Throughout this book, features that might comprise a pedagogy of teacher education have been described in detail based on such things as knowledge, actions, beliefs and understandings of practices of teaching *and* learning about teaching. Implicit in all such features is the recognition that both students *and* teachers of teaching can conceptualize teaching and learning about teaching in ways that extend beyond the technical if views about practice are thoughtfully questioned and re-considered (and therefore better informed), rather than simply being viewed as taken for granted. Therefore, in developing a pedagogy of teacher education, individuals matter.

At one level then, this book is an attempt to encourage individual teacher educators to reconsider that which comprises their practice and to begin to focus more attention on the manner in which that practice might be purposefully shaped and conducted. In so doing, the manner in which individuals might conceptualize their teaching about teaching and, the way in which they create and construct possibilities for their students' learning about teaching may positively be impacted. Hence, developing a pedagogy of teacher education is a professional responsibility for all those teacher educators committed to deeper understandings of teaching, learning and teaching about teaching and learning.

Beyond the individual, though, there are two other important levels at which developing a pedagogy of teacher education matters. First is the institutional level whereby the practices inherent in a pedagogy of teacher education need to be explicitly played out not only through individual teacher educators' practice, but also in the manner in which program organization and structure reflect the way in which a pedagogy of teacher education is inherently intended to shape teacher education as a whole. Finally, there is the collective responsibility of the community of teacher educators, for it is through the teacher education community that ideas, issues, concerns and conceptualizations might be developed, debated, articulated and portrayed in ways that will progress the field of teacher education.

Just as the S-STEP community has progressed ideas of self-study in teacher education, so too the teacher education community as a whole needs to focus attention on what teacher educators know and are able to do; one tangible response is through the development of a pedagogy of teacher education.

How quality teaching about teaching is conducted, how students of teaching are encouraged to learn about and better value the knowledge, skills and abilities that are inherent in good teaching, matter in shaping ways in which such practices might be portrayed, shared, built upon and extended through the teacher education community. Developing a pedagogy of teacher education begins with individuals but is enhanced through scholars working together at the institutional level as well as within the community of teacher educators at large. Real action at all three levels then matters in developing a pedagogy of teacher education that might truly shape the manner in which teaching and learning about teaching is conducted in our teacher education programs.

Overview

The growing momentum for a sustained focus on the development of a pedagogy of teacher education is well encapsulated in what Korthagen and Lunenberg (2004) describe as the four dimensions of congruency between teacher education reform and self-study. They note the shift from: (i) a focus on expert knowledge to an emphasis on authority of practice; (ii) a focus on academic theory to an emphasis on personal practical theory; (iii) a focus on generalization to a focus on unique situations in their contexts; and, (iv) an exclusive focus on individual learning toward an emphasis on both individual and collaborative learning and their inter-relatedness.

The challenge for all of those concerned with teaching and learning about teaching is to ensure that these shifts are positive supports for better articulating, informing and shaping a pedagogy of teacher education. Striving for an appropriate balance in these dimensions may well be the key to constructing a pedagogy of teacher education that is meaningful to individual teacher educators, the community of teacher educators, their students of teaching, and ultimately their students. A search for balance may well comprise the journey, finding harmony is not doubt the challenge.

References

Allender, J. S. (2001). *Teacher Self: The Practice of Humanistic Education*. Lanham, Maryland: Rowman and Littlefield Publishers, Inc.

Austin, T., and Senese, J. (2004). Self-study in school teaching: Teachers' perspectives. In J. J. Loughran, M. L. Hamilton, V. K. LaBoskey and T. Russell (eds), *International Handbook of Self-study of Teaching and Teacher Education Practices* (Vol. 2, pp. 1231–1258). Dordrecht: Kluwer Academic Publishers.

Baird, J. R., (1992). Collaborative reflection, systematic enquiry, better teaching. In T. Russell and H. Munby (eds), *Teachers and Teaching: From Classroom to Reflection* (pp. 33–48). London: Falmer Press.

Baird, J. R., and Mitchell, I. J. (eds). (1986). *Improving the Quality of Teaching and Learning: An Australian Case Study – The PEEL Project*. Melbourne: Monash University Printing Service.

Baird, J. R., and Northfield, J. R. (eds). (1992). *Learning from the PEEL Experience*. Melbourne: Monash University Printing Service.

Barnes, D. (1992). The significance of teachers' frames for teaching. In T. Russell and H. Munby (eds), *Teachers and Teaching: From Classroom to Reflection* (pp. 9–32). London: Falmer Press.

Bass, L. (2002). Self-study and issues of privilege and race. In C. Kosnik, A. Freese and A. Samaras (eds), *Making a Difference in Teacher Education Through Self-study*. *Proceedings of the Fourth International Conference on Self-study of Teacher Education Practices*. Herstmonceux, East Sussex, U.K. (Vol. 1, pp. 20–25). Toronto: OISE, University of Toronto.

Baumann, J. F. (1996). Conflict or compatibility in classroom inquiry?: One teachers struggle to balance teaching and research. *Educational Researcher*, 25(7), 29–36.

Beck, C., Freese, A., and Kosnick, C. (2004). The preservice practicum: Learning through self-study in a professional setting. In J. J. Loughran, M. L. Hamilton, V. K. LaBoskey and T. Russell (eds), *International Handbook of Self-study of Teaching and Teacher Education Practices* (Vol. 2, pp. 1259–1293). Dordrecht: Kluwer Academic Publishers.

Bell, B., and Gilbert, J. (1996). *Teacher Development: A Model from Science Education*. London: Falmer Press.

Berry, A. (2001, September). *Making the Private Public: Using the WWW as a Window into one Teacher Educator's Thinking about her Practice*. Paper presented at the International Study Association of Teachers and Teaching Conference, Faro, Portugal.

Berry, A. (2004a). Self-study in teaching about teaching. In J. Loughran, M. L. Hamilton, V. LaBoskey and T. Russell (eds), *International Handbook of Self-study of Teaching and Teacher Education Practices* (Vol. 2, pp. 1295–1332). Dordrecht: Kluwer.

Berry, A. (2004b). Making the private public: Giving preservice teachers access to their teacher educators' thinking via an electronic journal. *Didaktisk Tidskrift: För practiker och forskare (Nordic Journal of Teaching and Learning: For Practitioners and Researchers)*, 14(1), 17–24.

Berry, A. (2004c). Confidence and uncertainty in teaching about teaching. *Australian Journal of Education*, 48(2), 149–165.

Berry, A., and Loughran, J. J. (2002). Developing an understanding of learning to teach in teacher education. In J. Loughran and T. Russell (eds), *Improving Teacher Education Practices Through Self-study* (pp. 13–29). London: RoutledgeFalmer.

Berry, A., and Loughran, J. J. (2004, April). *Modeling in Teacher Education: Making the Unseen Clear*. Paper presented at the American Educational Research Association, San Diego.

Berry, A., and Loughran, J. J. (2005). Teaching about teaching: The role of self-study. In S. Weber, C. Mitchell and K. O'Reilly-Scanlon (eds), *Just Who do We Think We Are?: Methodologies for Self-study in Teacher Education*. London: RoutledgeFalmer.

Berry, A., and Milroy, P. (2002). Changes that matter. In J. Loughran, I. Mitchell and J. Mitchell (eds), *Learning from Teacher Research* (pp. 196–221). New York: Teachers College Press.

Bodone, F., Gudjónsdóttir, H., and Dalmau, M. C. (2004). Revisioning and recreating practice: Collaboration in self-study. In J. J. Loughran, M. L. Hamilton, V. K. LaBoskey and T. Russell (eds), *International Handbook of Self-study of Teaching and Teacher Education Practices* (Vol. 1, pp. 743–784). Dordrecht: Kluwer Academic Publishers.

Boyer, E. L. (1990). *Scholarship Reconsidered: Priorities of the Professoriate*. Princeton, N.J.: Carnegie Foundation for the Advancement of Teaching.

Brandenburg, R. (2004). Roundtable reflections: (Re)defining the role of the teacher educator and the preservice teacher as 'co-learners'. *Australian Journal of Education*, 48(2), 166–181.

Brookfield, S. D. (1995). *Becoming a Critically Reflective Teacher*. San Francisco: Jossey-Bass Publishers.

Bulfin, S. (2003). *Learning to Learn Against the Grain: Beginning English Teaching and the Processes of Professional Learning*. Unpublished Honours thesis in Education, Monash University, Melbourne.

Bullough, R. V. Jr (1989). *First Year Teacher: A Case Study*. New York: Teachers College Press.

Bullough, R. V. Jr (1991). Exploring personal teaching metaphors in preservice teacher education. *Journal of Teacher Education*, 42(1), 43–51.

Bullough, R. V. Jr (1994). Personal history and teaching metaphors: A self-study of teaching as conversation. *Teacher Education Quarterly*, 21(1), 107–120.

Bullough, R. V. Jr (1997). Practicing theory and theorizing practice in teacher education. In J. Loughran and T. Russell (eds), *Teaching About Teaching: Purpose, Passion and Pedagogy in Teacher Education* (pp. 13–31). London: Falmer Press.

Bullough, R. V. Jr, and Gitlin, A. (1995). *Becoming a Student of Teaching: Methodologies for Exploring Self and School Context*. (1st edn). New York: Garland.

Bullough, R. V. Jr, and Gitlin, A. (2001). *Becoming a Student of Teaching: Linking Knowledge Production and Practice* (2nd edn). London: RoutledgeFalmer.

Bullough, R. V. Jr, Young, J., and Draper, R. J. (2004). One-year teaching internships and the dimensions of beginning teacher development. *Teachers and Teaching: Theory and Practice*, 10(4), 365–394.

Burn, K., Hagger, H., Mutton, T., and Everton, T. (2000). Beyond concerns with self: The sophisticated thinking of beginning student teachers. *Journal of Education for Teaching*, 26, 259–278.

Burn, K., Hagger, H., Mutton, T., and Everton, T. (2003). The complex development of student-teachers' thinking. *Teachers and Teaching: Theory and Practice*, 9(4), 309–331.

Calderhead, J. (1988). The development of knowledge structures in learning to teach. In J. Calderhead (ed.), *Teachers' Professional Learning* (pp. 51–64). London: Falmer Press.

Calderhead, J., and Shorrock, S. B. (1997). *Understanding Teacher Education: Case Studies in the Professional Development of Beginning Teachers*. London: Falmer press.

Carter, K. (1990). Teachers' knowledge and learning to teach. In W. R. Houston (ed.), *Handbook of Research on Teacher Education* (pp. 291–310). New York: MacMillan.

Chin, P. (1997). Teaching and learning in teacher education: Who is carrying the ball? In J. Loughran and T. Russell (eds), *Teaching About Teaching: Purpose, Passion and Pedagogy in Teacher Education* (pp. 117–129). London: Falmer press.

Clandinin, D. J. (1995). Still learning to teach. In T. Russell and F. Korthagen (eds), *Teachers Who Teach Teachers* (pp. 25–31). London: Falmer press.

Clandinin, D. J., and Connelly, F. M. (eds), (1995). *Teachers' Professional Knowledge Landscapes*. New York: Teachers College Press.

Clandinin, D. J., and Connelly, F. M. (2000). *Narrative Inquiry*. San Francisco: Jossey-Bass.

Clark, C., and Peterson, P. (1986). Teachers' thought processes. In M. C. Wittrock (ed.), *Handbook of Research on Teaching* (3rd edn, pp. 255–296). New York: MacMillan.

Clarke, A. (1997). Advisor as coach. In J. Loughran and T. Russell (eds), *Teaching About Teaching: Purpose, Passion and Pedagogy in Teacher Education* (pp. 164–180). London: Falmer Press.

Clarke, A., and Erickson, G. (2004). Self-study: The fifth commonplace. *Australian Journal of Education*, 48(2), 199–211.

Clift, R. T. (2004). Self-study research in the context of teacher education programs. In J. J. Loughran, M. L. Hamilton, V. K. LaBoskey and T. Russell (eds), *International Handbook of Self-study of Teaching and Teacher Education Practices* (Vol. 2, pp. 1333–1366). Dordrecht: Kluwer Academic Publishers.

Cochran-Smith, M., and Lytle, S. (1999). Relationships of knoweldge and practice: Teacher learning communities. In A. Iran-Nejad and P. D. Pearson (eds), *Review of Research in Education* (Vol. 24, pp. 249–305). Washington D.C.: American Educational Research Association.

Cochran-Smith, M., and Lytle, S. (2004). Practitioner inquiry, knowledge, and university culture. In J. J. Loughran, M. L. Hamilton, V. K. LaBoskey and T. Russell (eds), *International Handbook of Self-study of Teaching and Teacher Education Practices* (Vol. 1, pp. 601–649). Dordrecht: Kluwer Academic Press.

Cole, A., and Knowles, G. (1995). Methods and issues in a life history approach to self-study. In T. Russell and F. Korthagen (eds), *Teachers Who Teach Teachers: Reflections on Teacher Education* (pp. 130–151). London: Falmer Press.

Cole, A., and Knowles, G. (1996). Reform and being true to oneself: Pedagogy, professional practice, and the promotional process. *Teacher Education Quarterly*, 23(3), 19–26.

Cole, A., and Knowles, G. (1998a). Reforming teacher education through self-study. In A. Cole, R. Elijah and G. Knowles (eds), *The Heart of the Matter: Teacher Education and Teacher Education Reform* (pp. 41–54). San Francisco: Caddo Gap Press.

Cole, A., and Knowles, G. (1998b). The self-study of teacher education practices and the reform of teacher education. In M. L. Hamilton (ed.), *Reconceptualizing Teaching Practice: Self-study in Teacher Education* (pp. 224–234). London: Falmer Press.

Cooley, W. W., Gage, N. L., and Scriven, M. (1997). The vision thing: Educational research and AERA in the 21st Century. Part 1: Competing visions of what educational researchers should do. *Educational Researcher*, 26(4), 18–21.

Dalmau, M. C., and Gudjónsdóttir, H. (2002). Framing professional discourse with teachers: Professional working theory. In J. Loughran and T. Russell (eds), *Improving Teacher Education Practices Through Self-study* (pp. 109–129). London: RoutledgeFalmer.

Dewey, J. (1929). *The Sources of Science Education*. New York: Horace Liveright.

Dewey, J. (1933). *How We Think*. Lexington, Massachusetts: D.C. Heath and Company.

Dewey, J. (1938). *Experience and Education*. Chicago: Henry Regnery.

Dewey, J. (ed.). (1964). *John Dewey on Education: Selected Writings*. Chicago: University of Chicago Press.

Dinkleman, T. (1999, April). *Self-study in Teacher Education: A Means and Ends Tool for Promoting Reflective Teaching*. Paper presented at the Annual Meeting of the American Educational Research Association, Montreal, Quebec.

Dinkelman, T., Margolis, J., and Sikkenga, K. (2001, April). *From Teacher to Teacher Educator: Experiences, Expectations and Expatriation*. Paper presented at the American Educational Research Association, Seattle.

Ducharme, E. (1993). *The Lives of Teacher Educators*. New York: Teachers College Press.

Duckworth, E. (1991). Twenty-four, forty-two, and I love you: Keeping it complex. *Harvard Educational Review*, 61(1), 1–24.

Elbaz, F. (1991). Research on teachers' knowledge: The evolution of a discourse. *Journal of Curriculum Studies*, 23(1), 1–19.

Elijah, R. (1998). Questioning tenets of teacher education through an examination of my practice: Extending notions of teacher education and practice? In A. L. Cole and S. Finley (eds), *Conversations in Community. Proceedings of the Second International Conference of the Self-study of Teacher Education Practices. Herstmonceux Castle, East Sussex, England* (Vol. 1, pp. 6–9). Kingston, Ontario: Queen's University.

Elliott, J. (1989, April). *Action Research and the Emergence of Teacher Appraisal in the United Kingdom*. Paper presented at the American Educational Research Association, San Francisco.

Feiman-Nemser, S. (2001). Helping novices learn to teach: Lessons from an exemplary support teacher. *Journal of Teacher Education*, 52(1), 17–30.

Fenstermacher, G. D. (1986). Philosophy of research on teaching: Three aspects. In Wittrock (ed.), *Handbook of Research on Teaching* (3rd edn, pp. 37–49). N.Y.: MacMillan.

Fenstermacher, G. D. (1994). The knower and the known: The nature of knowledge in research on teaching. In L. Darling-Hammond (ed.), *Review of Research in Education* (Vol. 20, pp. 3–56). Washington D.C.: American Educational Research Association.

Fenstermacher, G. D. (1997). Foreword. In J. Loughran and T. Russell (eds), *Teaching About Teaching: Purpose, Passion and Pedagogy in Teacher Education* (pp. viii–xiii). London: Falmer Press.

Fitzgerald, L. M., Farstad, J. E., and Deemer, D. (2002). What gets "mythed" in the student evaluations of their teacher education professors? In J. Loughran and T. Russell (eds), *Improving Teacher Education Practices Through Self-study* (pp. 208–221). London: RoutledgeFalmer.

Fox, D. (1997). What do I do with all these questions? In I. Mitchell and J. Mitchell (eds), *Stories of Reflective Teaching: A Book of PEEL Cases* (pp. 45–49). Melbourne: PEEL publishing.

Freidus, H. (2002). Through a murky mirror: Self-study of a program in reading and literacy. In C. Kosnik, A. Freese and A. Samaras (eds), *Making a Difference in Teacher Education Through Self-study. Proceedings of the Fourth International Conference on Self-study of Teacher Education Practices.* Herstmonceux, East Sussex, England (Vol. 1, pp. 81–86). Toronto, Ontario: OISE, University of Toronto.

Freire, P. (1972). *Pedagogy of the Oppressed.* New York: Herder and Herder.

Fullan, M. (1993). *Change Forces: Probing the Depths of Educational Reform.* London: Falmer Press.

Fullan, M., and Hargreaves, A. (1991). *What's Worth Fighting for in Your School?* Buckingham, U.K.: Open University Press.

Fuller, F. F. (1969). Concerns of teachers: A developmental conceptualization. *American Educational Research Journal,* 6(2), 207–226.

Fuller, F. F., and Bown, O. H. (1975). Becoming a teacher. In K. Ryan (ed.), *Teacher Education: The 74th Yearbook of the National Society for the Study of Education, Part 11* (pp. 25–52). Chicago: University of Chicago Press.

Furlong, J., and Maynard, T. (1995). *Mentoring Student Teachers: The Growth of Professional Knowledge.* London: Routledge.

Ginsburg, M. B., and Clift, R. T. (1990). The hidden curriculum of preservice teacher education. In W. R. Houston (ed.), *Handbook of Research on Teacher Education* (pp. 450–465). New York: Macmillan.

Goodlad, J. I. (1990). *Teachers for Our Nation's Schools.* San Francisco: Jossey-Bass.

Gordon, W. J. J. (1961). *Synectics: The Development of Creative Capacity.* New York: Harper.

Grimmett, P. P., and Erickson, G. (1988). *Reflection in Teacher Education.* New York: Teachers College Press.

Grimmett, P. P., and MacKinnon, A. M. (1992). Craft knowledge and the education of teachers. In G. Grant (ed.), *Review of Research in Education* (Vol. 18, pp. 385–456). Washington D.C.: American Educational Research Association.

Grossman, P. L. (1992). Why models matter: An alternate view on professional growth in teaching. *Review of Educational Research,* 62(2), 171–179.

Guilfoyle, K., Hamilton, M. L., Pinnegar, S., and Placier, M. (1995). Becoming teachers of teachers: The paths of four beginners. In T. Russell and F. Korthagen (eds), *Teachers Who Teach Teachers: Reflections on Teacher Education* (pp. 35–55). London: Falmer Press.

Guilfoyle, K., Hamilton, M. L., and Pinnegar, S. (1997). Obligations to unseen children. In J. Loughran and T. Russell (eds), *Teaching About Teaching: Purpose, Passion and Pedagogy in Teacher Education* (pp. 183–209). London: Falmer Press.

Gunstone, R. F. (1995). A teacher educator's view. In J. Baird and J. Northfield (eds), *Learning from the PEEL Experience* (2nd edn, pp. 283–291). Melbourne: Monash University Printing Services.

Hagger, H., and McIntyre, D. (2000). What can research tell us about teacher education? *Oxford Review of Education*, 26(3 and 4), 483–494.

Hall, G. E., and Hord, S. M. (1987). *Change in Schools: Facilitating the Process*. New York: State University of New York Press.

Hall, G. E., and Loucks, S. (1977). A developmental model for determining whether the treatments is actually implemented. *American Educational Research Journal*, 14(3), 263–276.

Hamilton, M. L. (2004). Professional knowledge, teacher education and self-study. In J. J. Loughran, M. L. Hamilton, V. K. LaBoskey and T. Russell (eds), *International Handbook of Self-study of Teaching and Teacher Education Practices* (Vol. 1, pp. 375–419). Dordrecht: Kluwer Academic Publishers.

Hamilton, M. L., with, Pinnegar, S., Russell, T., Loughran, J., and LaBoskey, V. (eds) (1998). *Reconceptualizing Teaching Practice: Self-study in Teacher Education*. London: Falmer Press.

He, A. E., Walker, L., Mok, A., Bodycott, P., and Crew, V. (eds). (2000). *Back to School: Lecturer Attachment Experiences*. Hong Kong: Department of English, Hong Kong Institute of Education.

Heaton, R. M., and Lampert, M. (1993). Learning to hear voices: Inventing a new pedagogy of teacher education. In D. K. Cohen, M. W. McLaughlin and J. Talbert. (eds), *Teaching for Understanding: Challenges for Policy and Practice* (pp. 43–83). San Francisco: Jossey-Bass.

Hoban, G. (1997). Learning about learning in the context of a science methods course. In J. Loughran and T. Russell (eds), *Teaching About Teaching: Purpose, Passion and Pedagogy in Teacher Education* (pp. 133–149). London: Falmer Press.

Hoban, G. F. (2002). *Teacher Learning for Educational Change: A Systems Thinking Approach*. Buckingham: Open University Press.

Hoban, G. F. (2004). Seeking quality in teacher education design: A four-dimensional approach. *Australian Journal of Education*, 48(2), 117–133.

Hoban, G. F. (ed.). (2005). *The Missing Links in Teacher Education Design: Developing a Multi-linked Conceptual Framework*. Berlin: Springer.

Hord, S. M., Rutherford, W. L., Huling-Austin, L., and Hall, G. E. (1987). *Taking Charge of Change*. Austin TX: Southwest Educational Development Laboratory.

Hutchinson, N. (1998). Reflecting critically on teaching to encourage critical reflection. In M. Hamilton (ed.), *Reconceptualizing Teaching Practice: Self-study in Teacher Education* (pp. 124–139). London: Falmer Press.

Kagan, D. M. (1992). Professional growth among preservice and beginning teachers. *Review of Educational Research*, 62, 129–169.

Kessels, J., and Korthagen, F. A. J. (2001). The relation between theory and practice: Back to the classics. In F. A. J. Korthagen, with J. Kessels, B. Koster, B. Langerwarf and T. Wubbels (eds), *Linking Practice and Theory: The Pedagogy of Realistic Teacher Education* (pp. 20–31). Mahwah, New Jersey: Lawrence Erlbaum Associations, Publishers.

Kincheloe, J. L. (2003). *Teachers as Researchers: Qualitative Inquiry as a Path to Empowerment*. London: RoutledgeFalmer.

Kohnstamm, P. A. (1929). *De psychiater als opvoeder [The psychiatrist as pedagogue]*. Mededeelingen van het Nutsseminarium voor Paedagogiek aan de Universiteir van Amsterdam, 6 [Booklet].

Korthagen, F. A. J. (1988). The influence of learning orientations on the development of reflective thinking. In J. Calderhead (ed.), *Teachers' Professional Learning* (pp. 35–50). London: Falmer Press.

Korthagen, F. A. J. (2001a). Teacher education: A problematic enterprise. In K. F. A. J., with J. Kessels, B. Koster, B. Langerwarf and T. Wubbels (eds), *Linking Practice and Theory: The Pedagogy of Realistic Teacher Education* (pp. 1–19). Malhwah, New Jersey: Lawrence Erlbaum Associates, Publishers.

Korthagen, F. A. J. (2001b). The realistic approach: It's tenets, philosophical background, and future. In F. Korthagen, with J. Kessels, B. Koster, B. Langerwarf and T. Wubbels (eds), *Linking Theory and Practice: The Pedagogy of Realistic Teacher Education*. (pp. 254–274). Mahwah, New Jersey: Lawrence Erlbaum Associates Publishers.

Korthagen, F. A. J., (2001c). Building a realistic teacher education program. In F. A. J. Korthagen, with J. Kessels, B. Koster, B. Langerwarf and T. Wubbels (eds), *Linking Practice and Theory: The Pedagogy of Realistic Teacher Education* (pp. 69–87). Mahwah, New Jersey: Lawrence Erlbaum Associates.

Korthagen, F. A. J. (2004). In search of the essence of a good teacher: Towards a more holistic approach in teacher education. *Teaching and Teacher Education*, 20(1), 77–97.

Korthagen, F. A. J., and Kessels, J. (1999). Linking theory and practice: Changing the pedagogy of teacher education. *Educational Researcher*, 28(4), 4–17.

Korthagen, F. A. J., Loughran, J. J., and Lunenberg, M. (2005). Teaching teachers: Studies into the expertise of teacher educators. *Teaching and Teacher Education*, 21(2), 107–115.

Korthagen, F. A. J., and Lunenberg, M. (2004). Links between self-study and teacher education reform. In J. J. Loughran, M. L. Hamilton, V. K. LaBoskey and T. Russell (eds), *International Handbook of Self-study of Teaching and Teacher Education Practices* (Vol. 1, pp. 421–449). Dordrecht: Kluwer Academic Publishers.

Korthagen, F. A. J., with Kessels, J., Koster, B., Langerwarf, B., and Wubbels, T. (2001). *Linking Practice and Theory: The Pedagogy of Realistic Teacher Education*. Malhwah, New Jersey: Lawrence Erlbaum Associates, Publishers.

Koster, B., Brekelmans, M., Korthagen, F., and Wubbels, T. (2005). Quality requirements for teacher educators. *Teaching and Teacher Education*, 21(2), 157–176.

Kroll, L. R. (2004). Constructing constructivism: How student-teachers construct ideas of development, knowledge, learning and teaching. *Teachers and Teaching: Theory and Practice*, 10(2), 199–221.

Kroll, L. R., Crossey, R., Donahue, D. M., Galguera, T., LaBoskey, V. K., Richert, A. *et al.* (2005). *Teaching as Principled Practice: Managing Complexity for Social Justice*. Thousand Oaks: SAGE.

Kuzmic, J. J. (2002). Research as a way of knowing and seeing: Advocacy for the other. In J. Loughran and T. Russell (eds), *Improving Teacher Education Practices Through Self-study* (pp. 222–235). London: RoutledgeFalmer.

LaBoskey, V. K. (1991, April). *Case Studies of Two Teachers in a Reflective Teacher Education Program: "How do you know?"* Paper presented at the American Educational Research Association, Chicago.

LaBoskey, V. (1997). Teaching to teach with purpose and passion: Pedagogy for reflective practice. In J. Loughran and T. Russell (eds), *Teaching About Teaching: Purpose, Passsion and Pedagogy in Teacher Education* (pp. 150–163). London: Falmer press.

Lanier, J., and Little, J. (1986). Research on teacher education. In M. Wittrock (ed.), *Handbook of Research on Teaching* (3rd edn, pp. 527–569). New York: Macmillan.

Lortie, D. C. (1975). *Schoolteacher*. Chicago: Chicago University Press.

Loughran, J. (2001, April). *Learning to Teach by Embedding Learning in Experience*. Paper presented at the American Educational Research Association, Seattle.

Loughran, J., Mitchell, I., and Mitchell, J. (eds). (2002). *Learning from Teacher Research*. New York: Teachers College Press.

Loughran, J. J. (1995). Practicing what I preach: Modelling reflective practice to student teachers. *Research in Science Education*, 25(4), 431–451.

Loughran, J. J. (1996). *Developing Reflective Practice: Learning About Teaching and Learning Through Modelling*. London: Falmer Press.

Loughran, J. J. (1997a). Teaching about teaching: Principles and practice. In J. Loughran and T. Russell (eds), *Teaching About Teaching: Purpose, Passion and Pedagogy in Teacher Education* (pp. 57–69). London: Falmer Press.

Loughran, J. J. (1997b). An introduction to purpose, passion and pedagogy. In J. Loughran and T. Russell (eds), *Teaching About Teaching: Purpose, Passion and Pedagogy in Teacher Education* (pp. 3–8). London: Falmer Press.

Loughran, J. J. (1999). Professional development for teachers: A growing concern. *Journal of In-Service Education*, 25(2), 261–272.

Loughran, J. J. (2002). Effective reflective practice: In search of meaning in learning about teaching. *Journal of Teacher Education*, 53(1), 33–43.

Loughran, J. J. (2003, June). *Knowledge Construction and Learning to Teach*. Paper presented at the International Study Association of Teachers and Teaching, Leiden.

Loughran, J. J. (2004a). Learning through self-study. In J. J. Loughran, M. L. Hamilton, V. K. LaBoskey and T. Russell (eds), *International Handbook of Self-study of Teaching and Teacher Education Practices* (Vol. 1, pp. 151–192). Dordrecht: Kluwer Academic Publishers.

Loughran, J. J. (2004b). Informing practice: Developing knowledge of teaching about teaching. In D. Tidwell, L. Fitzgerald and M. Heston (eds), *The Fifth International Conference of Self-study of Teacher Education Practices*. Herstmonceux Castle, East Sussex, U.K. (pp. 186–189). Cedar Falls, Iowa: University of Northern Iowa.

Loughran, J. J. (2004c). Student teacher as researcher: Accepting greater responsibility for learning about teaching. *Australian Journal of Education*, 48(2), 212–220.

Loughran, J. J., Hamilton, M. L., LaBoskey, V. K., and Russell, T. L. (eds) (2004). *The International Handbook of Self-study of Teaching and Teacher Education Practices (Vol. 1 and 2)* Dordrecht: Kluwer Academic Publishers.

Loughran, J. J., Berry, A., and Tudball, L. (2005a). Collaborative learning in teaching about teaching. In C. Kosnik, C. Beck, A. Freese and A. Samaras (eds), *Making a Difference in Teacher Education Through Self-study: Studies of Personal, Professional, and Program Renewal*. Berlin: Springer.

Loughran, J. J., Berry, A., and Tudball, L. (2005b). Developing trust in teaching: Learning to help student-teachers learn about their practice. In G. Hoban (ed.), *The Missing Links in Teacher Education*. Berlin: Springer.

Loughran, J. J., and Northfield, J. R. (1996). *Opening the Classroom Door: Teacher, Researcher, Learner*. London: Falmer Press.

Lytle, S., and Cochran-Smith, M. (1991). Teacher research as a way of knowing. *Harvard Educational Review*, 62(4), 447–474.

MacKinnon, A. M. (1989, April). *Reflection in a Science Teaching Practicum*. Paper Presented at the Annual conference of the American Educational Research Association, San Francisco.

Mason, J. (2002). *Researching Your Own Practice: The Discipline of Noticing*. London: RoutledgeFalmer.

Mayeroff, M. (1971). *On Caring*. New York: Harper and Rowe.

McIntyre, D. (1988). Designing a teacher education curriculum from research and theory on teacher knowledge. In J. Calderhead (ed.), *Teachers' Professional Learning* (pp. 97–114). London: Falmer Press.

Minnett, A. M. (2003). Collaboration and shared reflections in the classroom. *Teachers and Teaching: Theory and Practice*, 9(3), 279–285.

Mitchell, C., and Weber, S. (1998). What can a teacher do with a camera. In A. L. Cole and S. Finley (eds), *Conversations in Community. Proceedings of the Second International Conference of the Self-study of Teacher Education Practices*. Herstmonceux Castle, East Sussex, England (Vol. 2, pp. 178–181). Kingston, Ontario: Queen's University.

Mitchell, C., and Weber, S. (1999). *Reinventing Ourselves as Teachers: Beyond Nostalgia*. London: Falmer Press.

Mitchell, C., and Weber, S. (2000). Prom dresses are us? Excerpts from collective memory work. In J. Loughran and T. Russell (eds), *Exploring Myths and Legends of Teacher Education. Proceedings of the Third International Conference on Self-study of Teacher Education Practices*. Herstmonceux Castle, East Sussex, England (Vol. 2, pp. 248–251). Kingston, Ontario: Queen's University.

Mitchell, I. (1992). The class level. In J. Baird and J. Northfield (eds), *Learning from the PEEL Experience* (pp. 61–104). Melbourne: Monash University Printing Service.

Mitchell, I., and Mitchell, J. (eds). (1997). *Stories of Reflective Teaching: A Book of PEEL Cases*. Melbourne: PEEL publishing.

Mitchell, I., and Mitchell, J. (2005). What do we mean by career long professional development and how do we get it? In D. Beijaard, P. Meijer, G. Morine-Dershimer and H. Tillema (eds), *New Directions in Teachers' Working and Learning Environment*. Berlin: Springer.

Munby, H., and Russell, T. (1994). The authority of experience in learning to teach: Messages from a physics method class. *Journal of Teacher Education*, 4(2), 86–95.

Munby, H., Russell, T., and Martin, A. K. (2001). Teachers' knowledge and how it develops. In V. Richardson (ed.), *Handbook of Research on Teaching* (4th edn, pp. 877–904). Washington D.C.: American Educational Research Association.

Myers, C. B. (2002). Can self-study challenge the belief that telling, showing and guided practice constitute adequate teacher education? In J. Loughran and T. Russell (eds), *Improving Teacher Education Practices Through Self-study* (pp. 130–142). London: RoutledgeFalmer.

Myers, C. B., and Simpson, D. J. (1998). *Re-creating Schools: Places Where Everyone Learns and Likes it*. Thousand Oaks, California: Corwin Press, Inc.

Nicol, C. (1997). Learning to teach prospective teachers to teach mathematics: Struggles of a beginning teacher educator. In J. Loughran and T. Russell (eds), *Teaching About Teaching: Purpose, Passion and Pedagogy in Teacher Education* (pp. 95–116). London: Falmer Press.

Noddings, N. (2001). The caring teacher. In V. Richardson (ed.), *Handbook of Research on Teaching* (4th edn, pp. 99–105). Washington D.C.: American Educational Research Association.

Northfield, J. R., (1996, April). *Quality and the Self-study Perspective on Research.* Paper presented at the American Educational Research Association, New York (ED 397034).

Northfield, J. R. (1997, July). *It is Interesting...but is it Research?* Paper presented at the Australasian Science Education Research Association, Adelaide, Australia.

Northfield, J. R., and Gunstone, R. F. (1997). Teacher education as a process of developing teacher knowledge. In J. Loughran and T. Russell (eds), *Teaching About Teaching: Purpose, Passion and Pedagogy in Teacher Education* (pp. 48–56). London: Falmer Press.

Pajares, M. F. (1992). Teachers' beliefs and educational research: Cleaning up a messy construct. *Review of Educational Research*, 62(3), 307–332.

Palmer, P. J. (1998). *The Courage to Teach: Exploring the Inner Landscape of a Teacher's Life.* San Francisco: Jossey-Bass publications.

Peck, R. F., and Tucker, J. A. (1973). Research on teacher education. In R. M. W. Travers (ed.), *Second Handbook of Research on Teaching* (pp. 940–978). Chicago: Rand McNally and Company.

Pereira, P. (2000). Reconstrucing oneself as a learner of mathematics. In J. Loughran and T. Russell (eds), *Exploring Myths and Legends of Teacher Education. Proceedings of the Third International Conference of the Self-study of Teacher Education Practices.* Herstmonceux Castle, East Sussex, England (pp. 204–207). Kingston, Ontario: Queen's University.

Perry, W. G. (1988). Different worlds in the same classroom. In P. Ramsden (ed.), *Improving Learning: New Perspectives.* East Brunswick, N.J.: Nicols.

Peterman, F. (1997). The lived curriculum of constructivist teacher education. In V. Richardson (ed.), *Constructivist Teacher Education: Building a World of New Understandings* (pp. 154–163.). London: Falmer Press.

Pinnegar, S. (1995). (Re)Experiencing student teaching. In T. Russell and F. Korthagen (eds), *Teachers Who Teach Teachers: Reflections on Teacher Education* (pp. 56–67). London: Falmer Press.

Polanyi, M. (1962). *Personal Knowledge: Towards a Post-critical Philosophy.* London: Routledge and Kegan Paul.

Polanyi, M. (1966). *The Tacit Dimension.* Garden City N.Y.: Doubleday.

Posner, G. J., Strike, K. A., Hewson, P. W., and Gertzhog, W. A. (1982). Accommodation of a scientific conception: Toward a theory of conceptual change. *Science Education*, 66(2), 211–227.

Richardson, V. (1992). The evolution of reflective teaching and teacher education. In R. T. Clift, R. W. Houston and M. C. Pugach (eds), *Encouraging Reflective Practice in Education: An Analysis of Issues and Programs.* New York: Teachers College Press.

Richardson, V. (1994). Conducting research on practice. *Educational Researcher*, 23(5), 5–10.

Richardson, V. (1997). Constuctivist teaching and teacher education: Theory and practice. In V. Richardson (ed.), *Constructivist Teacher Education: Building a World of New Understandings* (pp. 3–14). London: Falmer Press.

Richardson, V., and Placier, M. (2001). Teacher change. In V. Richardson (ed.), *Handbook of Research on Teaching* (4th edn, pp. 905–947). Washington D.C.: American Educational Research Association.

Richert, A. (1992). The content of student teachers' reflections with different structures for facilitating the reflective process. In T. Russell and H. Munby (eds), *Teachers and Teaching: From Classroom to Reflection* (pp. 171–191). London: Falmer Press.

Rogers, W. A. (1990). *You Know the Fair Rule: Strategies for Making the Hard Job of Discipline in School Easier*. Melbourne: ACER publishing.

Rogers, W. A. (1998). *You Know the Fair Rule and Much More: Strategies for Making the Hard Job of Discipline in School Easier*. Melbourne: ACER publishing.

Russell, T. (1986, April). *Beginning Teachers' Development of Knowledge-in-action*. Paper presented at the American Educational Research Association, San Francisco.

Russell, T. (1995). Returning to the physics classroom to re-think how one learns to teach physics. In T. Russell and F. Korthagen (eds), *Teachers Who Teach Teachers: Reflections on Teacher Education* (pp. 95–109). London: Falmer press.

Russell, T. (1997). Teaching teachers: How I teach IS the message. In J. Loughran and T. Russell (eds), *Teaching About Teaching: Purpose, Passion and Pedagogy in Teacher Education* (pp. 32–47). London: Falmer Press.

Russell, T. (1998). Introduction to part 1: Philosophical perspectives. In M. L. Hamilton (ed.), *Reconceptualising Teaching Practice: Self-study in Teacher Education* (pp. 5–6). London: Falmer Press.

Russell, T. (2002). Guiding new teachers' learning from classroom experience: Self-study of the faculty liaison role. In J. Loughran and T. Russell (eds), *Improving Teacher Education Practices Through Self-study* (pp. 73–87). London: RoutledgeFalmer.

Russell, T. (2004). Tracing the development of self-study in teacher education research and practice. In J. J. Loughran, M. L. Hamilton, V. K. LaBoskey and T. Russell (eds), *International Handbook of Self-study of Teaching and Teacher Education Practices* (Vol. 2, pp. 1191–1210). Dordrecht: Kluwer Academic Publishers.

Russell, T., and Bullock, S. (1999). Discovering our professional knowledge as teachers: Critical dialogues about learning from experience. In J. Loughran (ed.), *Researching Teaching: Methodologies and Practices for Understanding Pedagogy* (pp. 132–151). London: Falmer Press.

Schön, D. A. (1983). *The Reflective Practitioner: How Professionals Think in Action*. New York: Basic Books.

Schuck, S., and Segal, G. (2002). Learning about our teaching from our graduates, learning about our learning with critical friends. In J. Loughran and T. Russell (eds), *Improving Teacher Education Practices Through Self-study* (pp. 88–101). London: RoutledgeFalmer.

Schwab, J. J. (1978). The practical: A language for the curriculum. In I. Westbury and J. Wilkof (eds), *Joseph J. Schwab: Science, Curriculum and Liberal Education – Selected Essays* (pp. 287–321). Chicago: University of Chicago Press.

Segall, A. (2002). *Disturbing Practice: Reading Teacher Education as Text*. New York: Peter Lang Publishing Inc.

Senese, J. (2002). Opposites attract: What I learned about being a classroom teacher by being a teacher educator. In J. Loughran and T. Russell (eds), *Improving Teacher Education Practices Through Self-study* (pp. 43–55). London: RoutledgeFalmer.

Senese, J. (2004). The accidental curriculum. In D. Tidwell, L. Fitzgerald and M. Heston (eds), *The Fifth International Conference of Self-study of Teacher Education Practices*. Herstmonceux Castle, East Sussex, U.K (Vol. 2, pp. 221–224). Cedar Falls, Iowa: University of Northern Iowa.

Shulman, J. H. (1992). *Case Methods in Teacher Education*. New York: Teachers College Press.

Shulman, L. S. (1986). Those who understand: Knowledge growth in teaching. *Educational Researcher*, 15(2), 4–14.

Shulman, L. S. (1987). Knowledge and teaching: Foundations of the new reform. *Harvard Educational Review*, 57(1), 1–22.

Shulman, L. S. (1999). Taking learning seriously. *Change*, 31(4), 10–17.

Sim, C. (2004). The personal as pedagogical practice. *Teachers and Teaching: Theory and Practice*, 10(4), 351–364.

Simon, B. (1981). Why no pedagogy in England? In B. Simon and W. Taylor (eds), *Education in the Eighties*. London: Batsford Academic and Educational Ltd.

Smith, K. (1997). Learing to teach: A story of five crises. In D. Featherstone, H. Munby and T. Russell (eds), *Finding a Voice While Learning to Teach* (pp. 98–108). London: Falmer Press.

Smith, K. (2003, April). *Teacher Educators' Professional Knowledge: How Does it Differ from Teachers' Professional Knowledge?* Paper presented at the American Educational Research Association, Chicago.

Stenhouse, L. (1975). *An Introduction to Curriculum Research and Development*. London: Heinemann.

Tabachnick, B. R., and Zeichner, K. M. (1991). *Issues and Practices in Inquiry-oriented Teacher Education*. London: Falmer Press.

Tickle, L. (1994). *The Induction of New Teachers*. London: Cassell.

Tidwell, D. (2002). A balancing act: Self-study in valuing the individual student. In J. Loughran and T. Russell (eds), *Improving Teacher Education Practices Through Self-study* (pp. 30–42). London: RoutledgeFalmer.

Torney-Purta, J. (1985). Linking faculties of education with classroom teachers through collaborative research. *Journal of Educational Thought*, 19(1), 71–77.

Trumbull, D. (2004). Factors important for the scholarship of self-study of teaching adn teacher education practices. In J. J. Loughran, M. L. Hamilton, V. K. LaBoskey and T. Russell (eds), *International Handbook of Self-study of Teaching and Teacher Education Practices* (Vol. 2, pp. 1211–1230). Dordrecht: Kluwer Academic Publishers.

Tudball, L. (2004). Listening and responding to the views of my students: Are they ready to teach in a diverse world? Risking self-study of the internationalization of teacher education. In D. Tidwell, L. Fitzgerald and M. Heston (eds), *The Fifth International Conference of Self-study of Teacher Education Practices*. Herstmonceux Castle, East Sussex, U.K. (Vol. 2, pp. 250–254). Cedar Falls, Iowa: University of Northern Iowa.

van Manen, M. (1991). *The Tact of Teaching: The Meaning of Pedagogical Thoughtfulness*. Albany, New York: State University of New York Press.

van Manen, M. (1999). The language of pedagogy and primacy of student experience. In J. Loughran (ed.), *Researching Teaching: Methodologies and Practices for Understanding Pedagogy* (pp. 13–27). London: Falmer Press.

Westbury, I., and Wilkof, J. (eds). (1987). *Joseph J. Schwab: Science, Curriculum, and Liberal Education – Selected Essays*. Chicago: Chicago University Press.

Wheatley, M. J. (1992). *Leadership and the New Science*. San Francisco, CA: Berrett-Koehler Publishers.

White, B. C. (2002). Constructing constructivist teaching: Reflection as research. *Reflective Practice*, 3(3), 307–326.

Whitehead, J. (1993). *The Growth of Educational Knowledge: Creating Your Own Living Educational Theories*. Bournemouth: Hyde publications.

Wideen, M., Mayer-Smith, J., and Moon, B. (1998). A critical analysis of the research on learning to teach: Making the case for an ecological perspective on inquiry. *Review of Educational Research*, 68(2), 130–178.

Wilkes, G. (1996). What I have learned so far: Paradoxes in teaching. In J. Richards and T. Russell (eds), *Empowering Our Future in Teacher Education. Proceedings of the First International Conference of the Self-study of Teacher Education Practices*. Herstmonceux Castle, East Sussex, England (Vol. 1, pp. 120–123). Kingtson, Ontario: Queen's University.

Wilkes, G. (1998). Seams of paradoxes in teaching. In M. L. Hamilton (ed.), *Reconceptualizing Teaching Practice: Self-study in Teacher Education* (pp. 198–207). London: Falmer press.

Williams, A., Prestage, S., and Bedward, J. (2001). Individualism to collaboration: The significance of teacher culture to the induction of newly qualified teachers. *Journal of Education for Teaching*, 27(3), 253–267.

Winter, R. (2004). Genuine tasks as academic assessment: Dilemmas in meeting both student and institutional requirements. In D. Tidwell, L. Fitzgerald and M. Heston (eds), *The Fifth International Conference of Self-study of Teacher Education Practices*. Herstmonceux Castle, East Sussex, U.K. (pp. 266–269). Cedar Falls, Iowa: University of Northern Iowa.

Wong, E. D. (1995). Challenges confronting the researcher/teacher. *Educational Researcher*, 24(3), 22–28.

Zanting, A., Verloop, N., and Vermunt, J. D. (2003). How do student teachers elicit their mentor teachers' practical knowledge? *Teachers and Teaching: Theory and Practice*, 9(3), 197–211.

Zeichner, K. M. (1995). Reflections of a teacher educator working for social change. In T. Russell and F. Korthagen (eds), *Teachers Who Teach Teachers* (pp. 11–24). London: Falmer Press.

Zeichner, K. M., and Liston, D. P. (1996). *Reflective Teaching: An Introduction*. Mahwah, New Jersey: Lawrence Erlbaum Associates.

Zeichner, K. M., and Noffke, S. (2001). Practitioner research. In V. Richardson (ed.), *Handbook of Research on Teaching* (4th edn, pp. 298–330). Washington D.C.: American Educational Research Association.

Index